Rick Joy

Desert Works

Graham Foundation / Princeton Architectural Press series

NEW VOICES IN ARCHITECTURE

presents first monographs on emerging designers from around the world

Rick Joy
Desert Works

Foreword by Steven Holl
Introduction by Juhani Pallasmaa

Graham Foundation for Advanced Studies in the Fine Arts, Chicago
Princeton Architectural Press, New York

Published by
Princeton Architectural Press
37 East Seventh Street
New York, New York 10003

For a free catalog of books, call 1.800.722.6657.
Visit our web site at www.papress.com.

Printed in Hong Kong
05 04 03 5 4 3 2

Publication of this book has been supported by a grant from the Graham Foundation for Advanced Studies in the Fine Arts.

Photo Credits
Bill Timmerman: 6, 24–35, 38–50, 52–64, 71, 74, 77ur, 77lr, 78l, 79l, 80–84, 92ul, 92ll, 94, 98l, 99, 104, 106r, 107, 108, 110, 111, 114, 118, 119, 121, 122r, 123, 125ul, 125r, 126–132, 134, 136, 139, 140, 142l, 143–146, 150, 152–154, 156–160, 167, 172
Wayne Fuji: 66, 70, 72, 73, 76, 77, 78r, 85, 86
Andy Tinucci: 67ul, 67ll, 95, 112r
Tim Hursley: 67r, 75, 79r, 87
Jeff Goldberg: 88, 90, 91, 93, 96, 97, 98r, 102, 103, 105, 106l, 109, 112l, 113, 115
Jerry Sieve: 92lr
James McGoon: 116, 122l, 124, 125ll, 133
Undine Prohl: 137, 141, 142r, 147
Maartje Steenkamp: 173
Nick Berezenko: 176

Editing: Clare Jacobson
Design: Evan S. Schoninger

Special thanks to: Nettie Aljian, Ann Alter, Nicola Bednarek, Janet Behning, Penny Chu, Jan Cigliano, Mark Lamster, Nancy Eklund Later, Linda Lee, Jane Sheinman, Lottchen Shivers, Katharine Smalley, Scott Tennent, Jennifer Thompson, and Deb Wood of Princeton Architectural Press
—Kevin C. Lippert, publisher

Library of Congress Cataloging-in-Publication Data
Joy, Rick, 1958-
Rick Joy : desert works / foreword by Steven Holl ; introduction by Juhani Pallasmaa.
p. cm.—(New voices in architecture)
Includes bibliographical references and index.
ISBN 1-56898-336-0
1. Joy, Rick, 1958- 2. Architecture—Arid regions—Southwest, New. 3. Architecture, Domestic—Southwest, New. I. Title: Desert works. II. Title.
NA737.J69 A4 2002
720'.92—dc21
2002000853

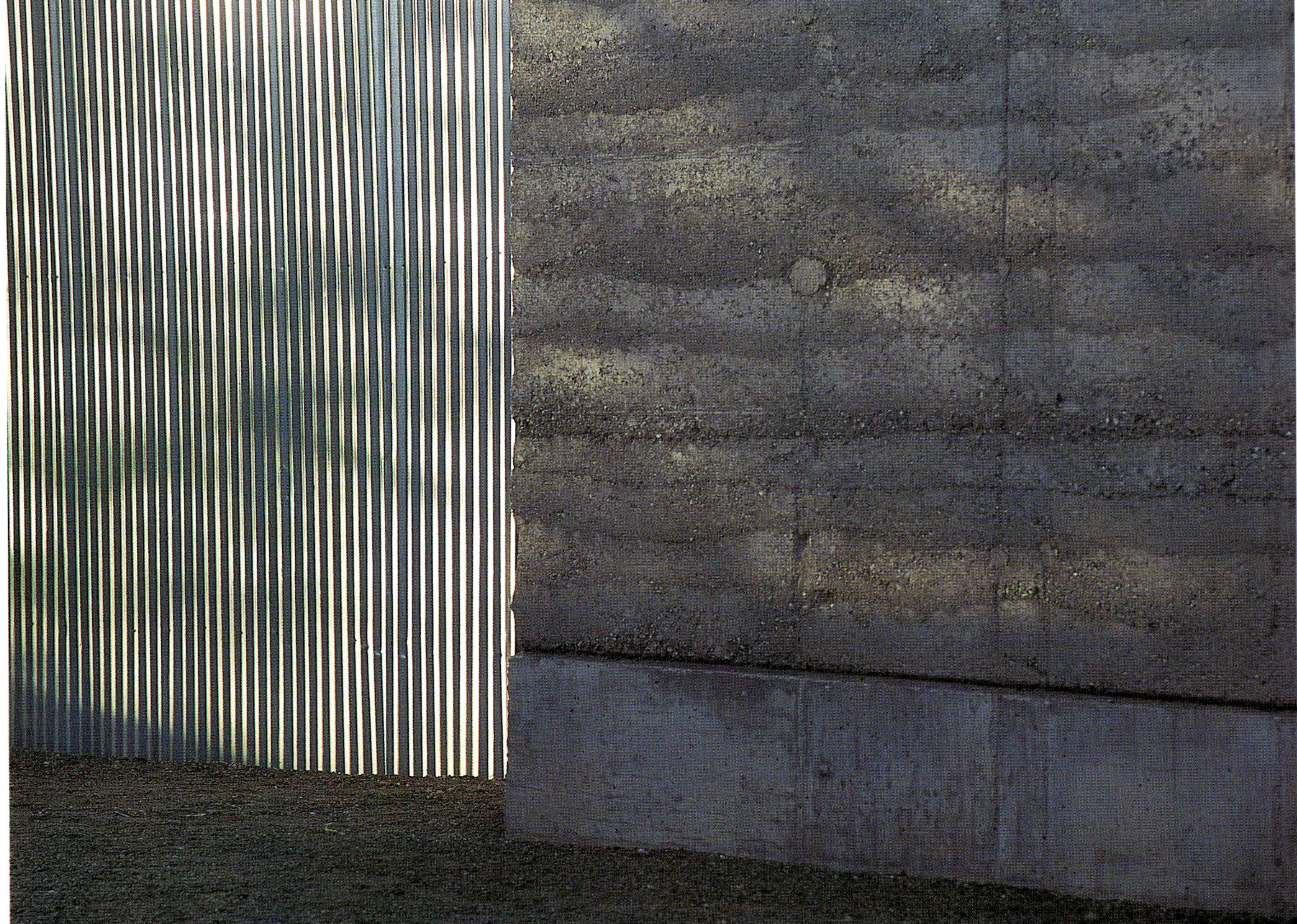

Foreword
Thickening the Light
Steven Holl

Experiential phenomena of a work of architecture encompass a silent meaning of things unseen. To seek meaning in these essences we might adopt a Zen aim, which places intuition before intellect. This subconscious perception—a kind of a priori knowledge—can be directly embodied and later perceived.

For an architect, unless he or she is to build the thing directly, intuitive action must be first translated into construction drawings, specifications, quantities, etc. Intuition is diluted. Intuition alternatively might be given the role of driving the form making of the design phase, however, by the time construction begins, typical specification standards and construction practices have taken over. The result is often an excessive form realized in banal details. The actual experience of walking through such architecture is often quite less enjoyable than the photographs.

To be directly engaged on the construction site and, in the case of Rick Joy, to build things directly allows a clear link to intuitive imagination. Experimentation with materials and details in orchestration of phenomenal and experimental spatial aims sets this work as the near opposite of empty formalism and banal execution. Not playing the game of corporate architecture or the routine of the academic publication exposure, Rick Joy remains on the fringe.

Four years ago while in Tucson, Arizona I met Rick Joy, visited his studio, and walked through three of his architectural works. In the rammed-earth walls I felt a concentration of materials—what I have often thought of as a hyphenated material-spirit or spirit-material. It is as if these two realms are pressed together into one, thickening the light. Surrounding spaces take on a particular density with textures animated in sunlight. The overall phenomenon, which is a result of material, detail, space, texture, light, and sound, allows architectural form to be almost negligible. I had a similar feeling when visiting the 1960 Church at the Bottom of the Lake by Sigurd Lewerentz—a feeling of solid materiality and blocks of carved light. I sensed in these small works a real engagement with the phenomenal architecture I have lectured on and sought to realize.

It is inspiring to discover fine architectural work outside of the visual channels of current fashion and politically manipulated publicity, and not surprising that the gestation period has been long. More than any other art, architecture takes time! Rick Joy worked as a carpenter/musician paving the foundation of his focus on architecture, which he finally came to at thirty. Further, these works were painstakingly constructed in some cases even by the hands that drew them. And yet in their sobriety, economy, and phenomenal mystery they are testaments to not playing the game... they are the wonderful prizes of being on the fringe.

Julio Cortazar, the enigmatic author of *Hopscotch* and *A Change of Light*, draws time and words together in the way space and light define architecture when he writes, "words lining themselves up in a notebook like congealed seconds, small sketches of time." In a similar intensity I hope to see future works of Joy, buildings with a "second sight."

Preface
Vivid Scenes
Rick Joy

On the weekend [mid-November 2001], I took my eleven-year-old son, Ethan, along with my two good friends and their sons to view the Leonids meteor shower. We traveled out to a very remote desert location, away from the city lights of Tucson. Two o'clock a.m. was identified by the astronomers as the best time to view it, so we arrived after midnight and stayed overnight. We chose a spot low in a desert wash, where we were surrounded by amazing specimens of Saguaro cactus that reached over thirty feet in height and were backlit by Tucson's distant glow. There was a slight bit of overcast to the south but the sky above us was totally clear and saturated with stars. Add the smells of desert sage and creosote, the sounds of a distant cargo train rumbling into Tucson, some coyote chatter to the west, a fine cigar and single malt scotch with my friends.

The light show was very dramatic and at times the sky was ablaze with dozens of burning meteors. Their colorful trails sometimes lasted minutes after the fireball had disappeared, creating a matrix of red, blue, orange, and green lines across the deep black sky. Later, as we bedded down in the soft sand, I looked over at my little boy who laid mesmerized by this fantastic fireworks-like display and I noticed the reflections in his eyes as he faded off to sleep. My son can't recall his dreams of that night, but I could see by the faint light of the stars that his eyes twitched continuously as he slept, indicating to me that he must have dreamt vivid scenes. It would be interesting for me to get a glimpse of how he will file away that experience compared to the perhaps more purely visually stimulating experiences he will have with the Xbox video gaming system he will get for Christmas.

Part of my motivation as an architect comes from an appreciation of very personal stories of life. The best tales are simple narratives that include descriptions of some of the more sensual aspects of our experiences. I feel that the greatest architectural achievements in the world can only truly be described in this way. This is how I think as an architect and it is how I see the world.

Architectural photography is of course a purely visual, two-dimensional art form, making it difficult to capture the more experiential aspects of the work. This is one of the reasons why we have chosen to show so many images in this book. At first glance, some images will seem similar to others. But with closer inspection they may evoke a different experiential mood as interpreted by the photographer. These intimate vignettes and details attempt to grasp the essences of the places better than the comprehensive photographs other collections provide.

I have been very fortunate in this early phase of my career to have been given the opportunity to work with some of the most gifted and prestigious architectural photographers in the world. Jeff Goldberg of Esto from New York, Tim Hursley from Arkansas, Wayne Fuji from Japan, James McGoon from Texas, and Undine Prohl from Germany have each given us some of their best work. It is truly an honor to have their images included here.

For the majority of the photographs in this book, however, I am most grateful to my friend Bill Timmerman. Not only are Bill's photographs very fine graphic images in and of themselves, but each one is for me a lesson in seeing and feeling that transcends simple description of architectural form. His images and our conversations about them have made a significant contribution to the deeper, more visceral explorations in my work. Thank you, Bill.

As I begin my ninth year as an architect, the nature of my practice has evolved to include not only the kind of wonderful private projects exhibited in this book, but also public projects of larger scale and work in places beyond the desert Southwest. As I work to maintain the small collaborative office that has worked so well thus far, the most significant change is in the ways our new projects are being built. Although we can now only serve as the contractor for the smallest of local residential projects, I can never let go of my passion for building and for the thrill of working collectively to synthesize our thinking with the real making of architecture.

The work has been graced by the caring hands and minds of many outstanding people. I was surprised to discover just how many as I compiled the list in the back of the book. All of these people have contributed something of themselves as thinkers and with their hands as makers and I thank them all. In particular, I would like to thank my most senior associate, Andy Tinucci. Andy came to my office from the University of Illinois just as we were beginning the construction of the Godat Design Studio and the Catalina House and has given of himself with selfless passion and full exuberance ever since. Although he has played a major role in nearly all of my work, my memories of the hundreds of hours we spent building our new studio together are some of the fondest of my career. Only in his mid-twenties, Andy is one of the very few exceptions to the widely accepted notion that youth is wasted on the young.

Finally, I would like to thank the people who have mattered most in my life as an architect: especially Will Bruder, who, since he first took that initial leap of faith in me in 1990, has been a consistent voice of optimism and encouragement; Jorges Silvetti, the Chairman of the Department of Architecture at the Harvard Graduate School of Design, for introducing me to the stimulating world of teaching; and Max Underwood, for helping me find my teaching voice and for encouraging its growth. I would also like to give a very special thank you to Steven Holl for his kind and eloquent words and to my new friend Juhani Pallasmaa, whose poetic and insightful writings in his introductory essay are deeply meaningful to me and very much appreciated. Many thanks as well to Clare Jacobson and Evan Schoninger for their patience and graceful management of the complex process of designing and making this book. Lastly and most significantly, thank you to Jean Millen, the love of my life, for helping me to understand that my persona as a man and a father defines who I am much more than my work.

Introduction
Thought and Experience in Rick Joy's Desert Architecture
Juhani Pallasmaa

The immense emptiness of desert landscapes, such as the African and Australian sand deserts or the all-white expanses of snow above the Polar Circle, radiate a strange appeal and emotional power. These settings erase the traces of man and evoke an experience of timelessness. The total absence of vegetation exposes the naked skin of the earth and turns the landscape into a tactile and muscular experience. Landscape becomes an extension of the human skin.

The Sonoran Desert of the American Southwest is a landscape of hidden drama. Its scarred and cracked soil is scorched by the merciless desert sun and eroded by attacks of desert rain. Its plants exhibit spectacular strategies for collecting and preserving water and even more striking means of defending the acquired stock of this basic substance of life. The life forms adapted to the conditions of the Sonoran Desert project an intriguing combination of aggression and beauty; the devices of defense and strategies of procreation turn into dazzling fireworks of color and form.

The radiant beauty of the desert extends from earthly phenomena to tones and colorations of the air and sky. John van Dyke, a professor of art history at the end of the nineteenth century, described the beauty of the desert air in his forgotten book, *The Desert*: "The desert air is practically colored air. Several times from high mountains I have seen it lying below me like an enormous tinted cloud or veil. A similar veiling of pink, lilac, or pale yellow is to be seen in the gorges.... Plain upon plain leads up and out to the horizon—far as the eye can see—in undulations of grey and gold; ridge upon ridge melts into the blue of the distant sky in lines of lilac and purple; fold upon fold over the mesas the hot air drops its veiling of opal and topaz. Yet, it is the kingdom of sun-fire. For every color in the scale is attuned to the key of flame, every airwave comes with the breath of flame, every sun-beam talks as a shaft of flame."[1]

The American desert has attracted numerous artists, writers, photographers, scholars, and observers from Georgia O'Keefe to Agnes Martin, John van Dyke to J. B. Jackson, Edward Weston to Richard Misrach, and Mary Austin to Reyner Banham. Gaston Bachelard, the French philosopher, wrote of "water poets"[2] attracted by images of water. We could, similarly, identify the opposite polarity of poetic sensibility, the desert poets. The desert has also seduced an entire generation of American landscape and earth artists, such as Robert Smithson, Donald Judd, Michael Heizer, James Turrell, and Walter de Maria. Even architects from Frank Lloyd Wright to William Bruder have been drawn to the south-western desert.

It is probably the sublime vastness and the sense of a divine void that has attracted these artists. The desert floor provides the *tabula rasa* for creative work that breaks from the confined and conditioned spaces of cities and museums. It gives a new context to the endeavors and products of modern man. A rusting carcass of a car appears brutal in a setting of lush greenery, but appears a fragile memento of human vulnerability and the vanity of human effort under the desert sun. The desert turns the metal of a tin can into a rusty lace reminiscent of an autumn leaf. The cemetery of American war planes on the outskirts of Tucson, Arizona, where B-52 bombers are dismembered like gargantuan locusts by an immense guillotine blade, elevates this confrontation of the desert and modern man to the scale of a frightening beauty.[3]

These are the sublime settings of Rick Joy's desert architecture.

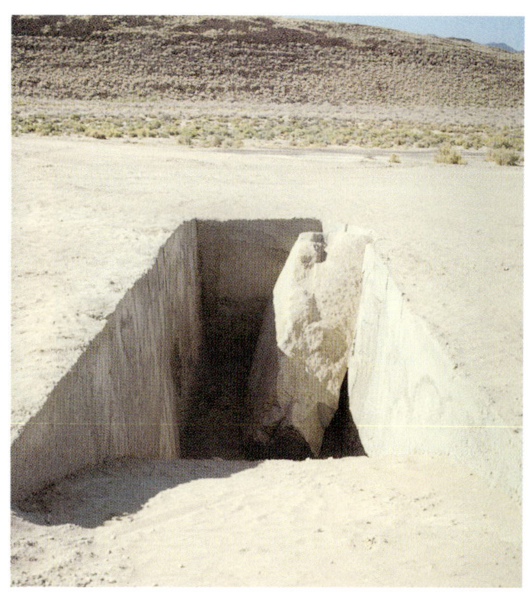

1. Michael Heizer, *Displaced/Replaced Mass 1:3*, 1969

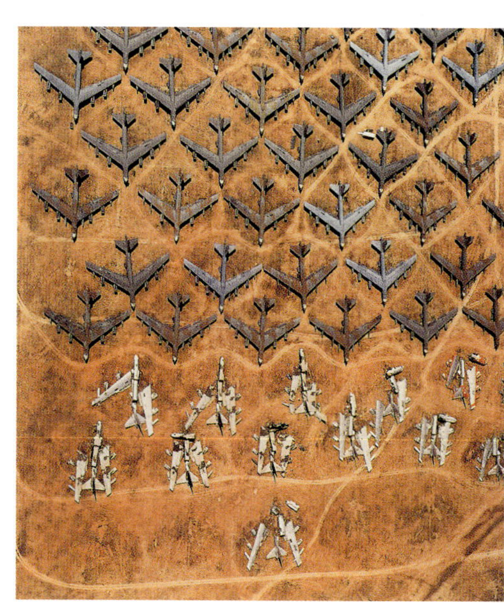

2. Alex S. MacLean, *Bone Yards*, 1996

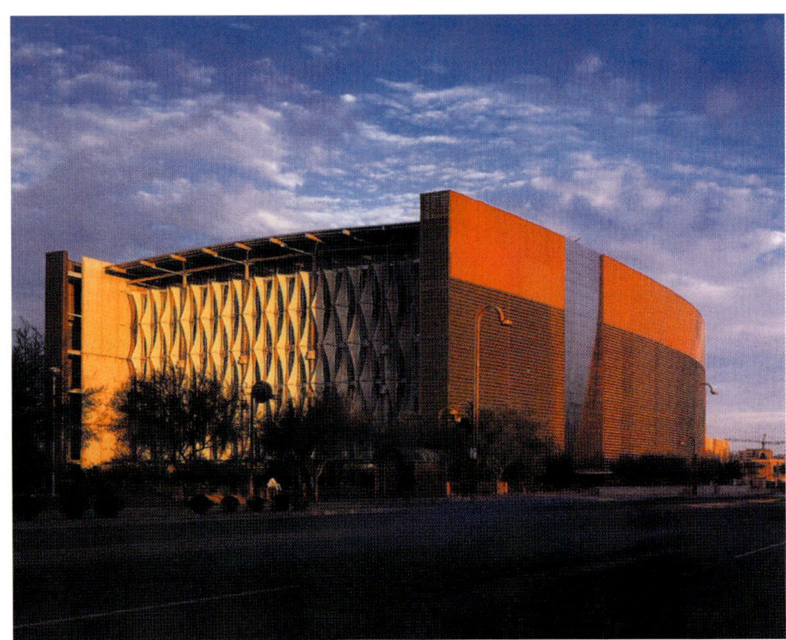

3. William Bruder, Phoenix Public Library, 1995

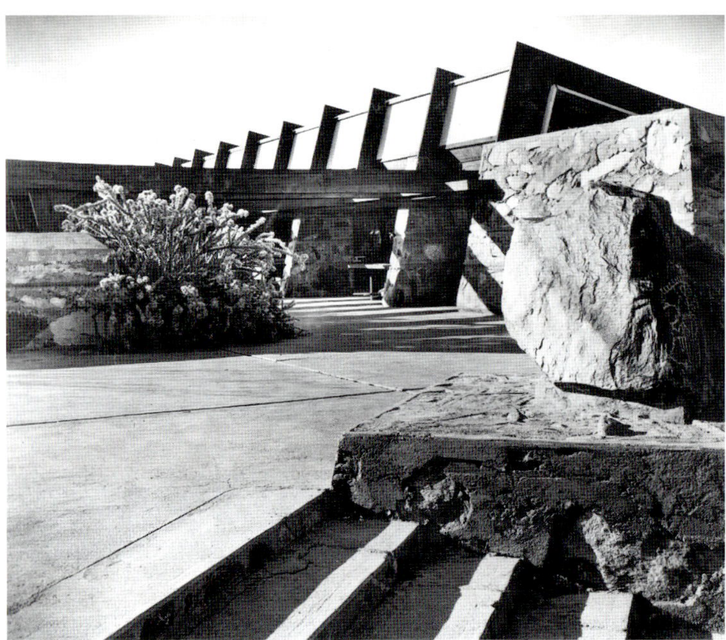

4. Frank Lloyd Wright, Taliesin West, Phoenix, Arizona, 1937

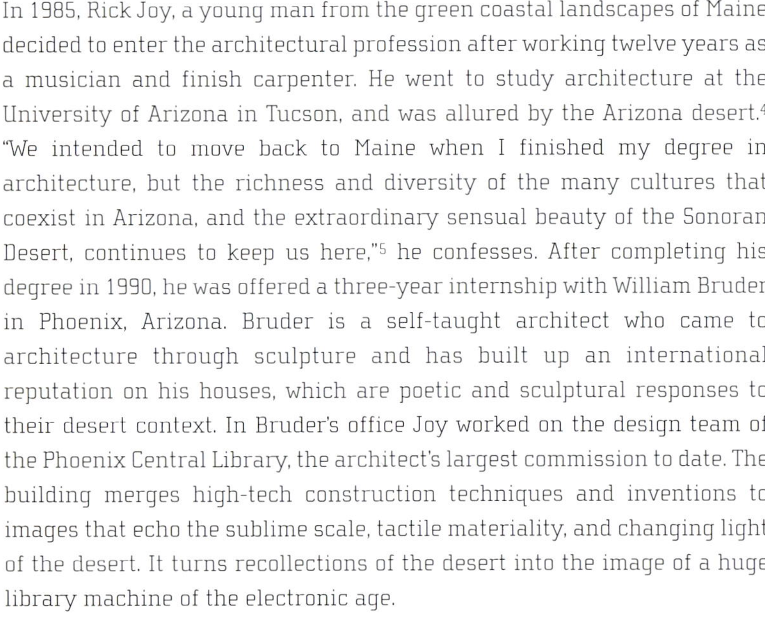

In 1985, Rick Joy, a young man from the green coastal landscapes of Maine decided to enter the architectural profession after working twelve years as a musician and finish carpenter. He went to study architecture at the University of Arizona in Tucson, and was allured by the Arizona desert.[4] "We intended to move back to Maine when I finished my degree in architecture, but the richness and diversity of the many cultures that coexist in Arizona, and the extraordinary sensual beauty of the Sonoran Desert, continues to keep us here,"[5] he confesses. After completing his degree in 1990, he was offered a three-year internship with William Bruder in Phoenix, Arizona. Bruder is a self-taught architect who came to architecture through sculpture and has built up an international reputation on his houses, which are poetic and sculptural responses to their desert context. In Bruder's office Joy worked on the design team of the Phoenix Central Library, the architect's largest commission to date. The building merges high-tech construction techniques and inventions to images that echo the sublime scale, tactile materiality, and changing light of the desert. It turns recollections of the desert into the image of a huge library machine of the electronic age.

The internship must have been significant to the formation of Joy's architectural sensibilities, particularly the interplay of rusticity and refinement, roughness of materials and technical sophistication, formal simplicity and concealed wealth of associations. It is interesting to realize the architectural lineage, which ties Joy to Frank Lloyd Wright. Bruder apprenticed with and learned the practice of architecture from Paolo Soleri, an immigrant from Turin, Italy who apprenticed with Wright in his Taliesin West desert studio in Scottsdale for three years at the end of the 1940s. Certain aspects of Wright's desert architecture—such as the use of thick walls that seem like protrusions of earth itself, the horizontality that defines a datum line for the reading of the undulations and rhythms of a landscape, as well as the juxtaposition of weight and lightness, opacity and transparency—can still be felt as distant tremors in Joy's buildings. Joy's allegiance to modernism, on the other hand, separates him from his predecessors. He is a constituent of the ongoing dialectics of modernity, which sets him in a perpetual process of questioning the accepted view of reality and the cultural convention.

A special quality of Joy's practice is his total engagement in the design and building process. During the past few decades, the design professions have distanced themselves from materials and processes of making; architects have become mere design specialists who are engaged in construction through the processes of intellectualization, conceptualization, and formalization. At the same time, construction has become increasingly geared to the methods, capabilities (often limited), choices, and economic objectives of contractors. These disappointing developments, coupled with the general conservatism of the architects' clientele, have given rise to a number of design-build practices across the United States.

Joy's decision to be involved in all aspects of the building process reestablishes the architect's venerable role as the true master of the construction work, but it also allows for greater quality control, experimentation, and use of craft. Most importantly, it re-creates the psychological advantages of truly collective work. Joy emphasizes the collaborative essence of architectural and construction work: "Our firm, like the work, strives for a higher ideal—that of a cooperative practice. To cooperate is to act or work with others with a shared vision and common aspiration. We see no disciplinary boundaries, only the boundaries of the problem under consideration. There lies the need to collectively strive to uncover the generative questions and discover answers through each person's contribution. That means involving clients, craftspeople, fabricators, friends, family, and staff every day in the creative process. It is for this reason (among others) we build (we are contractors for our local projects) our local residential projects utilizing a team consisting predominantly of recent architecture school graduates."[6] Joy's engagement in actual construction work as well as his employment of students and fresh graduates on his construction team echoes the practices of Wright's desert academy and Soleri's Cosanti and Arcosanti communities.

A significant aspect of collaboration in the realm of the arts is the collaboration with history. In his seminal essay "Tradition and the Individual Talent" (1919), T. S. Eliot wrote about this specific form of creative collaboration. He proposed "a historical sense," the artist's specific position in relation to the past, instead of the precise knowledge of historical facts of the historian. "Tradition is a matter of much wider significance. It cannot be inherited, and if you want it you must obtain it by great labor.... It involves in the first place, the historical sense... and the historical sense involves a perception, not only of the pastness of the past, but of its presence; the historical sense compels a man to write not merely with his own generation in his bones, but with a feeling that the whole of the literature... has a simultaneous existence and composes a simultaneous order."[7]

Joy's work seems to be informed by this kind of tacit wisdom of architecture, derived from vernacular and historical buildings as well as the entire heritage of modernity: "We are continually striving to create architecture that is regionally sympathetic and well grounded in the context and community of its place, wherever the place may be, and does not rely on responding to the superficial fads, historical styles, or the intellectual 'isms' that are so popular with architects today. I believe we can learn a lot from the buildings we have inherited, but imitating their forms without recognition of the original content degrades their importance, creates a skin-deep style, and limits the sense of wonder and inventiveness that is critical to creating memorable places."[8]

Joy's early projects were alterations and extensions of existing buildings. His engagement with the anatomies of old buildings must have sensitized him to issues of time and historical layering as well as to the inevitable ties of any architectural language with its own time and cultural condition. He is determined to maintain reverence for the integrity and autonomy of historical layers, and this position seems to put him in conflict with today's sentimental preservationist views.

Before his breakthrough into the awareness of a wider architectural public, Joy designed and executed a number of small but thoughtful projects. He built his own residence in Tucson (1991–1992), an extension of a plastered bungalow, during nine months at the same time that he was commuting daily between Tucson and Bruder's studio in New River, three

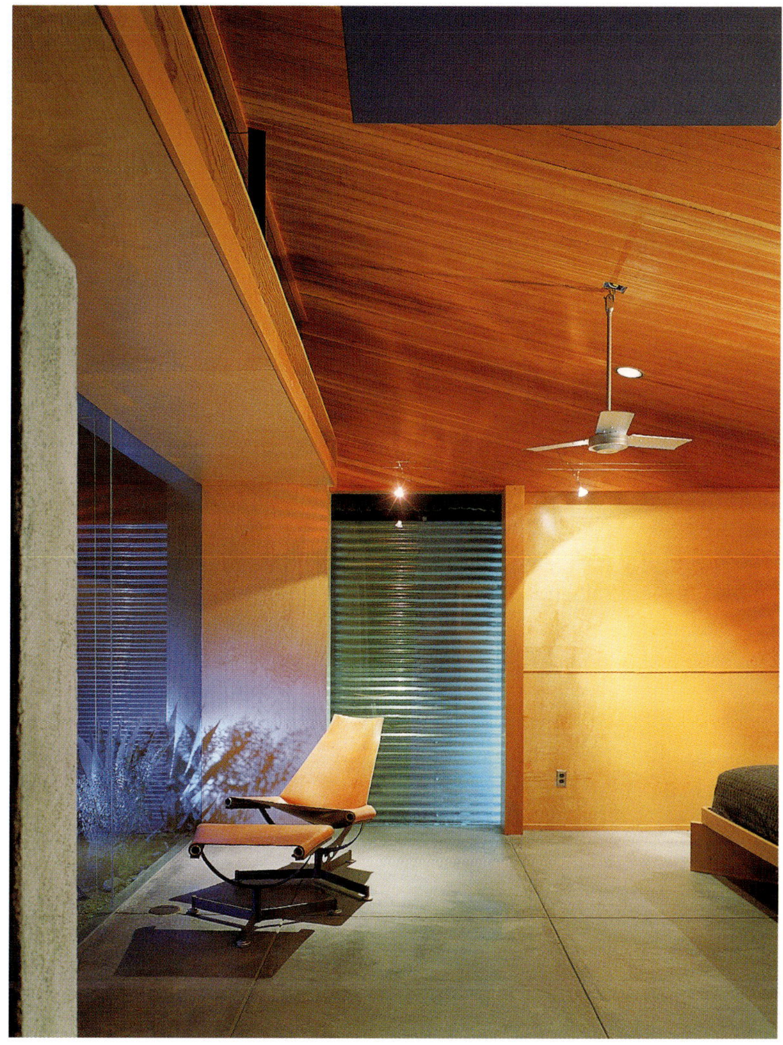

5. View of bedroom, Joy/Millen House, Tucson, Arizona, 1991–1992

hours away. The design reflects Bruder's influence, but it also displays some of Joy's basic later strategies and formal ideas, such as the interplay of simple *gestalt* and emotional density, indoors and outdoors, space and scale, materiality and color. The Bryant Residence (1993) and the Hoffman Residence (1996) remodelings contain delicate additions to existing buildings and developed the architect's sense of interior space, whereas the unexecuted Ahlquist Solar Retreat (1994), for a site seventy miles southeast of Tucson, is a minimal desert house underneath a single metal shed roof. The project incorporates environmentally progressive technologies, such as a photovoltaic electricity system, thermal water panels, composting toilets, and a gray-water system. The unbuilt project for the Birch/Slade Residence (1994) in Durango, Colorado is a more elaborate design with thick and protective masonry walls underneath a low horizontal gable roof. Two coffee houses (1994), one in Phoenix and one in Tucson, familiarized the architect early on with nonresidential design. The Aliso Spring Ranch (1995) in Tubac, Arizona, another unbuilt project, is a dynamic composition of three rectangular shed-roofed units of rammed earth, fitted gracefully within a group of mesquite trees. The project combines an air of modernity with a relaxed vernacular character.

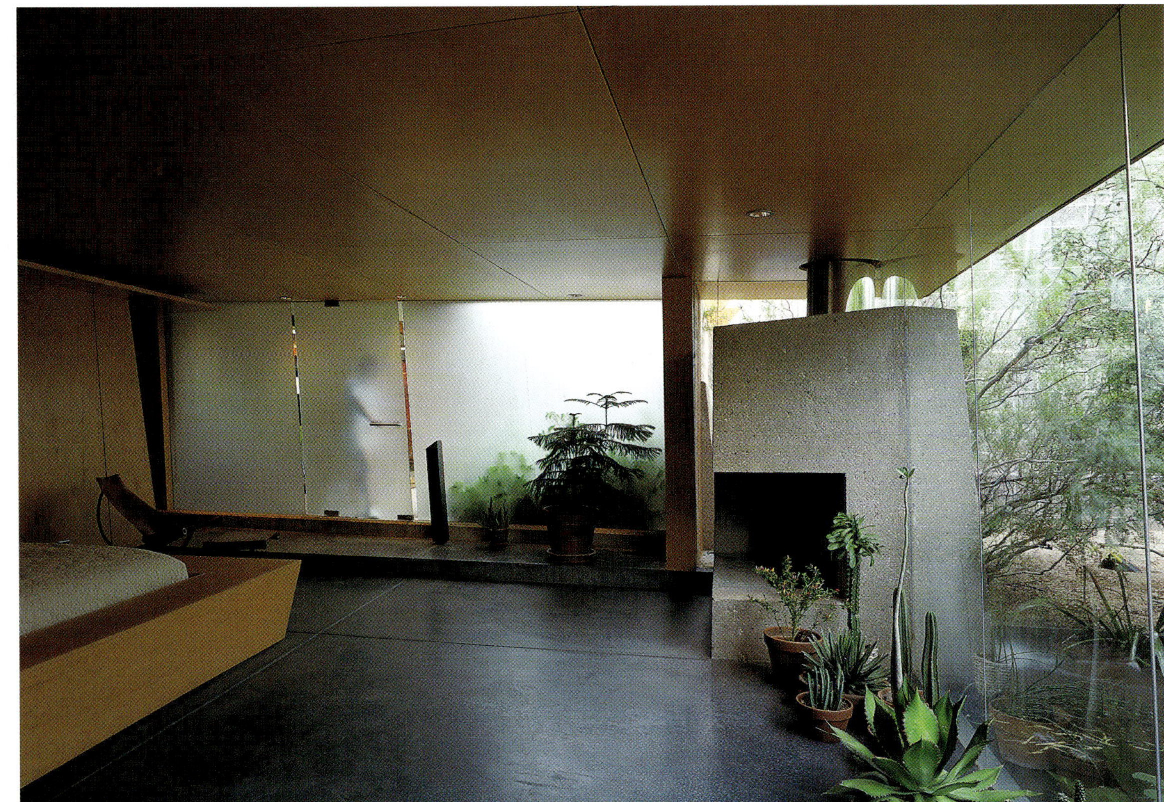

6. Hoffman Residence, Tucson, Arizona, 1996

Rick Joy's widening reputation as an architect with a personal message has been built up in the exceptionally short period of eight years, and on few fairly small residential projects. It is clear, however, that these houses will be the first chapter in the architect's future œuvre. His first work to awake national and international interest was his Convent Avenue Studios (1995–1997). It is located in the Barrio Histórico in Tucson, whose historical blocks fuse shops and businesses with residential functions and radiate a sense of integrated urban culture that has disappeared from American city centers.

When Joy began this project, the existing buildings on the site had already deteriorated to a state of ruins. His task was to restore the remains of the existing structures—essentially a wall, once a street front of a row of houses, and a fragment of one of the houses—and insert three modest loft studios. The new two-story wedge-shaped units—one turned around its axis 180 degrees—have a laconic shed roof of rusty corrugated sheets. The plan drawing makes the site look crowded, but visiting them turns crowdedness into a positive sense of density, mystery, and tactile intimacy. The site is entered through the renovated streetfront facade of the former buildings. Subtle gestures, such as the precisely framed wood door, elegant oxidized steel mailboxes, and randomly spaced iron bars, prepare the visitor for an interplay of tradition and novelty. In the entry courtyard, two aslant rusty Corten cubes containing water direct one's gaze down to earth and provide the welcoming and soothing gesture of refreshing water. The image of these water containers recalls Le Corbusier's "light canons" at La Tourette, Luis Barragán's troughs and chutes, and Richard Serra's heavy volumes of wrought iron. As one lifts one's eyes, the end wall of the nearest loft seems to rise to an unexpected height. The walls of the loft units, made of rammed earth[9] with a pinkish color (in fact, the coloration changes dramatically in accordance with the time of the day and weather), project sensations of a thick volume, weight, opacity, the tactility of earth, and the cool interior of its very mass.

Space meanders in a labyrinthine manner between the three studios, a weathered steel laundry unit, the boundary walls, and a freestanding landscape wall. The chartreuse green color of the landscape wall, next to the deep red brown of oxidized iron, exudes a surprising ambience of abstraction and organic association. The color brings to mind the astonishing yellow rectangles of pine or hazelnut pollen in Wolfgang Leib's floor installations. These are colors that vibrate with the sheer force of

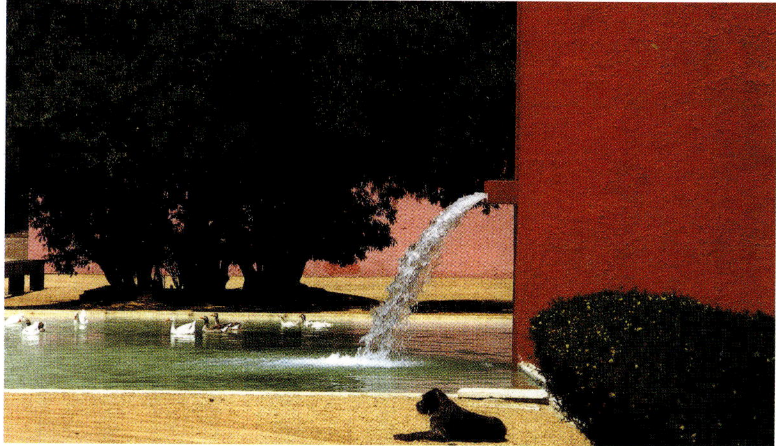

7. Luis Barragán, Cuadra San Cristóbal, Los Clubes, Mexico City, 1966–1968

growth and procreation. Joy's green evokes a sensation of taste and the memory of the maroon, pink, and violet walls of Luis Barragán. In the simple composition of the three wedges, order plays against randomness, as the visitor's mind oscillates between associations to vernacular constructions and modern images, anonymous tradition and idiosyncratic expression. Time turns into a deep time that has an archeological essence. Sharply contoured and thoughtful details, such as the concrete foundation extended upwards to form the window sill, or the thinness of the edges of rusty steel plates, create a counterpoint to the mass of rammed earth, with its associations to desert cliffs and layers of earth revealed by an excavation. One remembers Wright's desert concrete at Taliesin West and Le Corbusier's *beton brut*. The interiors of the loft spaces are rustic yet elegant. The windows, punctured through the thick walls, have a telescopic focusing effect, whereas a slit through the wooden roof structure unites the interior with the vastness of the sky.

Another intervention with an existing adobe building in the historic district of Tucson is Joy's interior design for the Godat Design Studio (1997). As the building's owner did not permit any alterations to the building, Joy's project is an architectural installation set respectfully within the context of the white-washed walls and tile floors of the original structure. The gypsum walls of the conference room, for instance, were leaned against walls of the house to provide display surfaces. Small square apertures in these walls create a sense of increased closure, at the same time that they regulate the amount of natural light. The interiors are articulated in two materials, plate steel and translucent glass, one evoking opacity and toughness, the other a glow of light and fragility. Regardless of their diminutive size, the rooms create a labyrinth-like space.

The Catalina House (1997–1998) in Tucson, oriented towards the Catalina Mountain Range to the northeast of the site, is another application of Joy's rammed-earth walls/undivided glass openings/weathered steel vocabulary. The butterfly roof and projecting gutters evoke rain even when dry heat is scorching the landscape. The house and the garage create a village-like cluster that has found its relaxed configuration in relation to the course of the sun as well as the near and distant views of Saguaro cacti. The opposite orientation of the two reversed gable roofs is surprisingly effective in creating an image of a conglomerate of volumes instead of a single house.

The Tubac House in Tubac, Arizona (1998–2000) is a more extensive residential design in smooth cast concrete and weathered steel. In comparison to Joy's earlier, more humble buildings, this house projects a complexity of spatial composition. The plan arrangement is reminiscent of certain Case Study Houses in California of the late 1940s and early fifties. Huge undivided glass walls flatten the landscape onto the window surface and turn it into a monumental painting; the house is not any more in a landscape setting, but the setting occupies the house. The architecture seems to set a dialogue between the opposite images of enrooting and abstracting, intimacy and distance—a dialogue that is an essential theme in all of Joy's architecture. While being structures of the desert, his buildings are also studies in the abstract and universal language of architecture. Joy himself emphasizes that, as a relative newcomer, he reads the desert landscape as an outsider.[10]

A couple of years after completing the Convent Avenue Studios, Joy began to design his own 400 Rubio Avenue (1998–1999) in a corner of the remaining site, and successfully expanded his labyrinthine ensemble in the center of modern Tucson. Located on a dusty service alley, the studio presents itself as a massive earth wall with a heavy wooden door, juxtaposed with rusting steel. The image expresses simultaneously ruggedness (the toughness of four-wheel-drives, farm machinery, and industrial settings) and an elegant design sensibility. Opening the door, which speaks of protection, authority, and domestic intimacy, one enters a wedge-form courtyard delineated by a rammed-earth wall on one side and a large diaphragm of glass on the other, terminating in the rusty darkness of a small reflecting pool. The courtyard directs one's attention to the sky above, which turns into a flattened picture framed by the edges of the space. The color tonalities of desert air, described by John van Dyke, come to play in Joy's reflective surfaces of water and glass, and his framed skies echo James Turrell's sky spaces. The sediments and cracks of the earth walls are contrasted with the high-tech suspension of huge sheets of glass flush with the earth wall. The juxtaposition makes one think of Sigurd Lewerentz's celebrated windows with glass elements clipped directly onto the surface of a brutally rough brick wall, making the windows appear as mere punctures through matter.

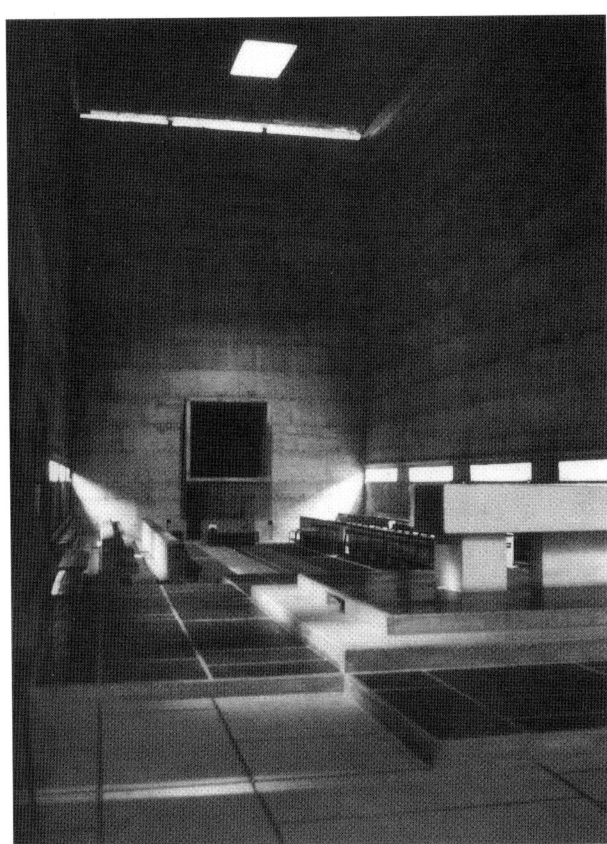

8. Le Corbusier, La Tourette, Eveux-sur-Arbresle, 1953–1957

The Tucson Mountain House (2000–2001) is a solitary architectural structure located in a valley surrounded by impressive ridges and gorgeous desert plants. Its concept is a variation of themes developed in the Catalina House a couple of years earlier. The plan consists of two parallel rows of rooms underneath a generous butterfly roof of weathered steel. The house is carefully sited and built without disturbing the fauna, which is fragile regardless of its aggressive appearance. In its combined rationality and emotional impact, the house brings to mind some of the clearheaded and poetic house designs of Glenn Murcutt in Australia. Characteristically to Joy's houses, the bathroom opens out to the desert scenery through a glass wall, contrasting intimacy and immensity, nakedness and roughness.

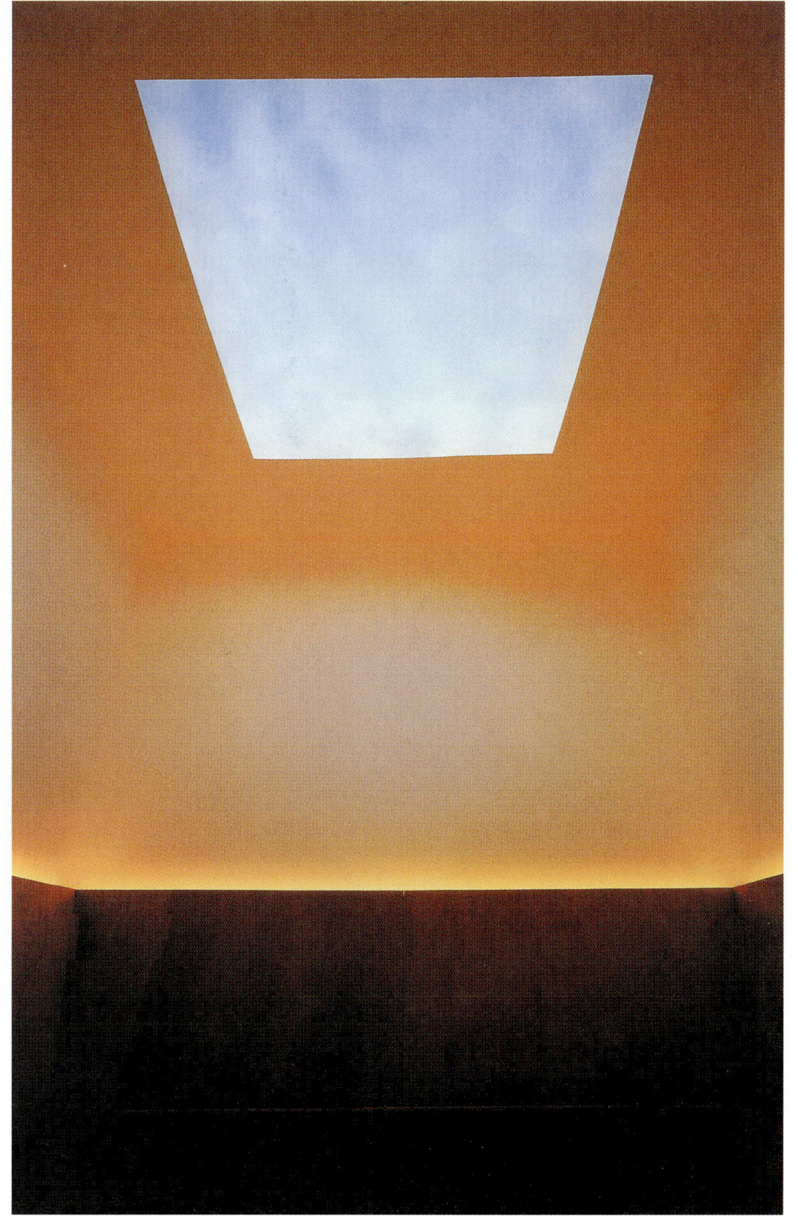

9. James Turrell, *Air Mass*, 1993

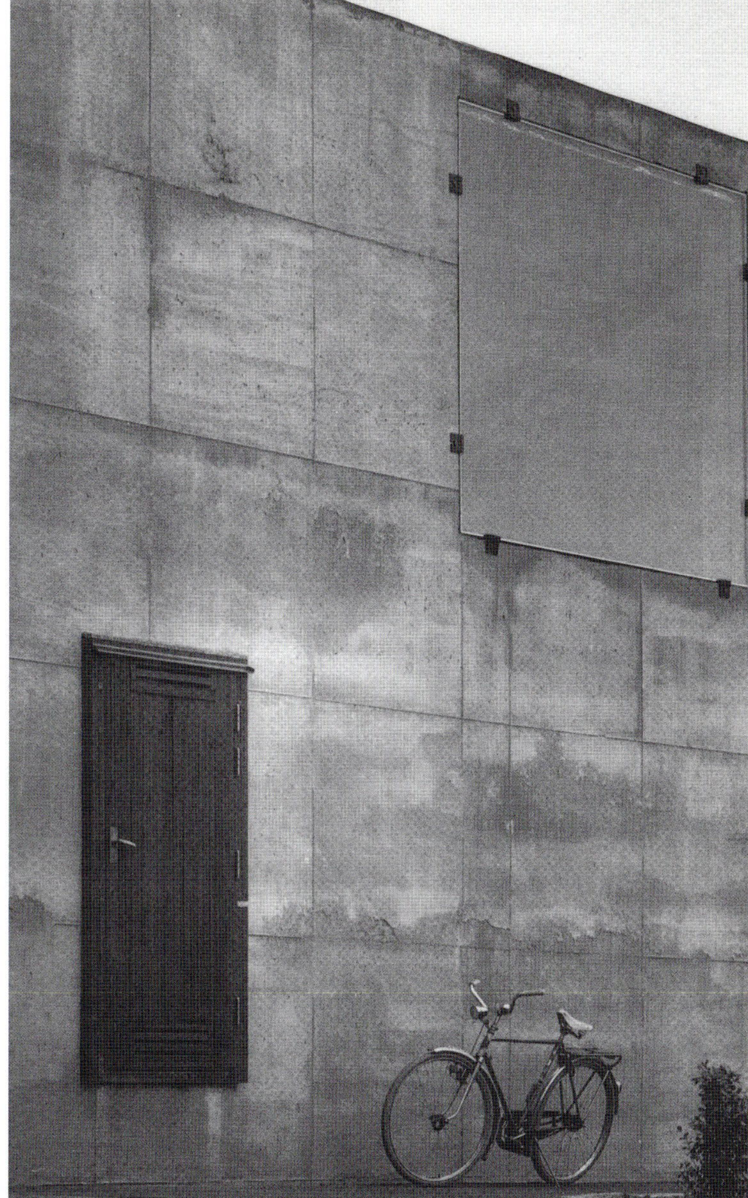

10. Sigurd Lewerentz, Flower Kiosk, Eastern Cemetery, Malmo, Sweden, 1969

The basic concept of the Casa Jax (1999–2002) of three boxes on a platform, set against the breathtaking desert backdrop and a distant mountain silhouette, has an explicit minimalist character akin to the aesthetics of Donald Judd and Carl Andre. In order to minimize the impact of construction on earth and vegetation, the units are elevated above the ground like pieces of sculpture on their bases. The flush wooden sleeping decks completely erase the image of a roof and further reinforce the sense of abstraction; the form is deliberately distanced from sentimental images of domesticity and comfort. The ensemble turns into an architectural still life reminiscent of Georgio Morandi's metaphysical compositions of a couple of timid bottles or cups in the desert of a table top. The counterpoint of the animistic gesturing of the huge saguaros and the restrained and pristine boxes is powerful, indeed. The fragmentation of the house into its basic functional components—living space, bedroom, and den—strengthens the sense of isolation in the middle of the desert, as the daily activities are interconnected only by gravel foot paths winding through cacti. The exterior, clad in plate steel, creates an ambience of defiant relentlessness (underlined by the exposed fasteners), whereas the maple veneer of the interior paneling projects an inviting domesticity. Translucent glass partitions add an image of fragility and pick up the slightest of light.

The Pima Canyon House (2000–2002) in Tucson is located in a gated community instead of Joy's usual setting, the open and limitless desert. The house is conceived as a monastic microcosm enclosed within its perimeter walls; the wall is interrupted only at the northeast corner, next to a flush pool of water, to open up a view to the mountains. The experiential encounter is richly articulated beginning with a dark entry space with its sound of dripping water. A revolving steel door protects the darkness of this space against the overpowering desert light and creates a mental distance between the world of vulgarity outside and the man-made paradise within (the ancient Persian word pari-dae'za means "walled garden"). This space of initiation slows down and tunes one's senses, and eventually the visitor is prepared to ascend to a glass entry pavilion and further into the textured plaster interior. Judging by the drawings, when finished, the house will have an emotional density akin to Luis Barragán's dreamlike architecture.

The Greer Cabin (2001–2002) in Greer, Arizona has taken Joy away from his beloved desert to an entirely different landscape, an aspen forest nine thousand feet above sea level. In the protective space of a forest, the house has a more fragile skin and softer appearance than when exposed to the shadeless desert. Like the individual units of the Casa Jax, the house is a box on a sloping field. Appropriately, the difference in the tone and plasticity of the landscape is reflected in the characteristics of the box; the vertical cedar slats of the facades create a subtle transparency and a dialogue

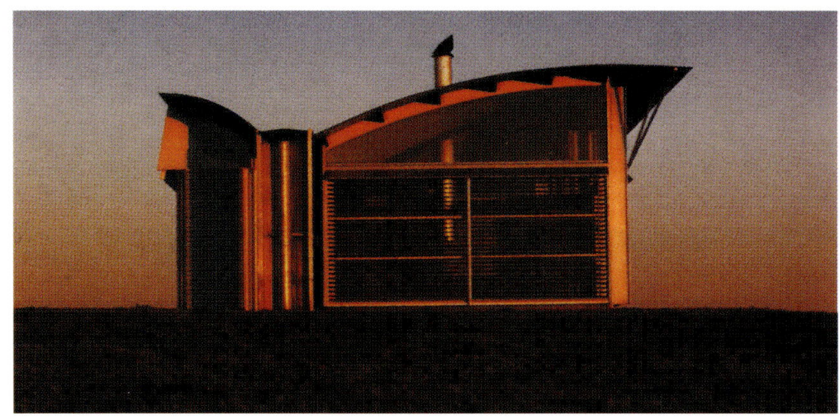

11. Glenn Murcutt, Magney House, Bingi Point, New South Wales, Australia, 1982–1984

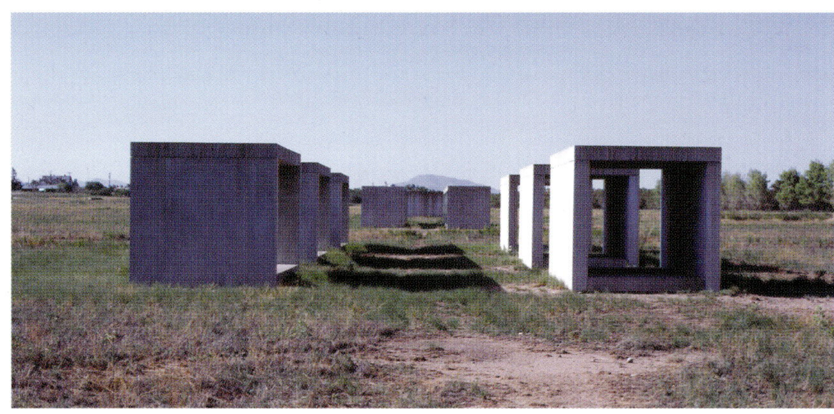

12. Donald Judd, 15 untitled works in concrete, 1980–1984, detail

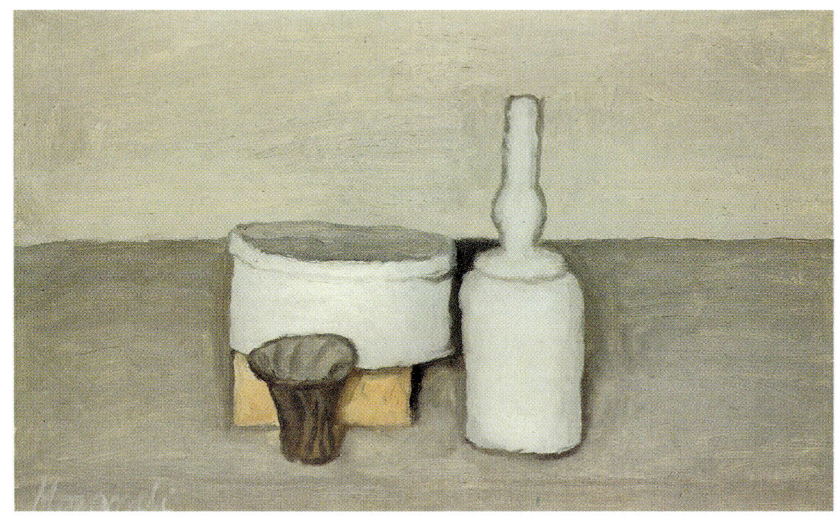

13. Giorgio Morandi, *Still Life*, 1956

with the rhythm of trees. The configuration recalls plan ideas of the 1950s and sixties; various units float in the undivided space and define zones of different domestic activities, while the thick wall on the north side contains service spaces and utilities. In Joy's design, the delightful utopian optimism of the mid-twentieth century fuses with the minimalist ideals of the early twenty-first century.

Regardless of its refined aesthetics, Joy's architecture is guided by an environmental and ecological concern. Joy's environmental attitudes are, however, based on reason and a sense of moderateness, instead of environmental fundamentalism. "Slowly emerging from our disposable society is an increasingly popular world view that helps us all to make life decisions in favor of the environment. At its simplest, I can only hope that by striving to design and build buildings that possess an enduring quality—buildings that are inherently sensual and soulful—I can have some positive impact on the issues of sustainable design. Bold, modern architecture that is rooted in the context and culture of its place and that is developed in combination with the basics of proper solar orientation and site protection, and the responsible use of sensible materials and fine craftsmanship, will have the quality to withstand the tests of time. In other words, we can increase the longevity of buildings and decrease the consumption of resources by simply doing a good job with the basics first. By creating an environmentally responsible architecture that in its simplicity and clarity is more attainable and desirable we can then bridge the gap between the environmental extremist fringe and popular culture."[11]

Today's ecologically oriented architecture often projects an air of aesthetic and technological conservatism. Joy does not accept compromises; even environmentally concerned architecture needs to look forward and aspire for aesthetic and technical perfection. Nature provides the model for this; natural selection works towards further refinement and efficiency of performance, not backwards to earlier, more archaic forms.

Rick Joy's architecture fuses reason and poetry into a single concept. His designs are illustrations of Joseph Brodsky's argument, "beauty can't be targeted... it is always a by-product of other, often very ordinary, pursuits."[12] Being a builder, Joy focuses on the technicalities and practicalities of construction, characteristics of the site, and principles of rationality and human perception, but these engagements result in qualities of purified beauty. Although his buildings also reflect an uncompromising aesthetic sensibility, his primary objectives seem to be beyond architecture, seen merely as a material and aestheticized object, in the experiential qualities of the encounter with the world of the real. His buildings are not architectural objects: they are existential instruments that frame, condition, and articulate the realm of experience.

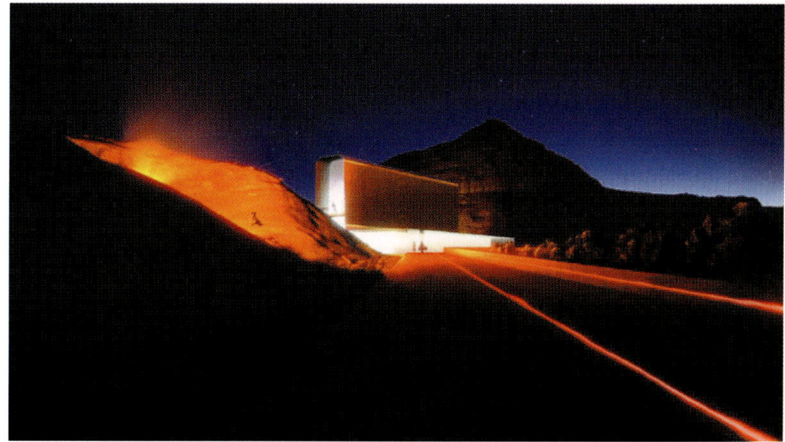

14. Entry building, Page One Resort Hotel

Joy emphasizes the importance of sensual experiences and an intuitive approach over theoretical speculations: "In the designs, a great deal of attention is given to the qualities of the sensual experiences. After achieving a thorough understanding of the owner's aspirations and the required functional aspects, I frequently enter into a realm of mindfulness that relies predominantly on intuition. This realm allows for a synthesis of the logical aspects of the design and a visceral understanding of the experiences—transcending the theoretical. This process is important to the overall development of ideas to such a great extent that it often preempts my consideration of the visual form. The more ethereal aspects of the intimate experiences—the sound, smells, tactile qualities, and moods—are often more important than the object itself. The act of seeing through the window or entering the door is considered first. An architecture develops that, in its deliberate simplicity, gently nudges people on to a more engaging multisensory experience and heightens the awareness of actually being there."[13]

One of Joy's current projects, the Page One Resort Hotel, is a step towards a larger scale and a further intensification and abstraction of expression. Designed as a collaborative project,[14] this luxury resort sits in a spectacular landscape in southern Utah. The images of the project have a primordial and futuristic atmosphere. In them architecture has been reduced to its minimum presence—one has a feeling that architecture enables us to confront the beauty of natural phenomena, in the sense that a mountain path, as a human artifact, leads us to places of extraordinary beauty. The guests of the resort are guided to the overwhelming context of nature, as the first man and woman confronted nature in their innocent nudity.

Joy's response to the client's question—How will this incredible site inform your approach to the design?—reveals the architect's objectives, but also illustrates his way of thinking: "The land is at once a place of respect for all its vitality and a place to inhabit and experience for all it ignites in our soul. The real allure of the land at Page One is quietly hidden in its wilderness. The land moves one to recall all that is pure and wild about the American West. With our twenty-first-century eyes we can see the beauty but from a perspective largely isolated from the land. To truly feel the land one must experience it up close. With every encounter with newly built elements one's perception of the wildness of the place will be altered. How can these man-made elements contribute to the maintenance of and perhaps the enhancement of the richness and wildness of the place? It is possible that, by giving people a more raw experience with the land/place, we can help them connect with the place, past and present, in a more profound way. Focusing primarily on the present and creating very pure sensual experiences can achieve this. Light—fire—mass—translucency—nature—earth—the moon—the sun—sound/quiet—protectiveness/ openness. By enhancing the experiences of these primal elements, we can create an architecture that in its simplicity will entice people to come to Page One and gently nudge them on to a more engaging encounter with the land."[15]

Joy's ethical stance is firm: the task of architecture is not to entertain us, or to suffocate us with impressions of witty formal inventions, but to create the silence, calmness, and concentration that enable us to experience the beauty of the world and life around us. He possesses a humility that is rare in today's architectural world of arrogance and self-centeredness: "I am thinking more and more these days about not just the making of architecture, but being an Architect. There are many architects in the world whose work I admire on a formal level, but their presence in the world is neither authentic nor giving of themselves as Architects."[16]

The literary description written for the Project Design Document focuses on a heightened sensory experience. The text is an experiential description of the still nonexistent building through the senses of a fictitious visitor to the resort, starting with one's impressions upon arrival: "Your car leaves the highway, the rumble of the dirt road is felt, and the indication that you have arrived at the resort is marked by a simple yet exquisite metal 'ranch' gate and a curving entry road that brings you up against the tall, mysterious sphinx-like rock formation that signals your arrival somewhere special. The sheer verticality of this rock formation mysteriously guards and screens the view beyond. Passing by a horse stable on your right, the guests arrive around the bend of this entry rock and suddenly a distant view to wider landscape reveals itself. The road then straightens out and heads towards a beautiful rock formation, an island in the midst of the 'rock garden.' A continuous fire emanates, sparkling reflections from up on the rock, luring the tired traveler to explore further."[17]

The description continues at length through the sequence of spaces, yet hardly mentions any architectural structures; instead it points out views, feelings, and sensations revealed and articulated by architecture. This literary account registers haptic experiences—sounds, smells, and temperature differences with the same weight as visual impressions. Joy's architecture creates a clear rhythm between active and passive, foreground and background, diminutive and grand. His sense of pause and restraint seems to derive from his experiences as a musician: "As a drummer I was always more interested in the ways to make the music 'feel' a certain way than in attempts to be flashy. Like in the music of Miles Davis—the silence is often more profound than the sound."[18]

During the fall of 2000, Joy taught a Studio at Harvard University entitled "The Five Senses," where he experimented with narrative writing as a means to communicate architectural intentions and experiences. "As the students prepared to bring their models and drawings into the review space, I told them they couldn't bring anything. They were required to verbally describe their projects as if they were telling a close friend about their fantastic encounter with the built reality. We later tested their verbal intentions with their progressing designs."[19]

Joy's current teaching and lecturing in widening circles is clearly launching him to another orbit. His personal design sensibility and authentic architectural language, developed and refined in the unique context of the Arizona desert, await the opportunity to be applied to completely new contexts, functions, and scales. The desert in his architectural equation will be replaced by new types of landscape or urban settings to generate profound and enticing architecture.

NOTES

1 John van Dyke, *The Desert: Further Studies in Natural Appearances* (New York: Scribner's Sons, 1901). As quoted in Reyner Banham, *Scenes in America Deserta* (Salt Lake City: Gibbs M. Smith, 1982), 154–5.

2 Gaston Bachelard, *Water and Dreams: An Essay on the Imagination of Matter* (Dallas: Pegasus Foundation, 1983), 5.

3 The demolition began in 1993 at the Davis-Monthan Air Force Base in Tucson, Arizona. The crushing of war planes is a way of complying with the Strategic Arms Reduction Treaty. The crushed planes are left on the site for ninety days to be observed and verified by Russian satellites. James Corner and Alex S. Mac Lean, *Taking Measures Across the American Landscape* (New Haven and London: Yale University Press, 1996), 96, 99.

4 Rick Joy studied art for two years before starting his studies in architecture, but he considers his experiences as a musician more important for his sensibilities as an architect. Rick Joy, telephone conversation with Juhani Pallasmaa, 17 November 2001.

5 Rick Joy, letter to Juhani Pallasmaa, 20 November 2001.

6 Excerpt from Rick Joy and Max Underwood, Rick Joy Architects Firm Profile, 2001.

7 T. S. Eliot, "Tradition and the Individual Talent," in *Selected Essays*, new edition (New York: Harcourt, Brace & World, 1984). As quoted in Colin St. John Wilson, "The Historical Sense," *Architectural Review* (October 1984): 68.

8 Rick Joy, letter to clients encouraging their consideration of modern experiential architecture, September 1994.

9 Rammed earth is composed of selected earth (without water-absorbing clays) mixed with three percent Portland cement. The mixture is compacted into formwork reminiscent of concrete forms. The walls require firm foundations because the slightest movement causes cracks in them. The interior surfaces are coated with a clear sealer in order to prevent dust from rubbing off. Joy credits his technique of employing rammed earth to Quentin Branch, who has refined the process and served as a consultant and contractor on the Convent Avenue Studios project. An eighteen-inch thickness of earth has proved ideal for the south, with thicker walls required for east and west, as the solar heat absorbed during the day is not radiated to the rooms until after sunset when the desert night temperature turns chilly.

10 Rick Joy, letter to Juhani Pallasmaa, 15 November 2001.

11 Rick Joy, interview with Paul Makovsky, *Metropolis* (April 2000): 75. Joy answered the questions, "How important is sustainable design to your work?" and "What do you see as major cultural challenges for architects in the new millennium?"

12 Joseph Brodsky, *Watermark* (London: Penguin Books, 1992), 70.

13 Rick Joy, "Designer Statement" written for the Chrysler Awards and National Design Awards submittals, 2001.

14 The project was co-designed by Rick Joy, Wendell Burnette, Marwan Al-Sayed, and Michael Boucher.

15 Rick Joy, letter to Bernt Kuhlman, Page One Resort Hotel client, 2000.

16 Rick Joy, letter to Juhani Pallasmaa, 31 October 2001; comments inspired by an article by Herbert Muschamp.

17 Descriptive text from the Page One Resort Hotel Preliminary Design Document, co-designed by Rick Joy, Wendell Burnette, Marwan Al-Sayed, and Michael Boucher.

18 Rick Joy, letter to Juhani Pallasmaa, 15 November 2001.

19 Ibid.

IMAGE CREDITS

1 Germano Celant, *Michael Heizer* (Milan: Fondazione Prada, 1997), 179.

2 James Corner and Alex S. MacLean, *Taking Measures Across the American Landscape* (New Haven: Yale University Press, 1996), 99.

3 Bill Timmerman

4 Bruce Brooks Pfeiffer and Robert Wojtowicz, ed., *Frank Lloyd Wright and Lewis Mumford: Thirty Years of Correspondence* (New York: Princeton Architectural Press, 2001), plate 5.

5 William Lesch

6 Bill Timmerman

7 Tim Street Porter, *Casa Mexicana* (New York: Stewart, Tabori & Chang, 1989), 183.

8 William J. R. Curtis, *Le Corbusier: Ideas and Forms* (London: Phaidon Press), 1986.

9 Peter Noever, editor, *James Turrell: The Other Horizon* (Vienna: MAK and Ostfildern-Ruit: Hatje Cantz Verlag), 1999.

10 Photo by Karl-Eric Olsson Snogerod in *Sigurd Lewerentz 1885–1975: The Dilemma of Classicism* (London: Architectural Association, 1988), 85.

11 Françoise Fromonot, *Glenn Murcutt: Buildings and Projects* (New York: Whitney Library of Design, 1995), 100.

12 Permanent collection of the Chinati Foundation, Marfa, Texas. Photograph by Florian Holzherr.

13 *Morandi* (New York: Rizzoli, 1988), 66.

14 Rick Joy, Wendell Burnette, Marwan Al-Sayed, and Michael Boucher.

PROJECTS

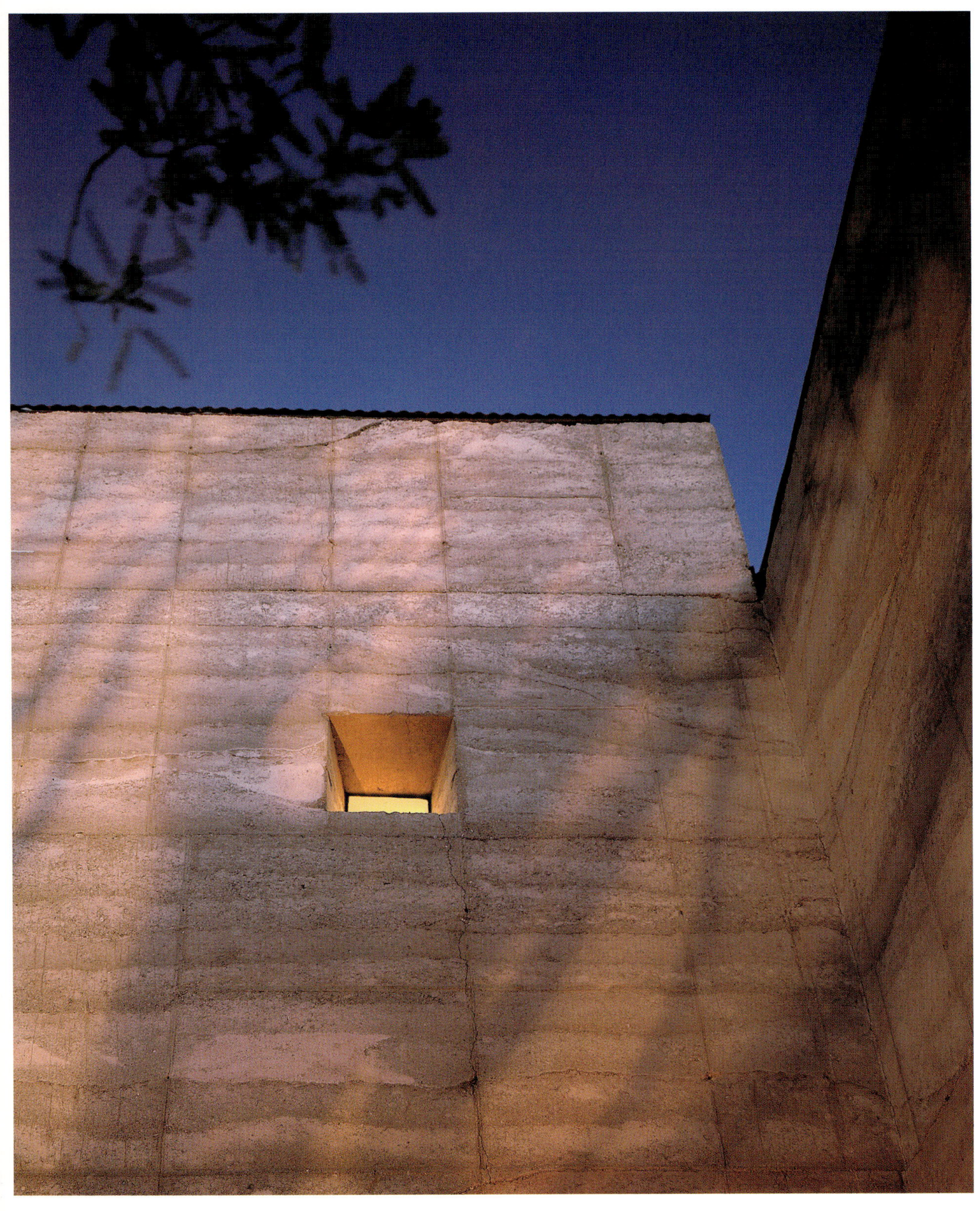

When I first walked the site, it was essentially a ruin, in fragile condition and in a fragile place. Convent Avenue is in one of the oldest neighborhoods in the Southwest, the Barrio Histórico listed on the National Register of Historic Places. First settled in the early 1800s, the area is rich with Mexican American culture. Tightly clustered courtyard residences and businesses share common walls and outside spaces. Mid-century "urban renewal" efforts reduced this neighborhood, among others, to only twenty blocks.

CONVENT AVENUE STUDIOS

Only a twelve-foot-high street wall, which was once the front of a series of historic row houses, and a portion of one of the houses remained on the site. The project involved restoring all that was left of the historic elements and carefully inserting three small loft houses and the required infrastructure. The project made a clear distinction between old and new throughout, being careful not to blur the historic record.

The restored street wall serves as the entry to the complex. Along the streetscape, passersby can see through the old door and window openings in the historic wall to new lush courtyards with fountains, large native mesquite trees, and creosote bush.

Each of the three new houses is a simple, wedge-shaped, two-story, shed-roofed building. These forms, when carefully placed on the site, create a matrix of private and semiprivate courtyards and pedestrian walkways. Their shapes help to resolve many of the encroachment and sun access issues their neighbors articulated. Landscape walls of chartreuse green, inspired by the color of new mesquite buds, serve as playful way-finding elements in this maze of external spaces.

The walls of the new houses are constructed of compacted earth. Rough-sawn wood elements complete the shell of each structure while more refined elements finish the interiors.

The little rusty steel laundry shed toward the rear of the property is my first stand-alone building as an architect.

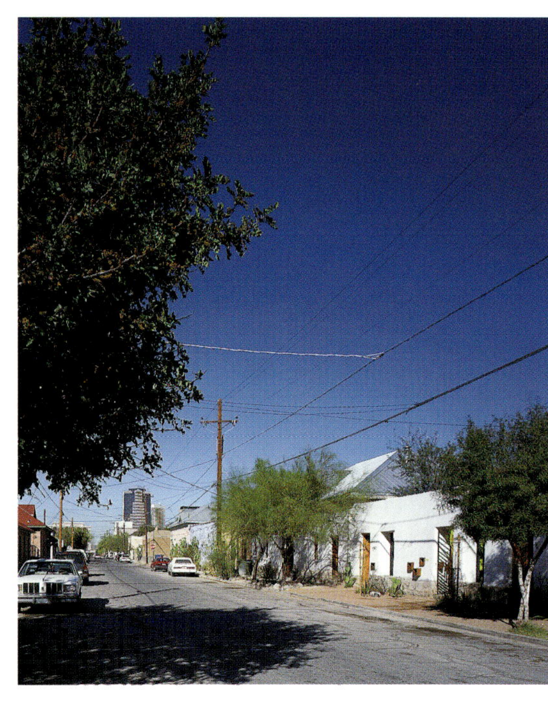

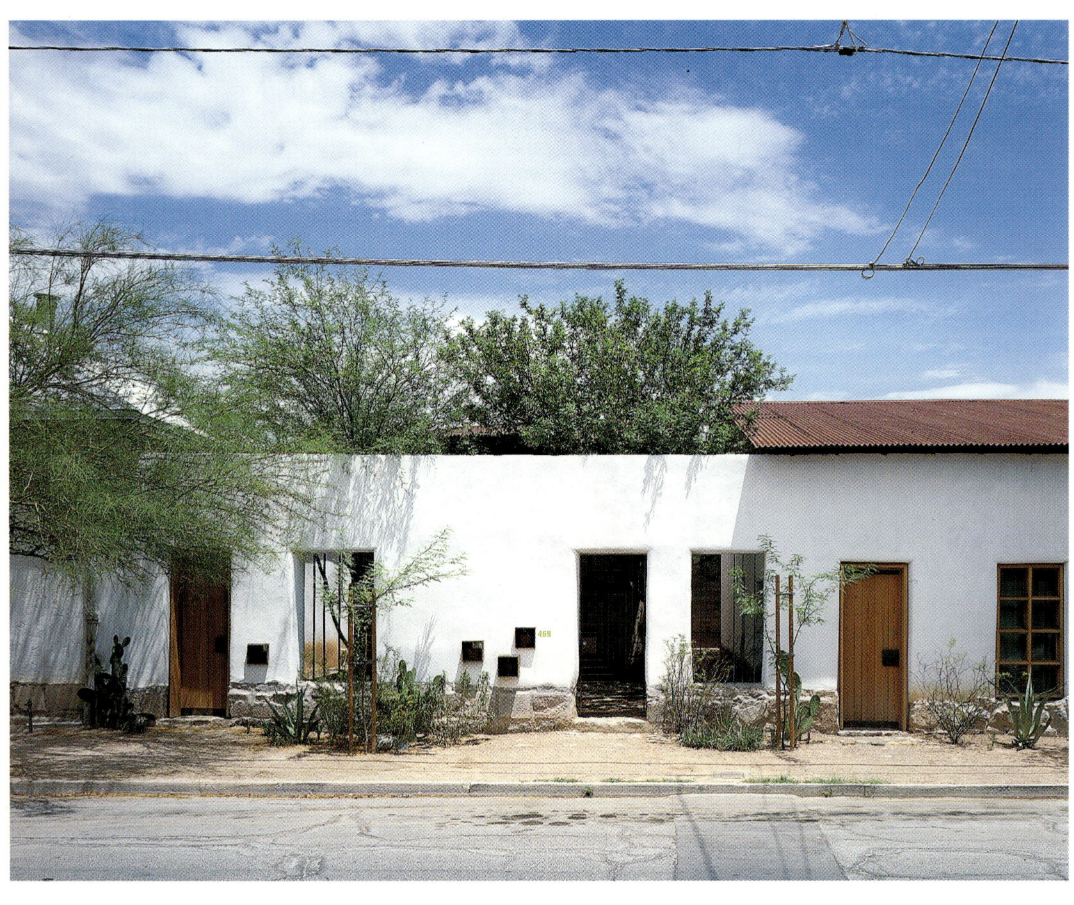

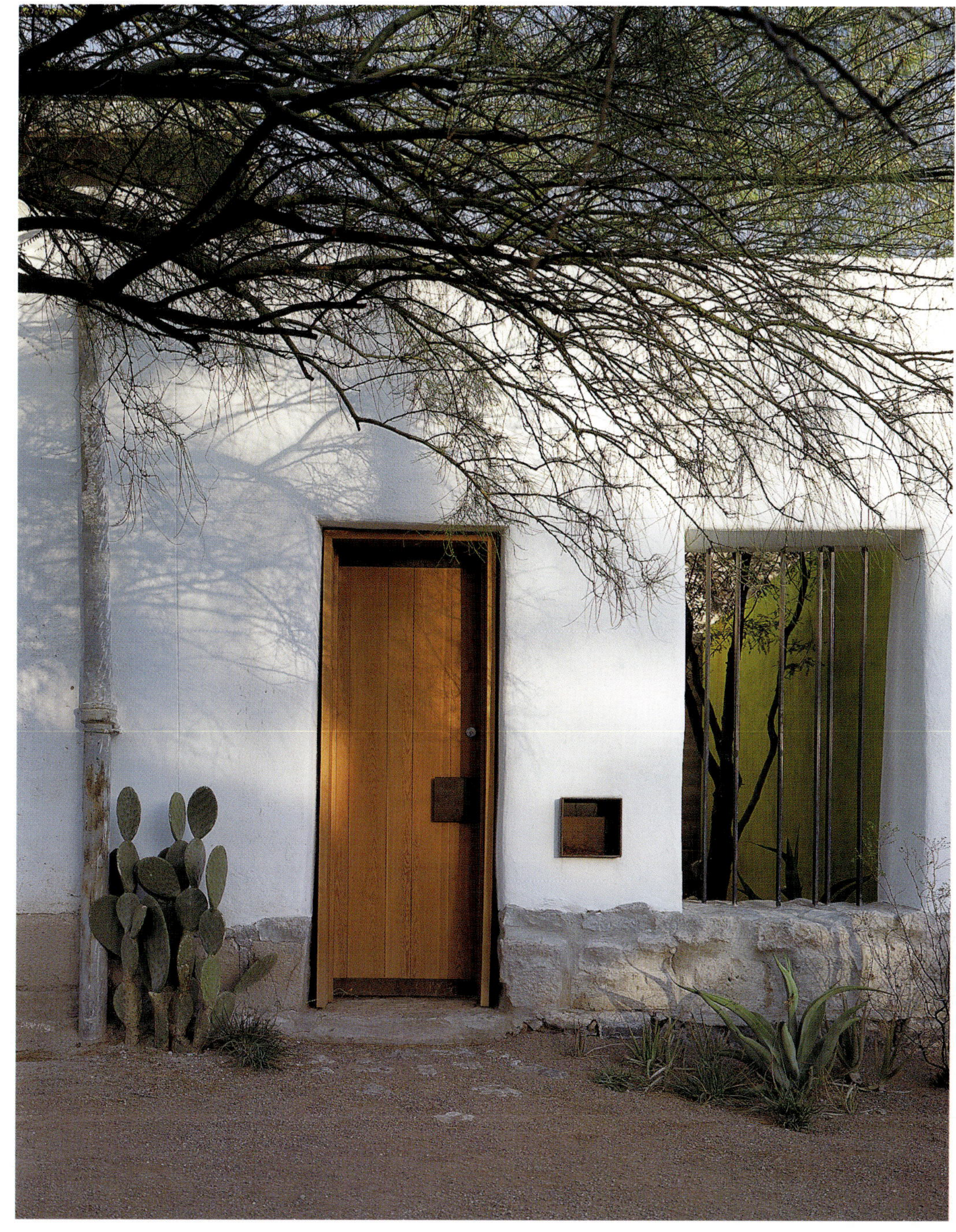

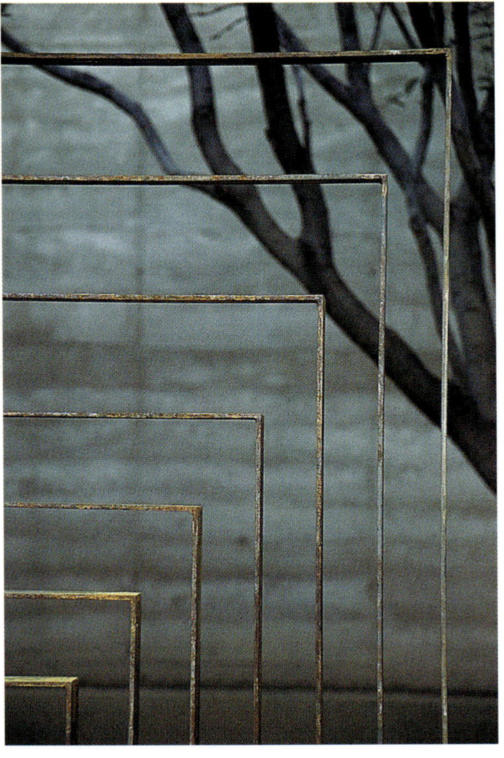

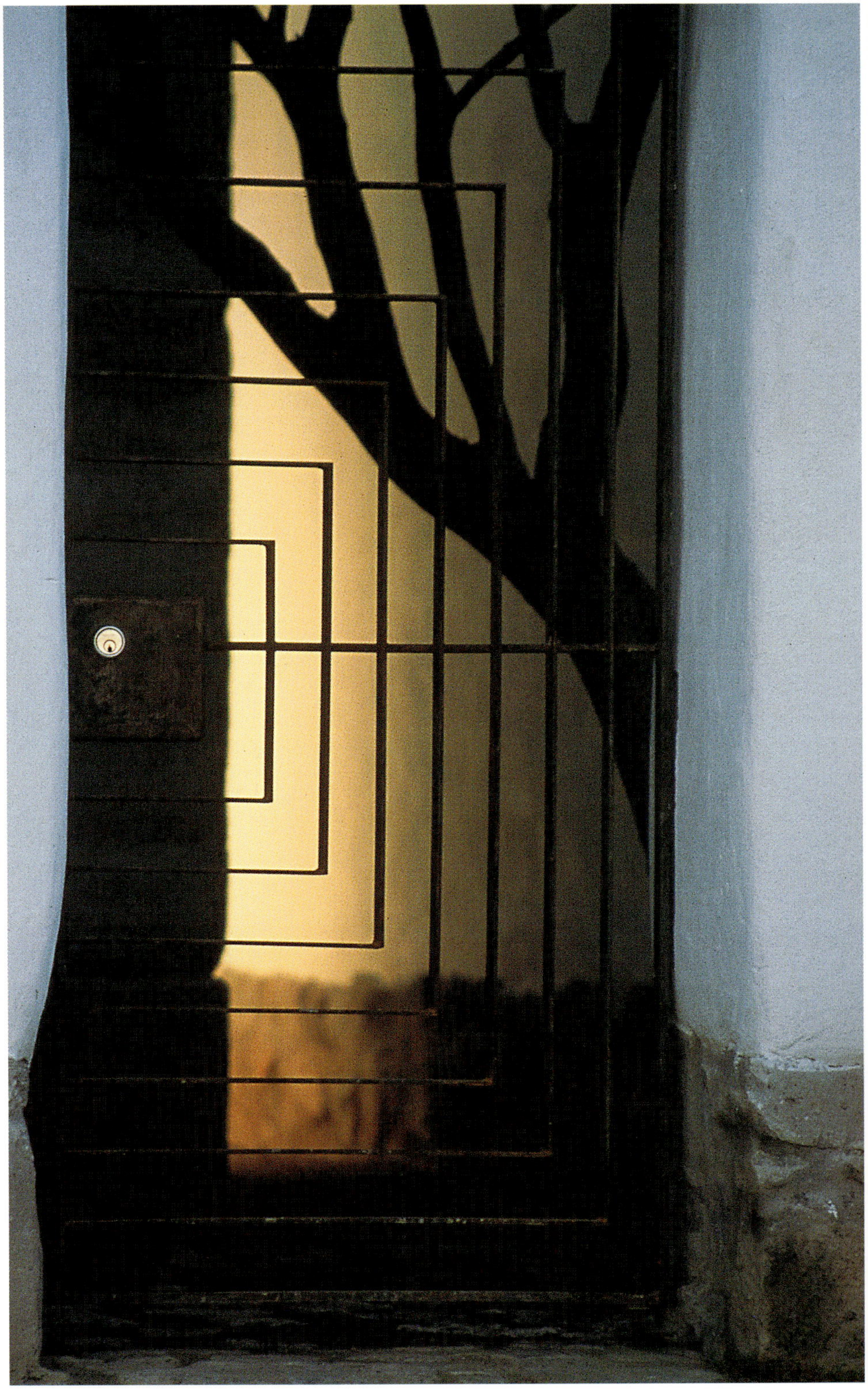

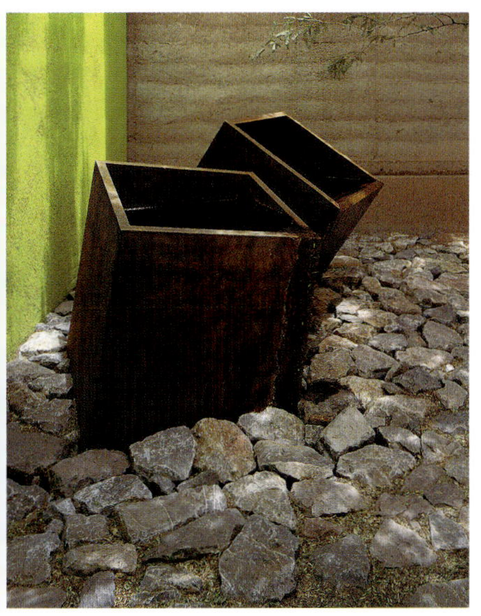

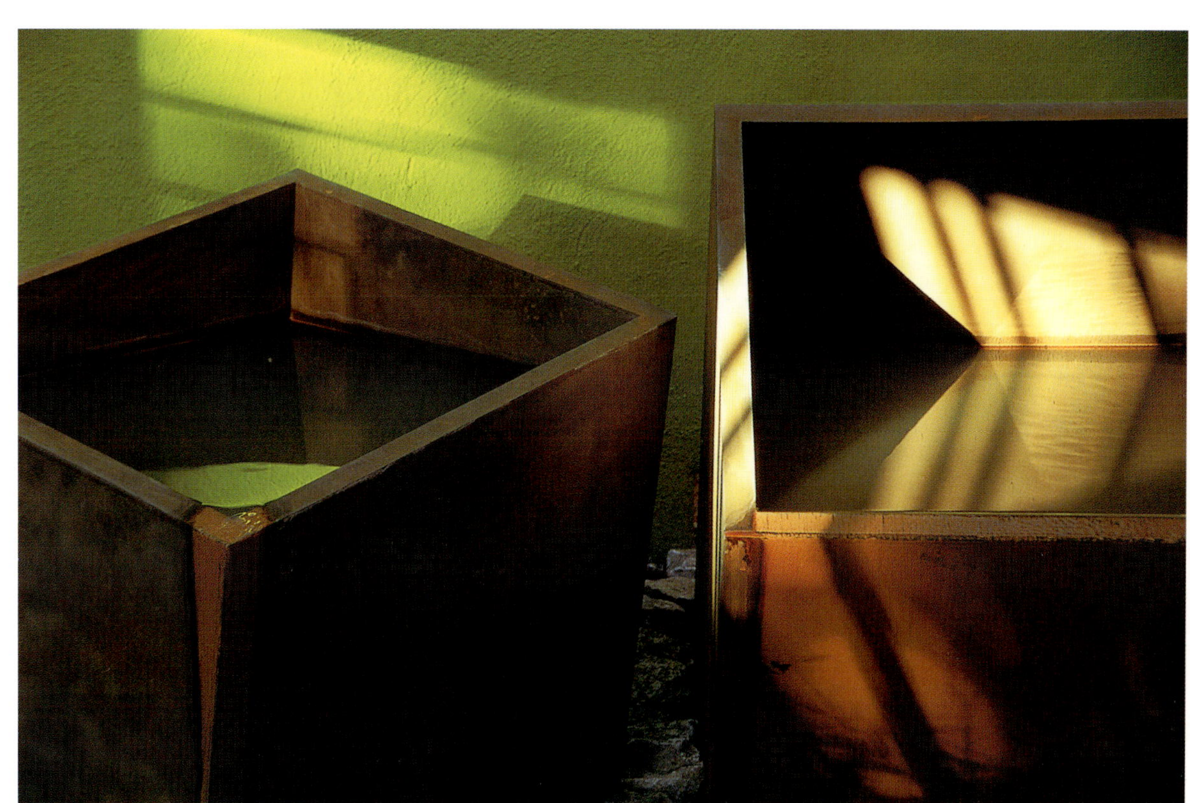

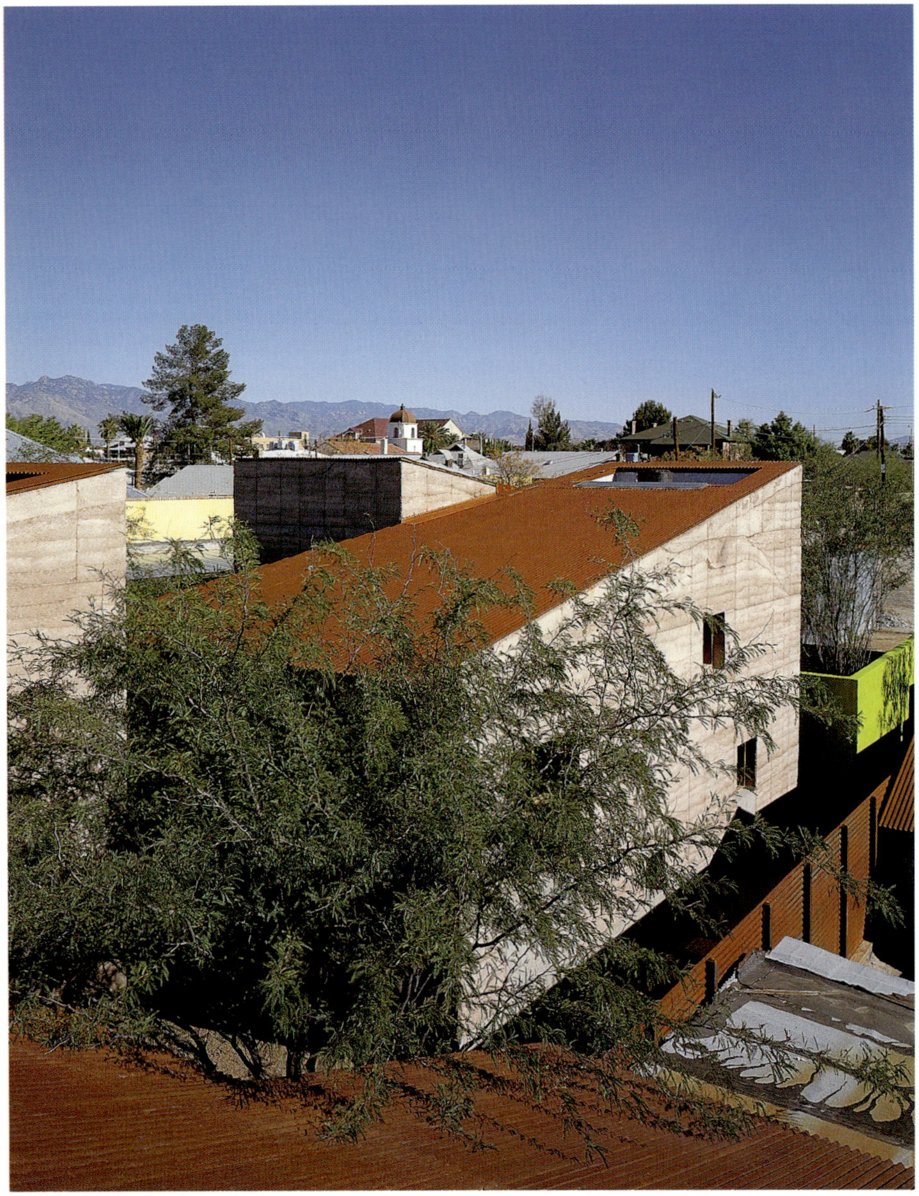

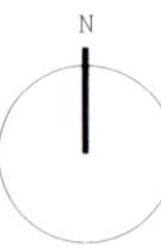
N

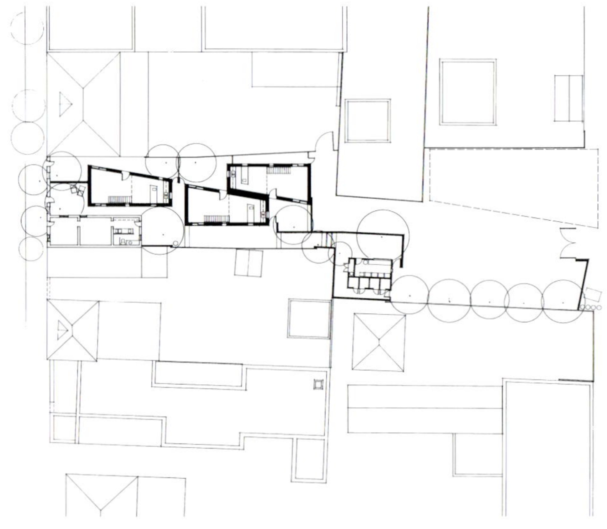

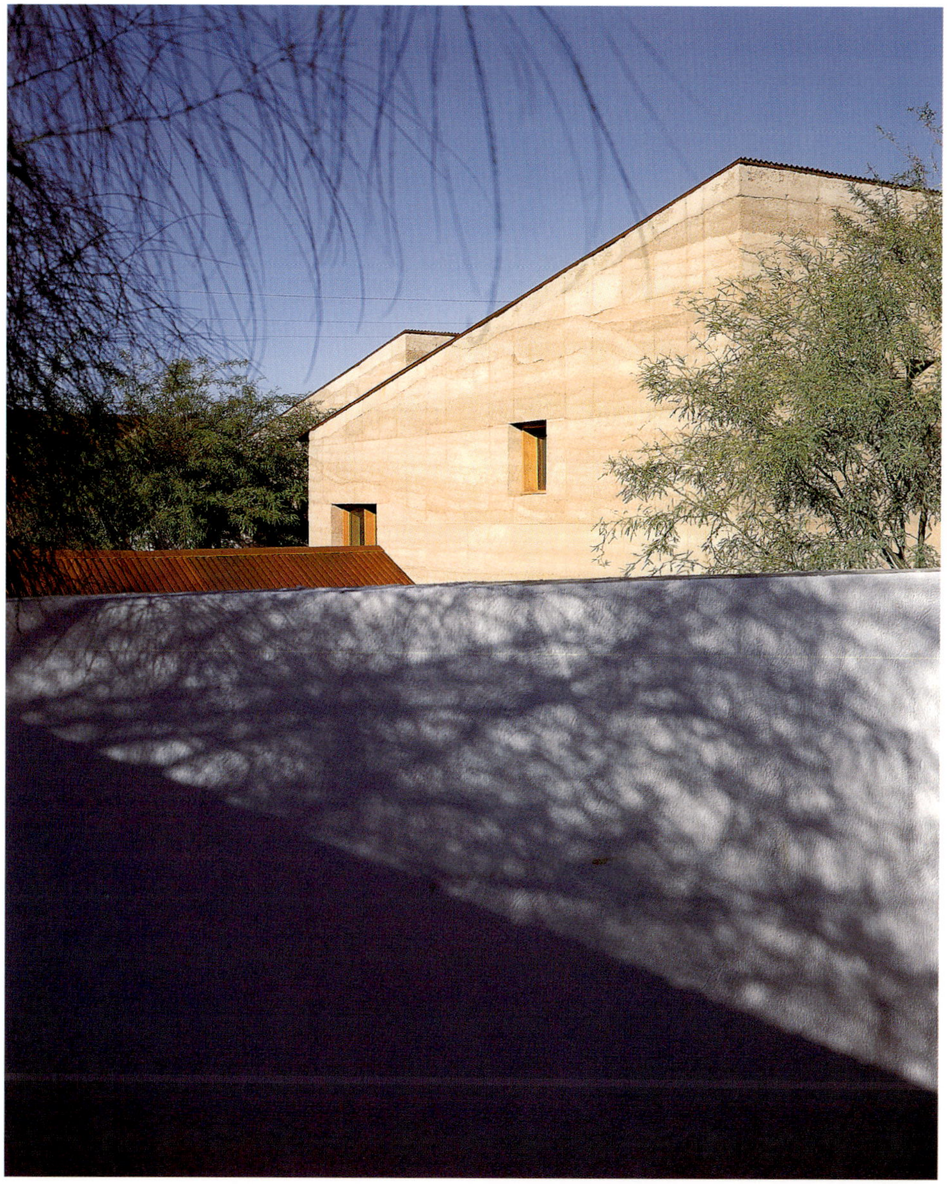

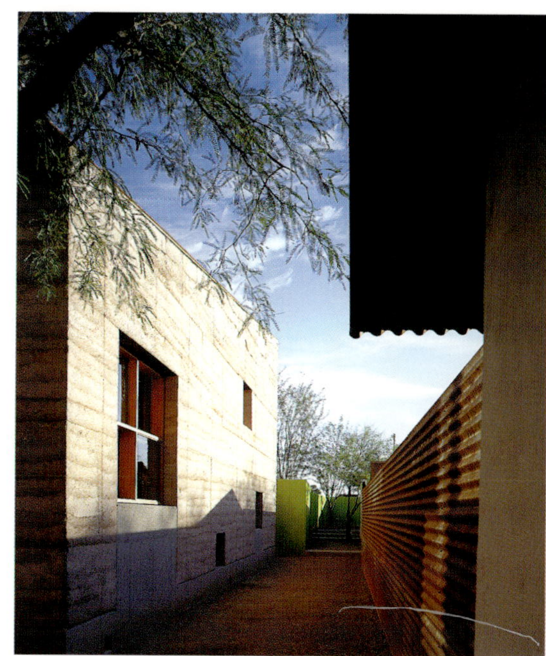

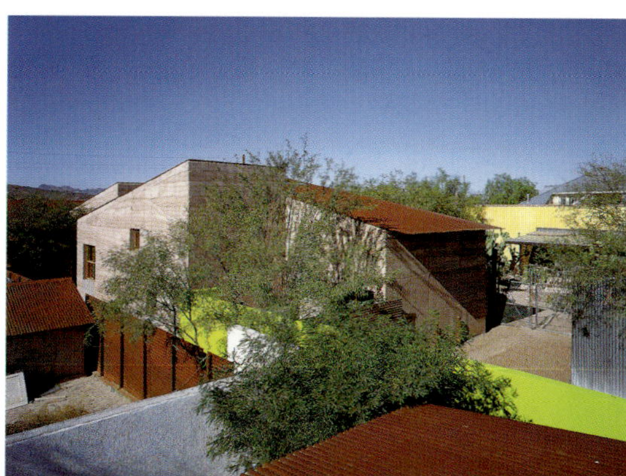

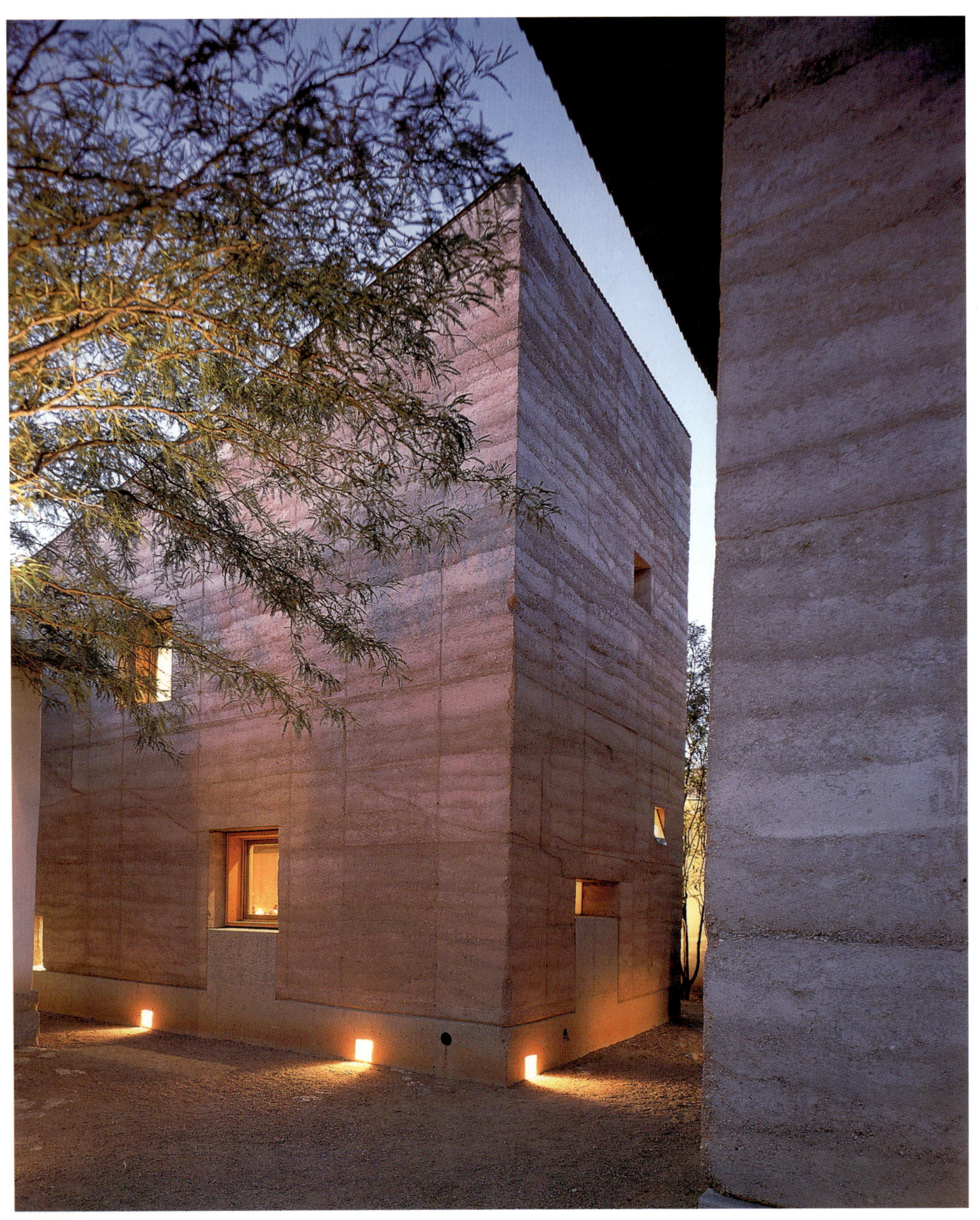

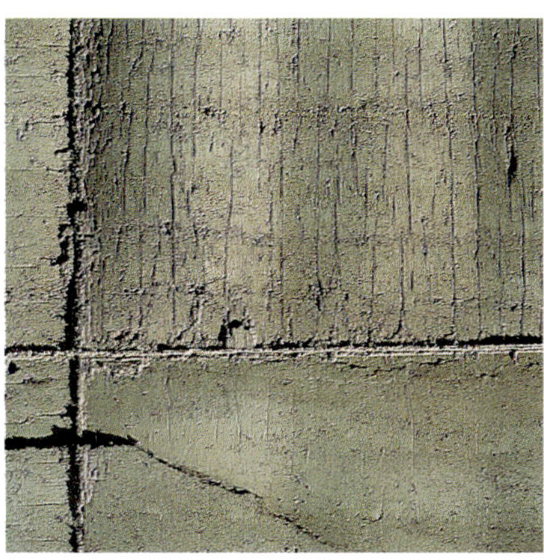

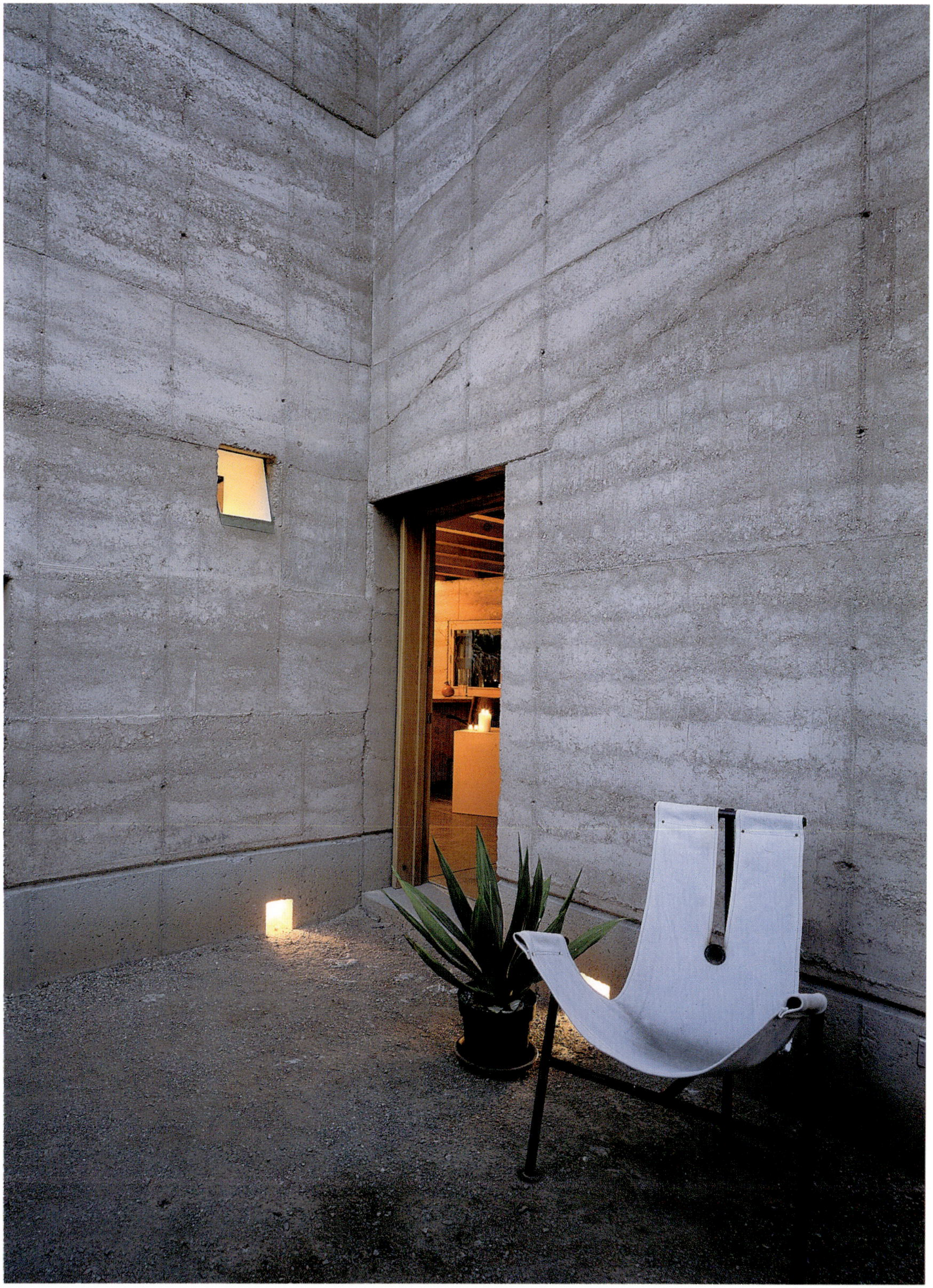

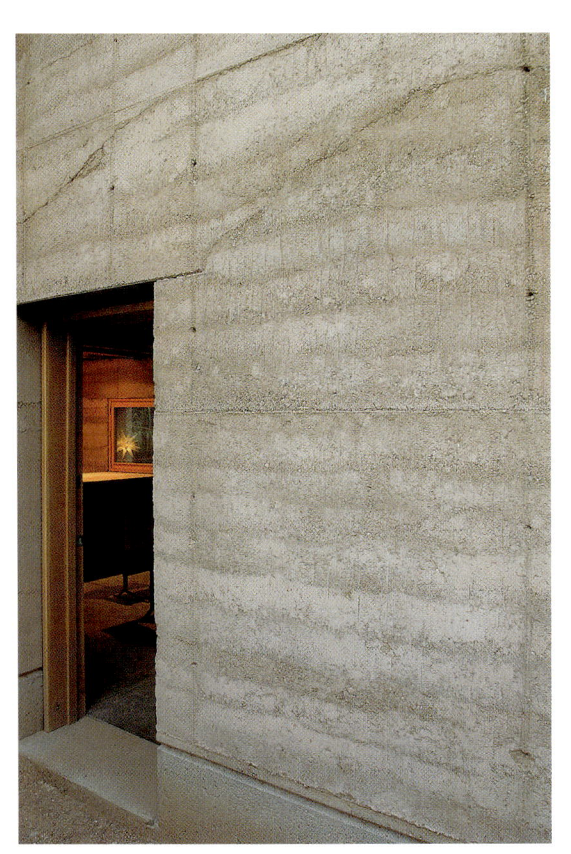

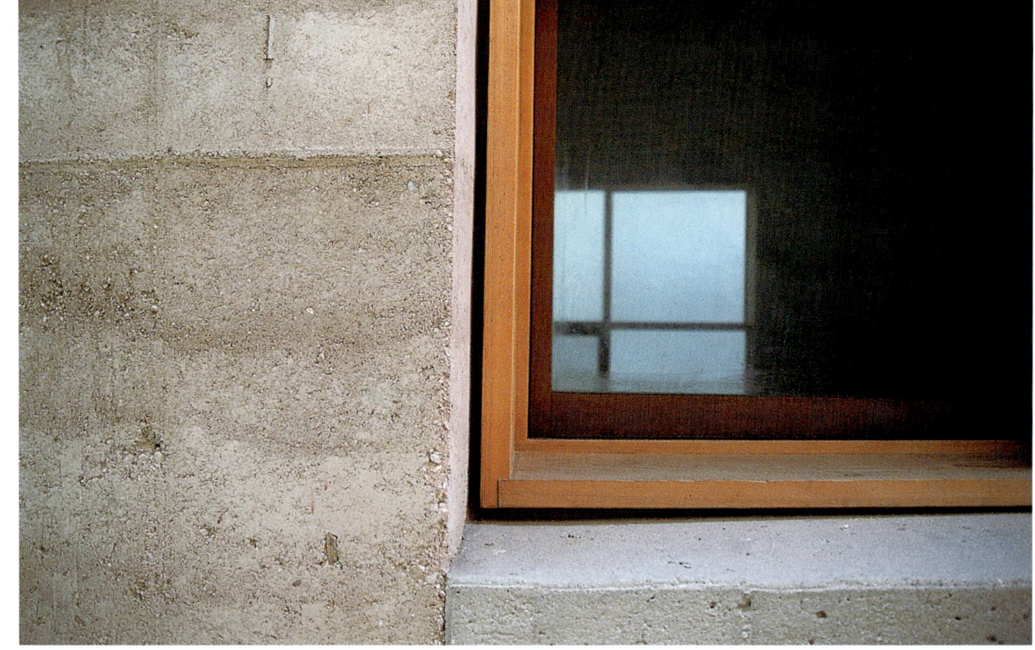

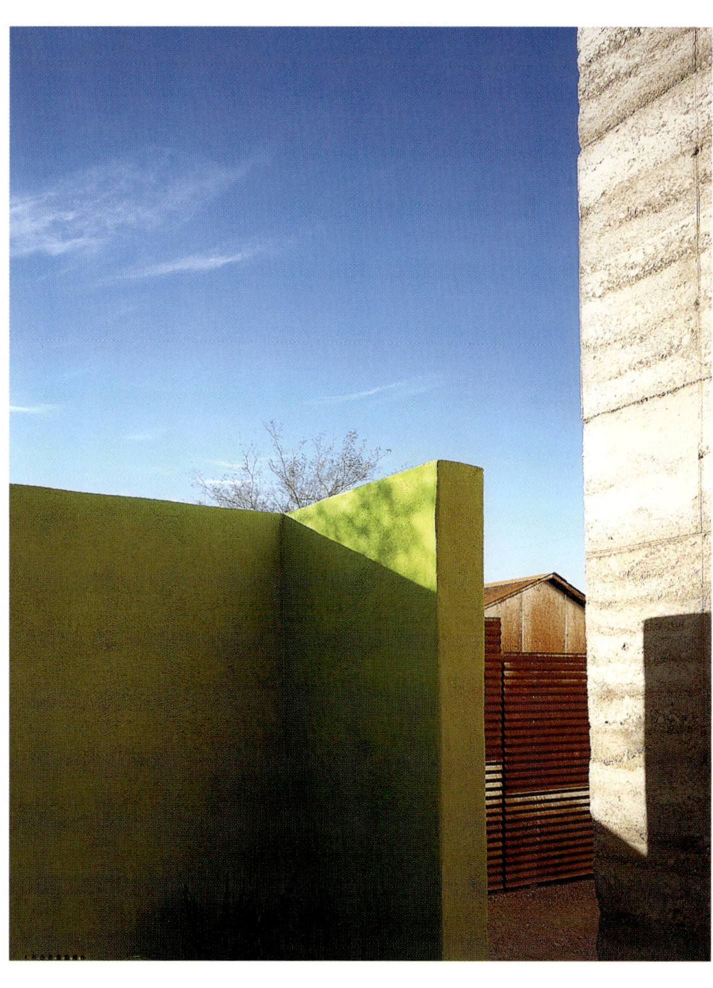

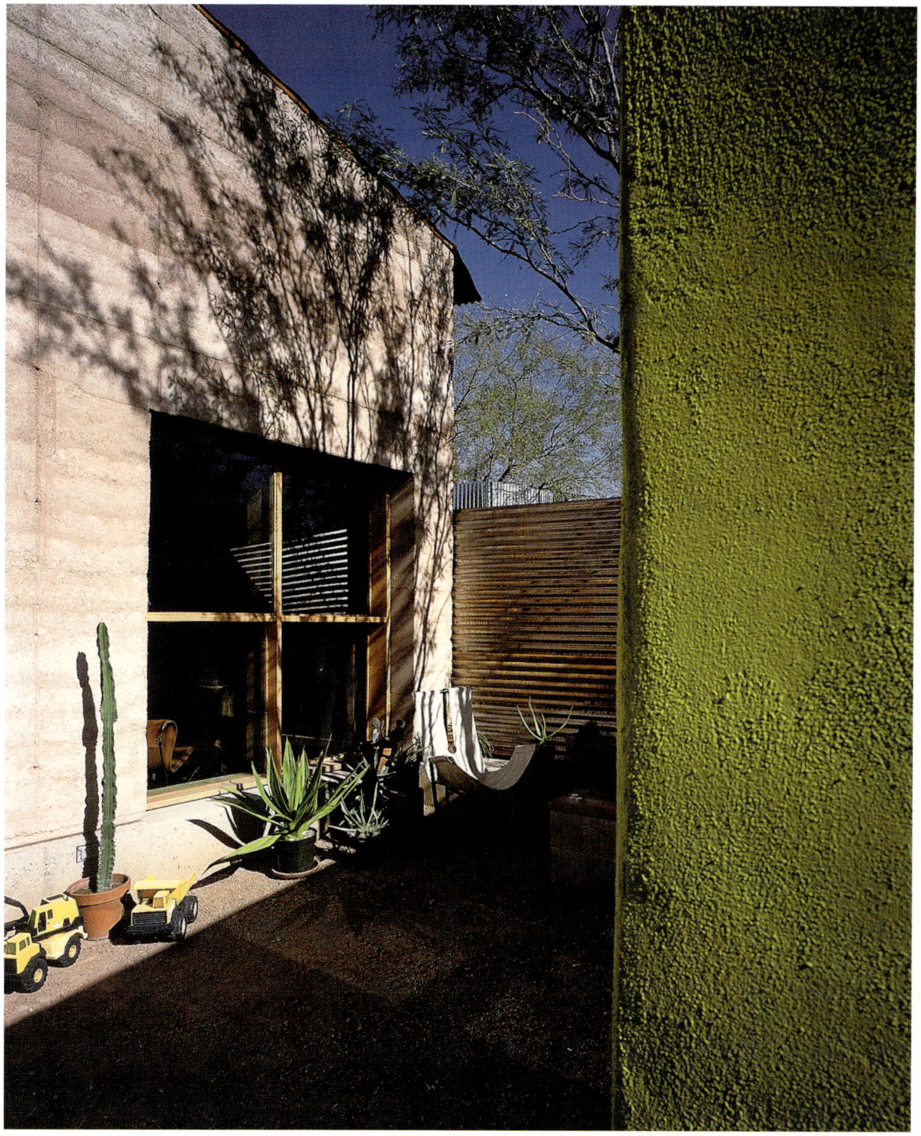

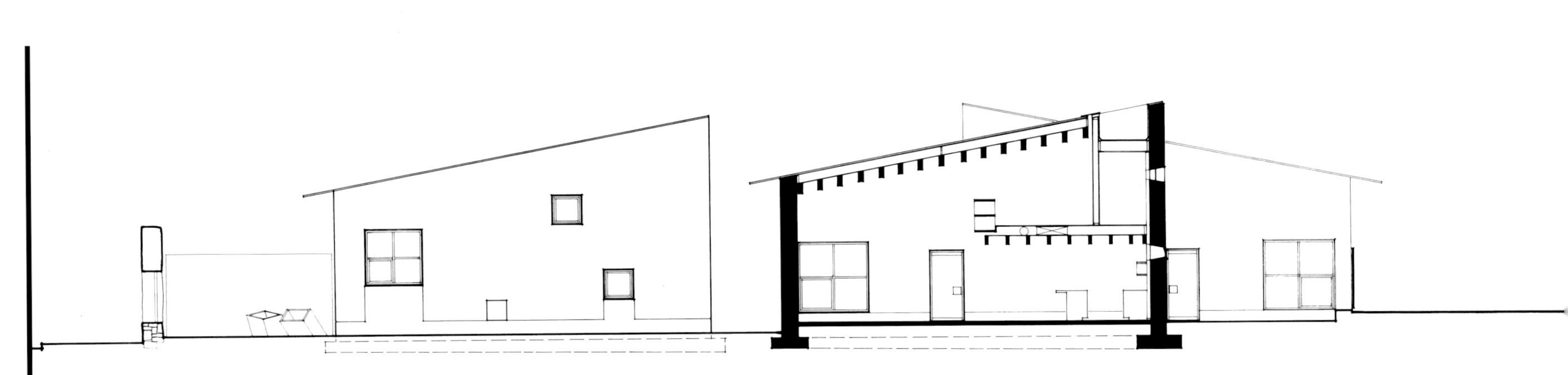

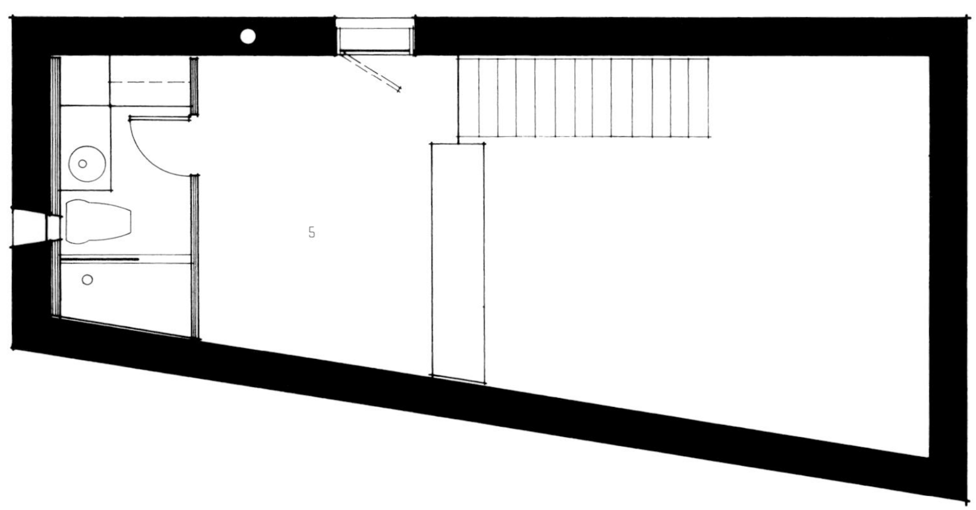

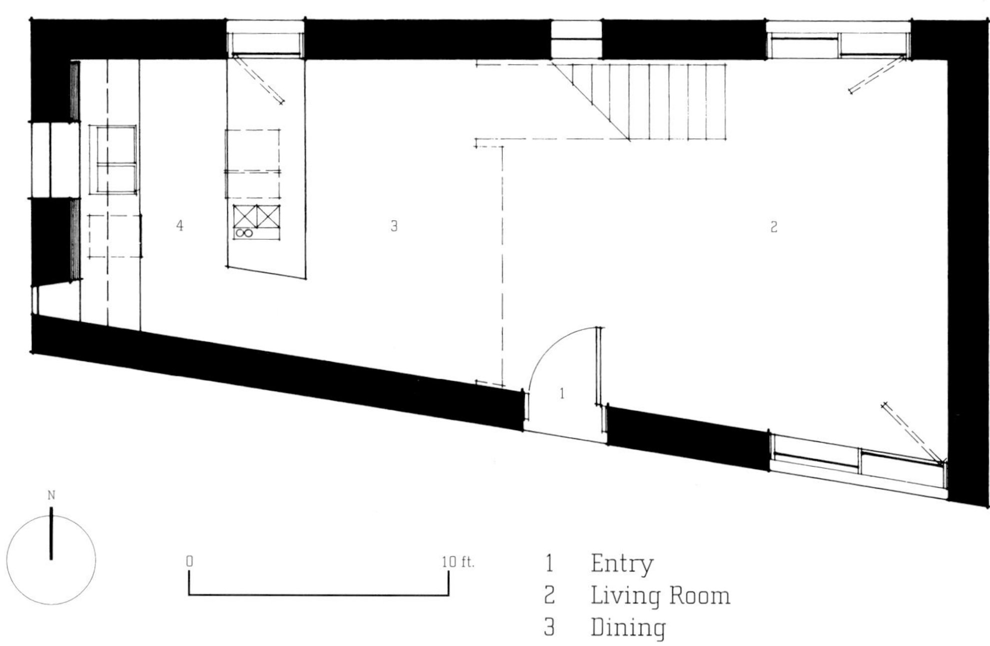

1 Entry
2 Living Room
3 Dining
4 Kitchen
5 Sleeping Loft

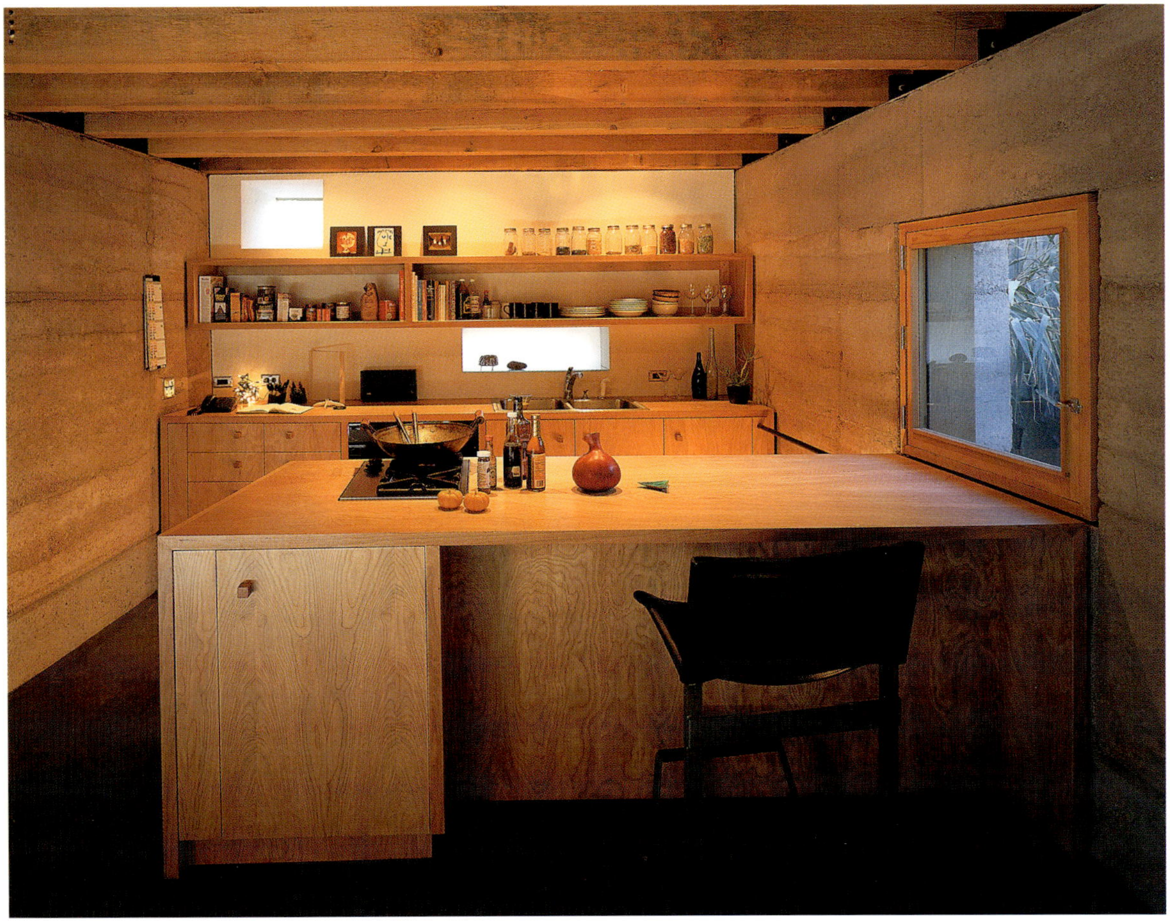

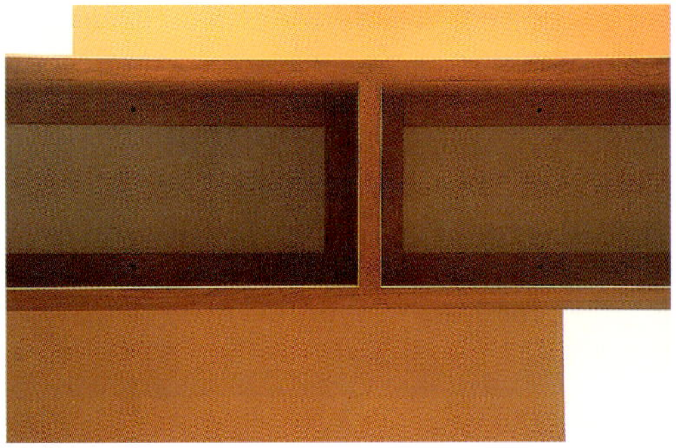

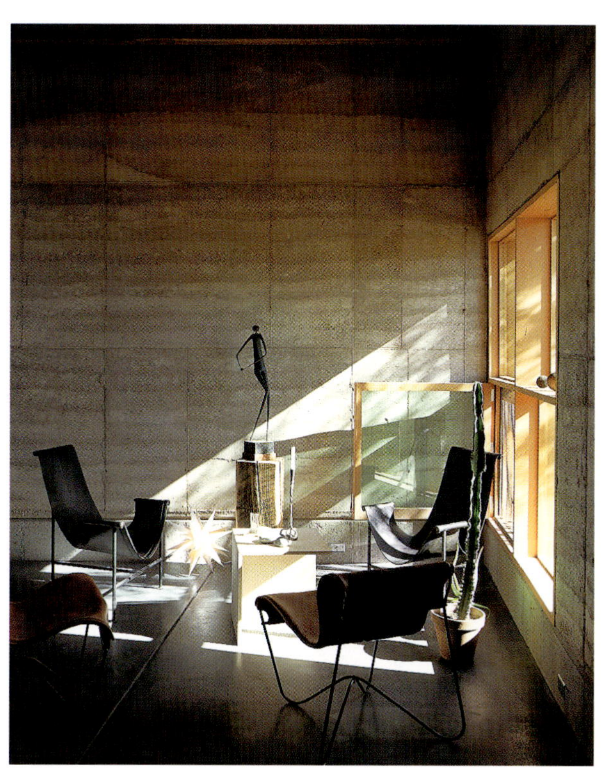

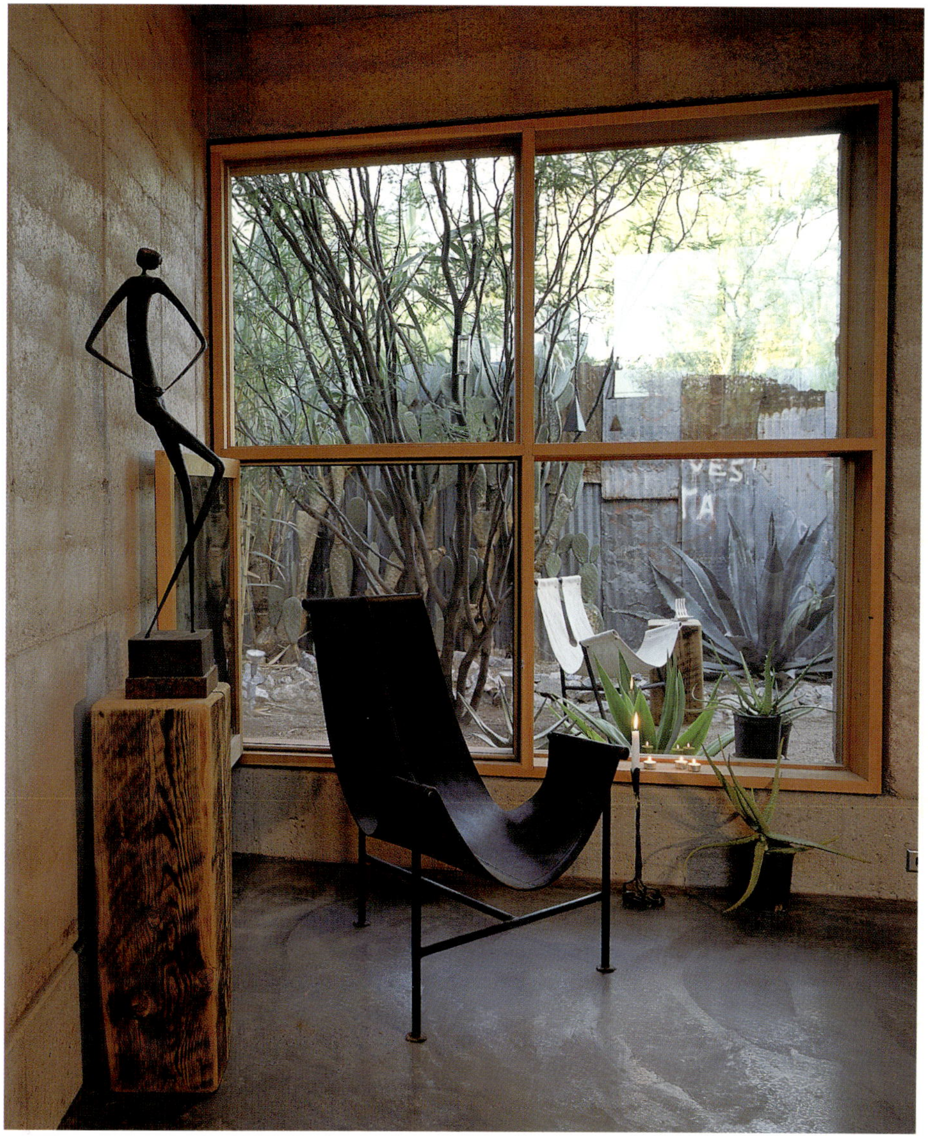

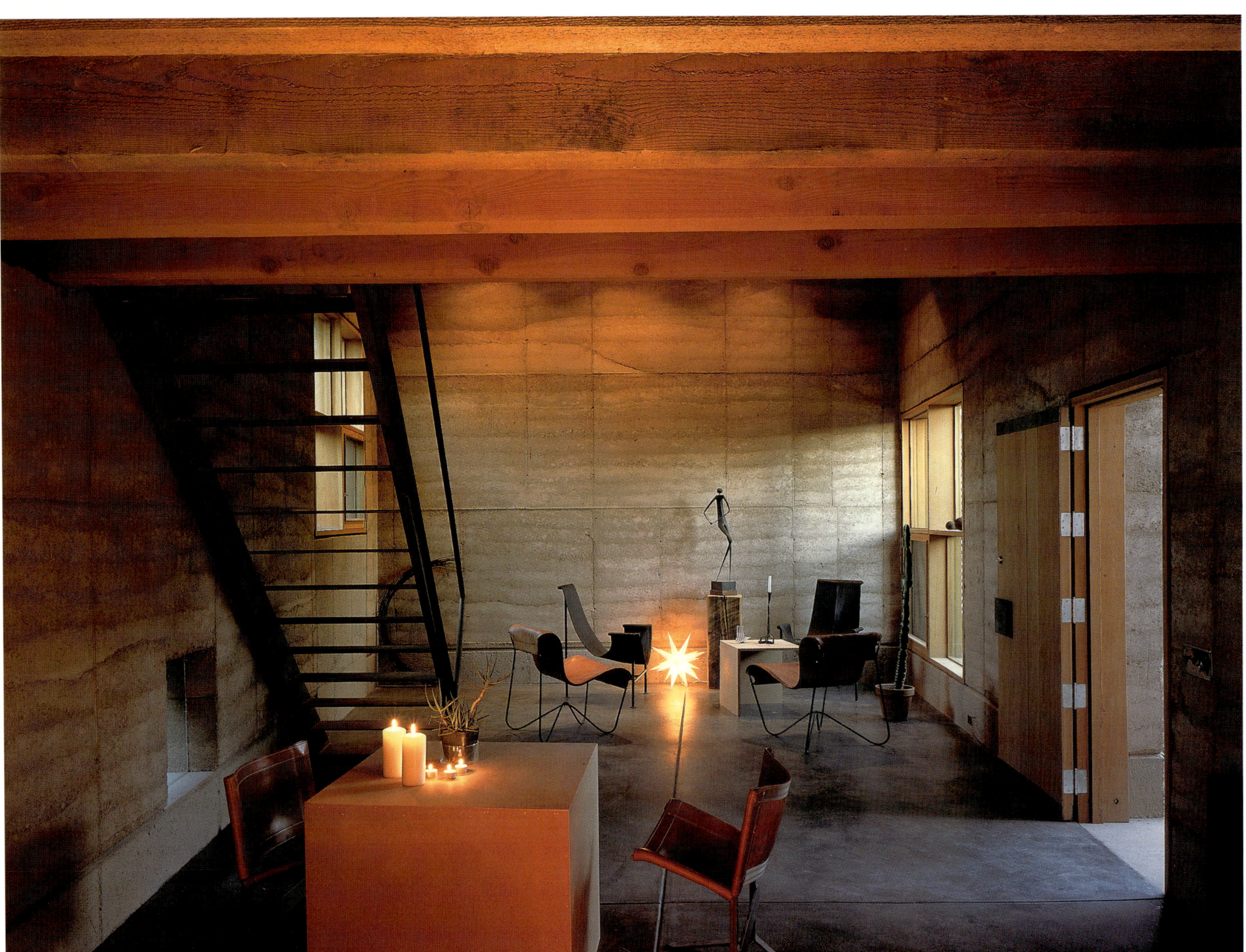

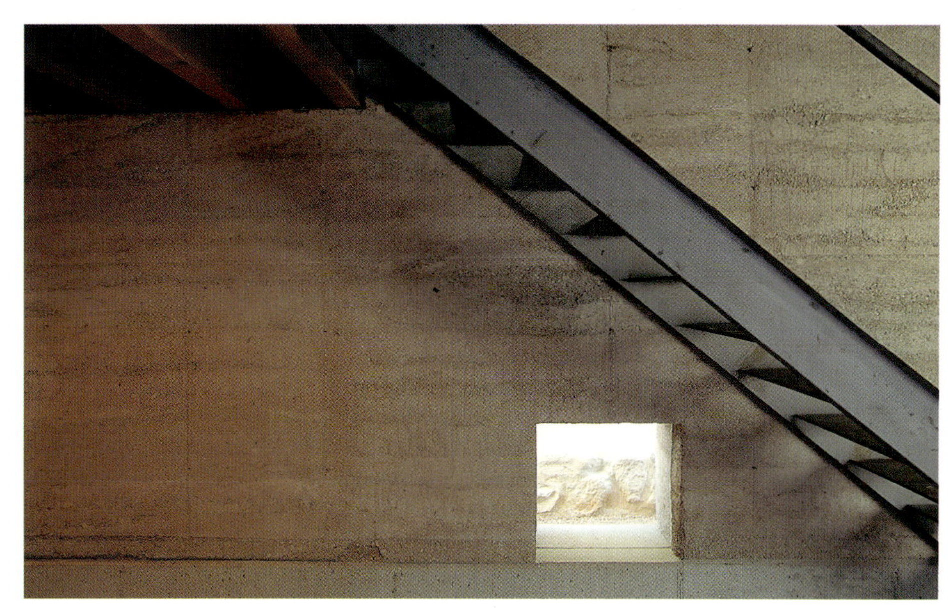

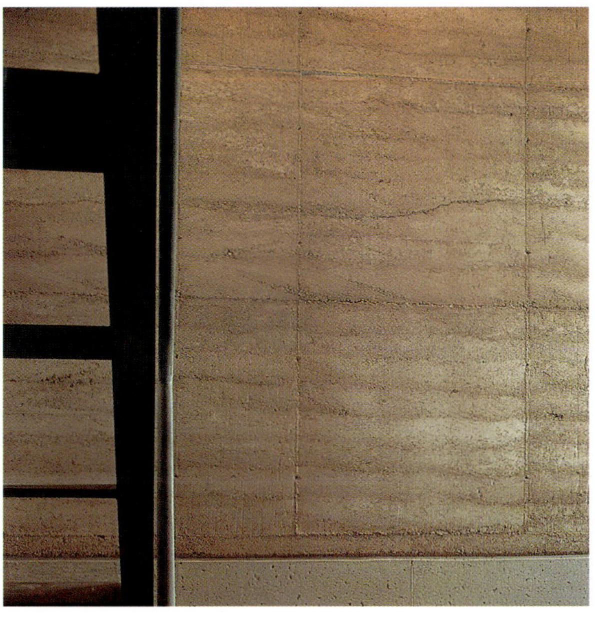

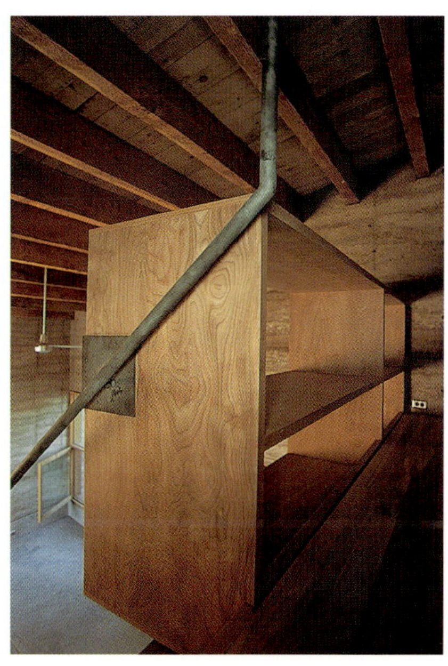

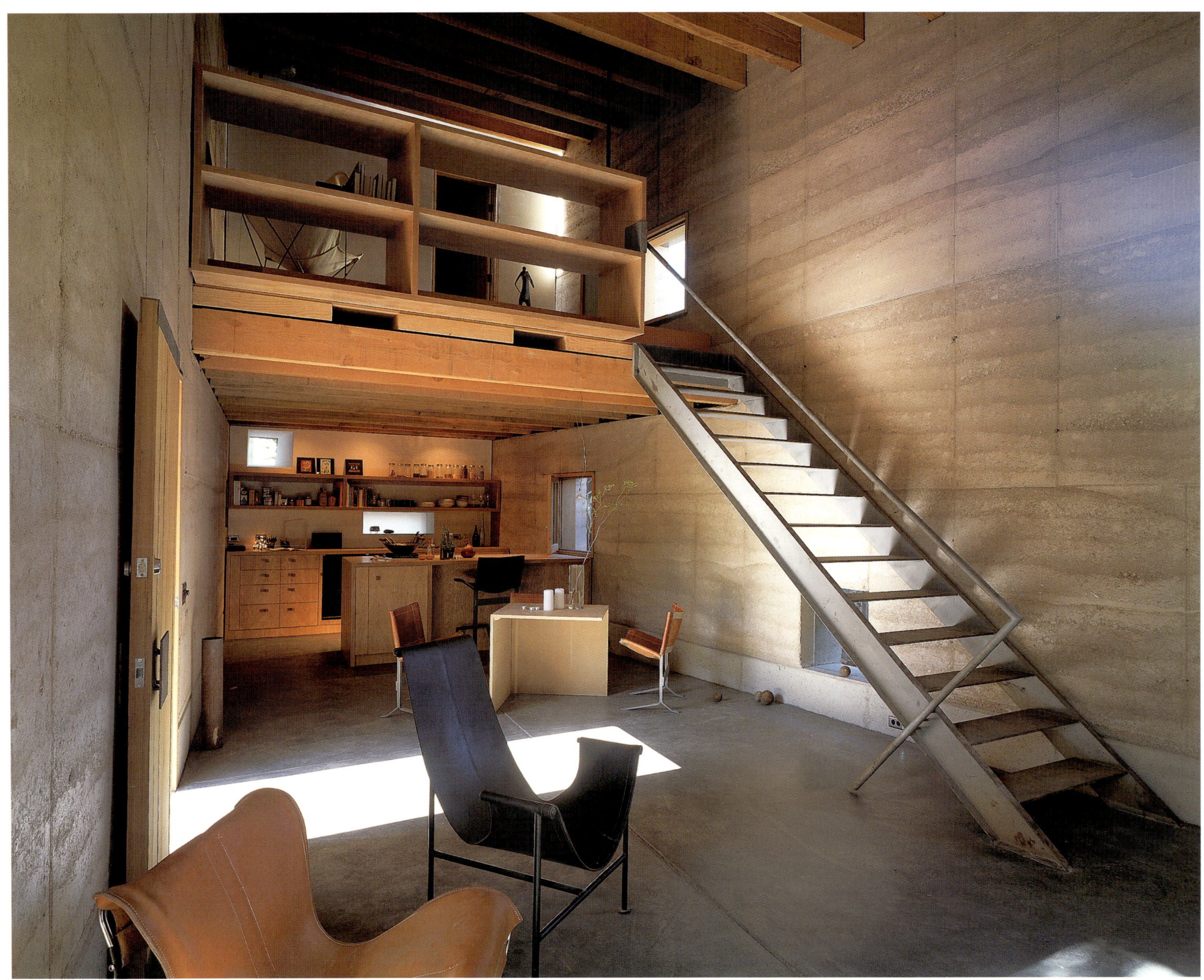

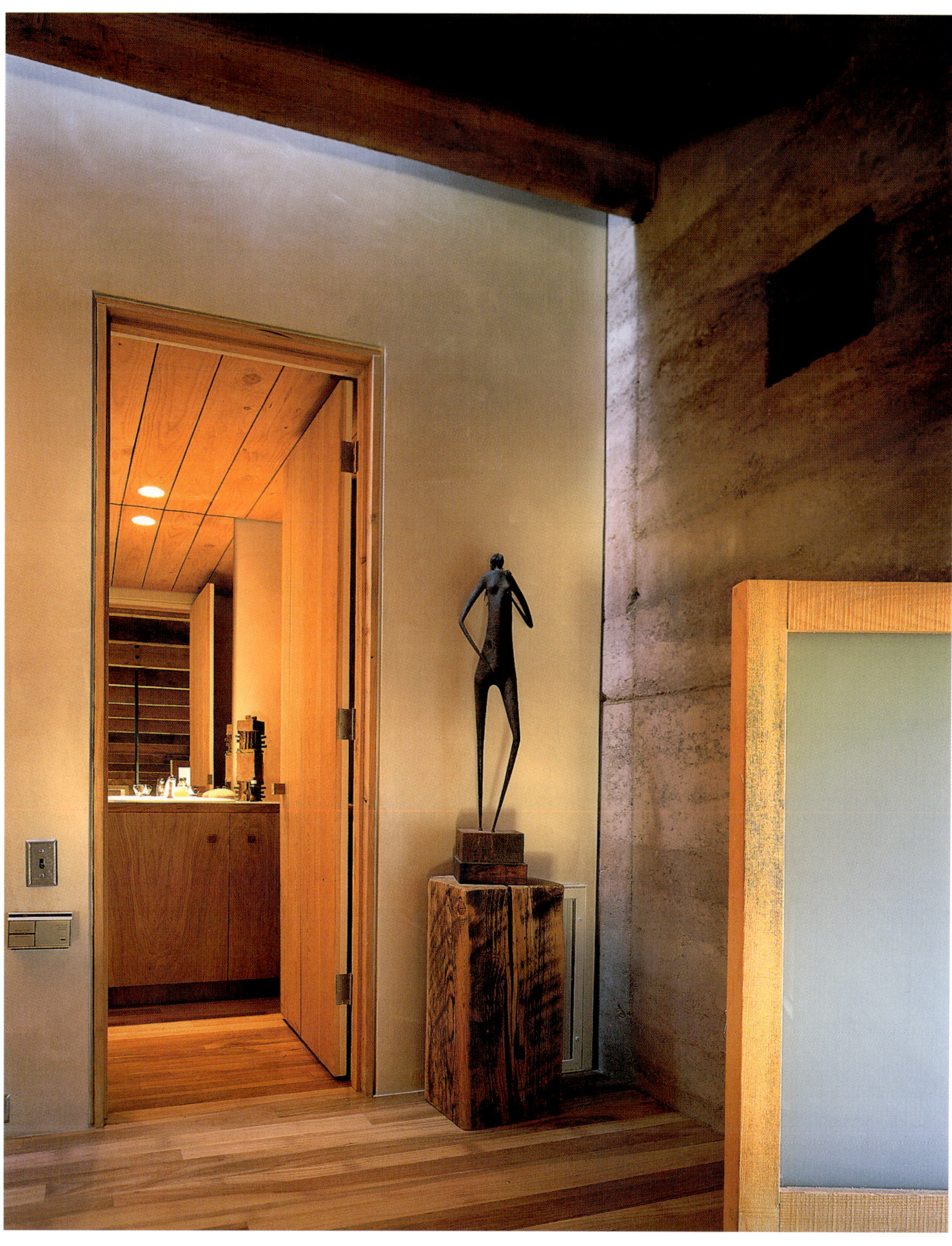

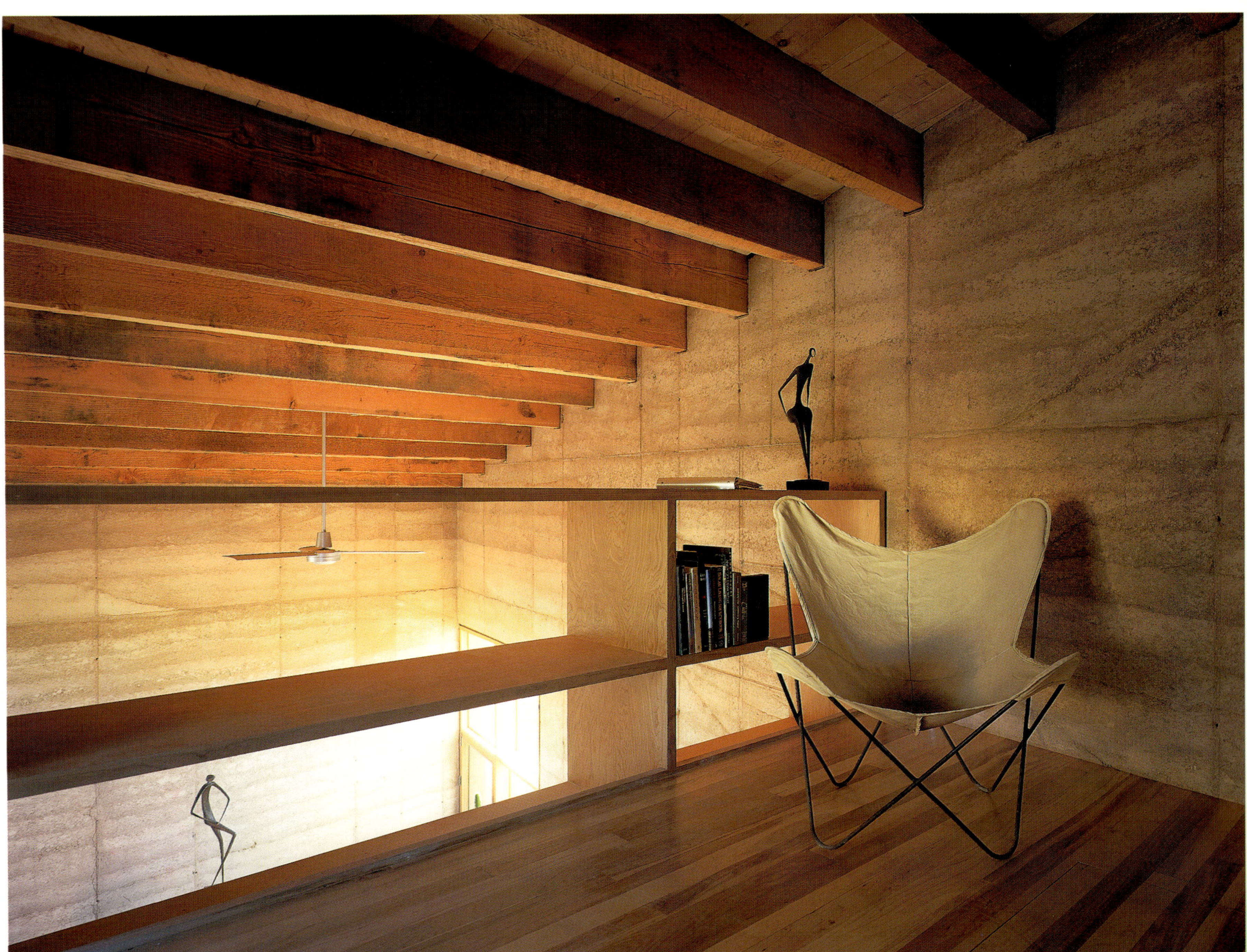

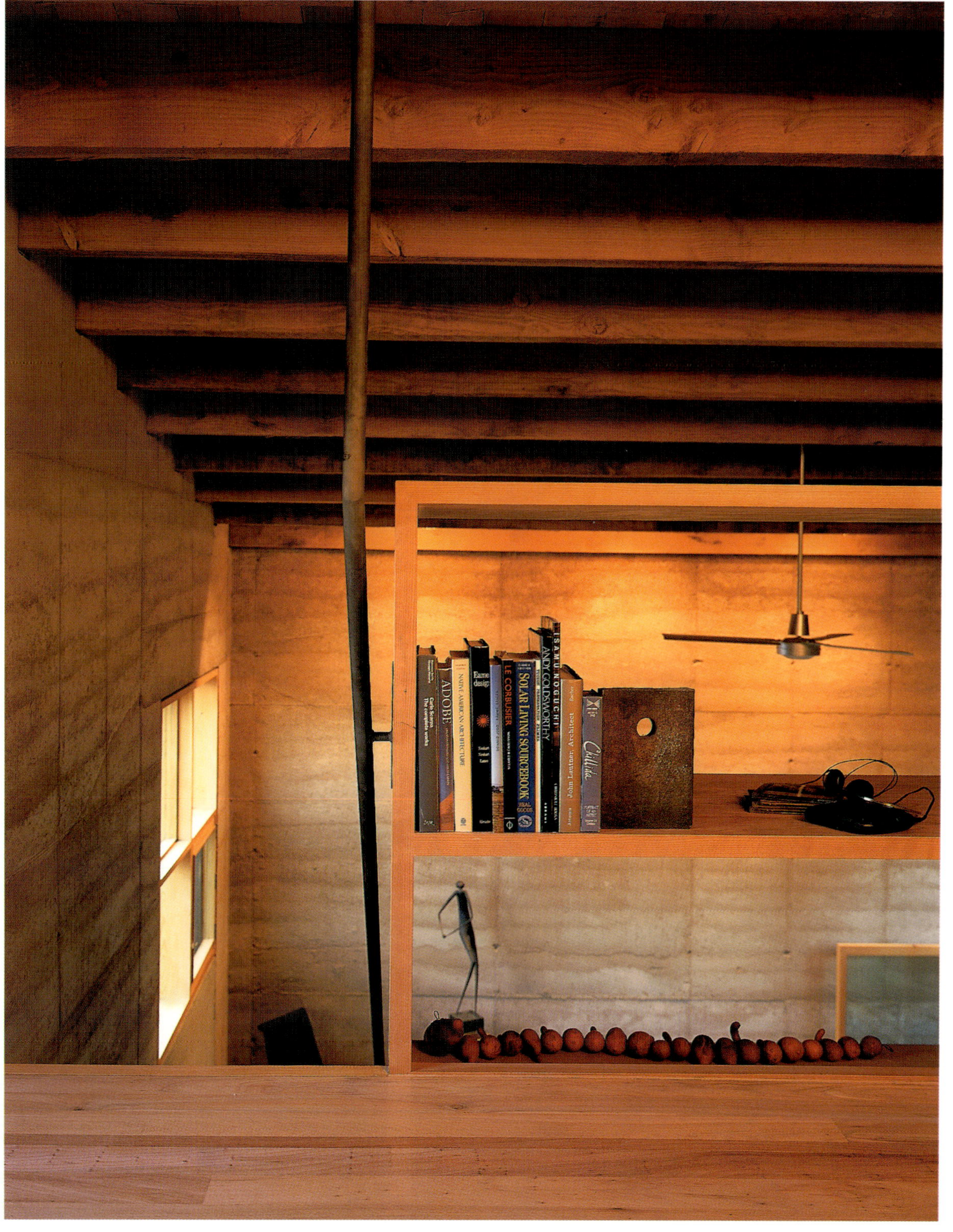
ADOBE
NATIVE AMERICAN ARCHITECTURE
LE CORBUSIER
SOLAR LIVING SOURCEBOOK
ISAMU NOGUCHI
ANDY GOLDSWORTHY
John Lautner, Architect
Chillida

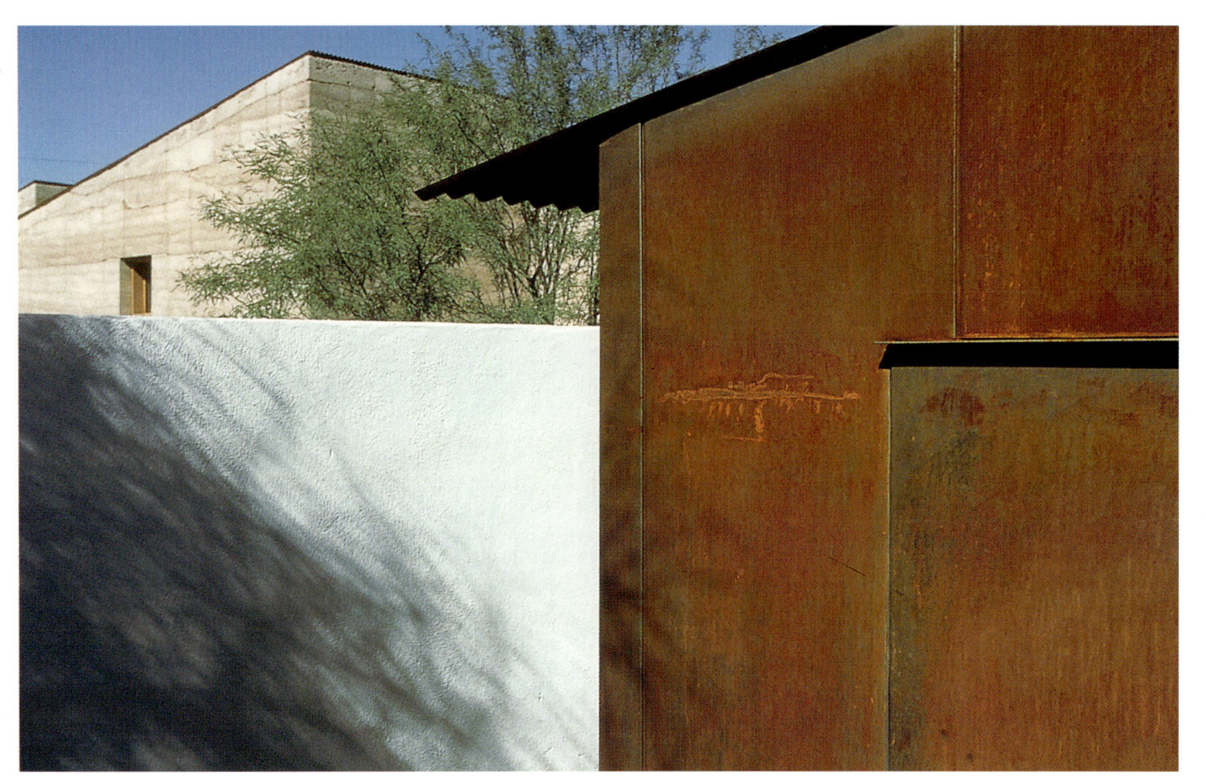

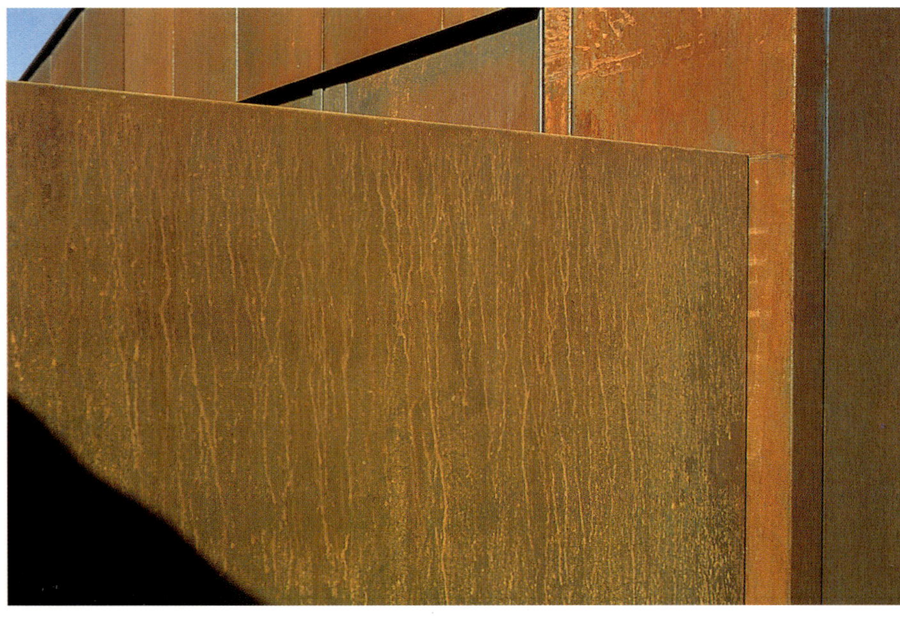

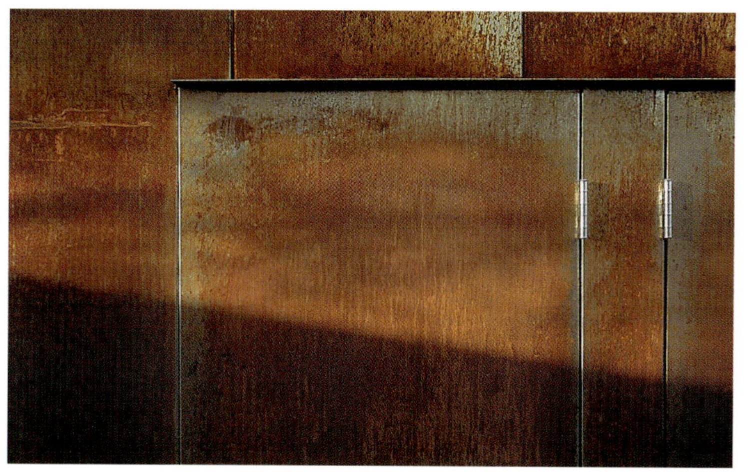

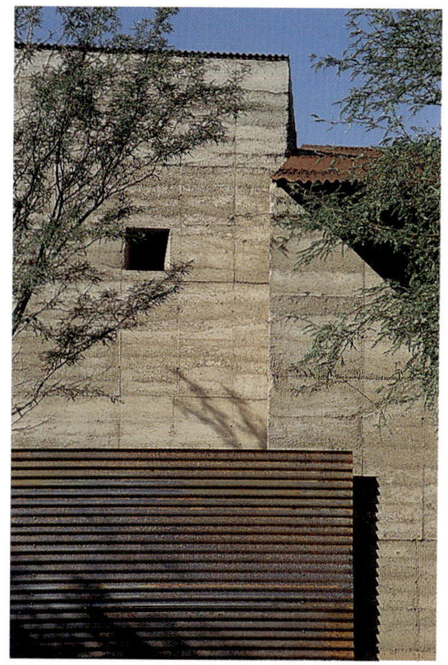

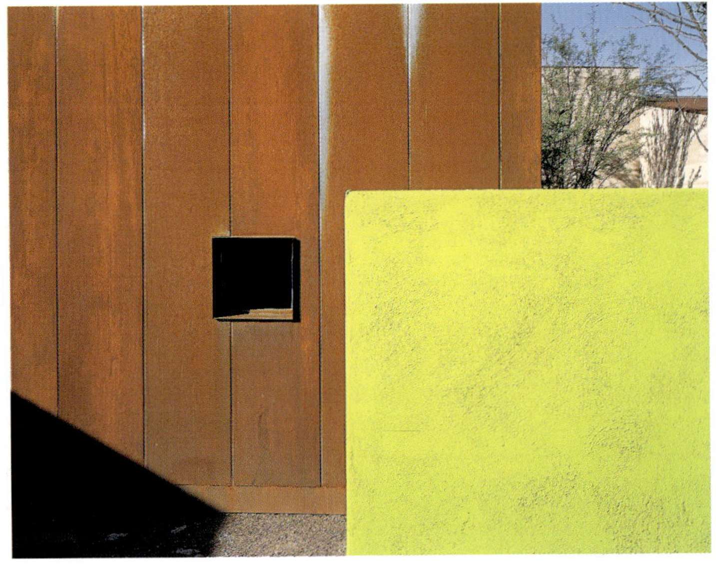

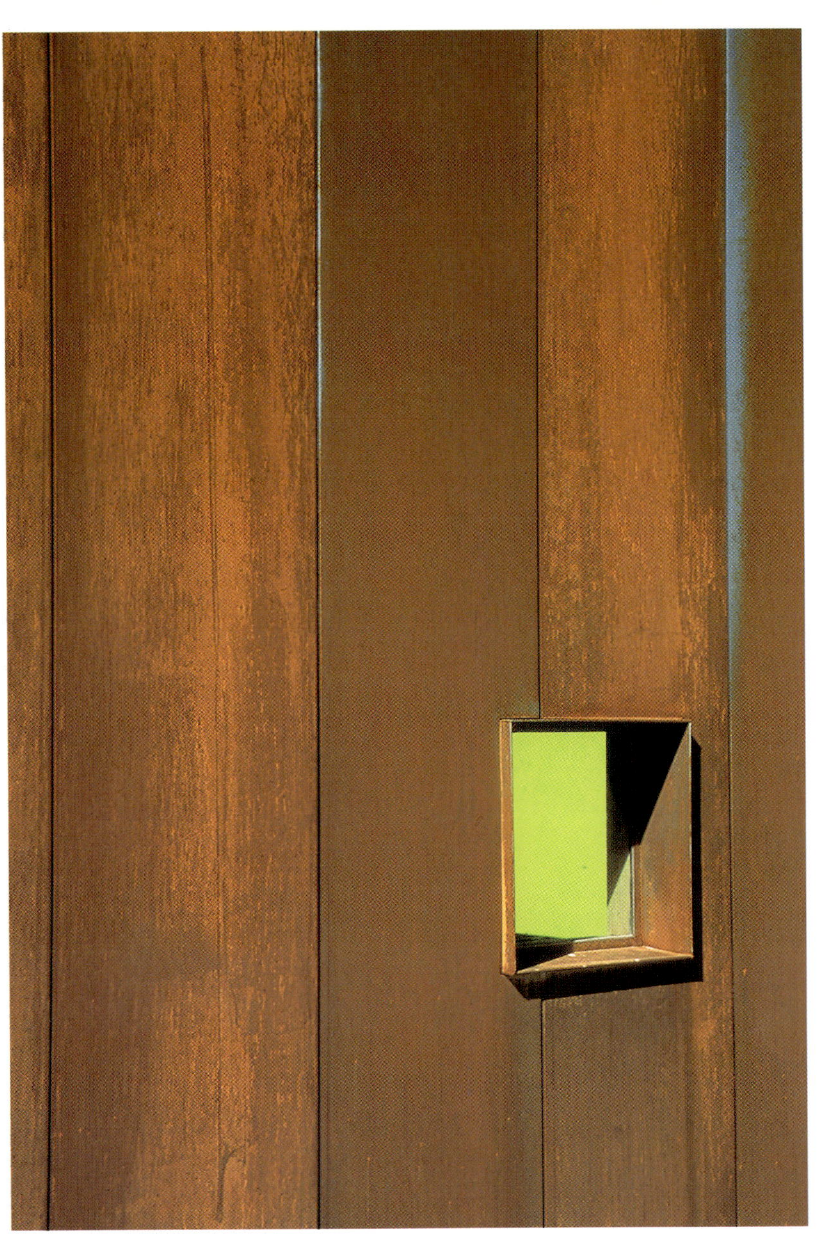

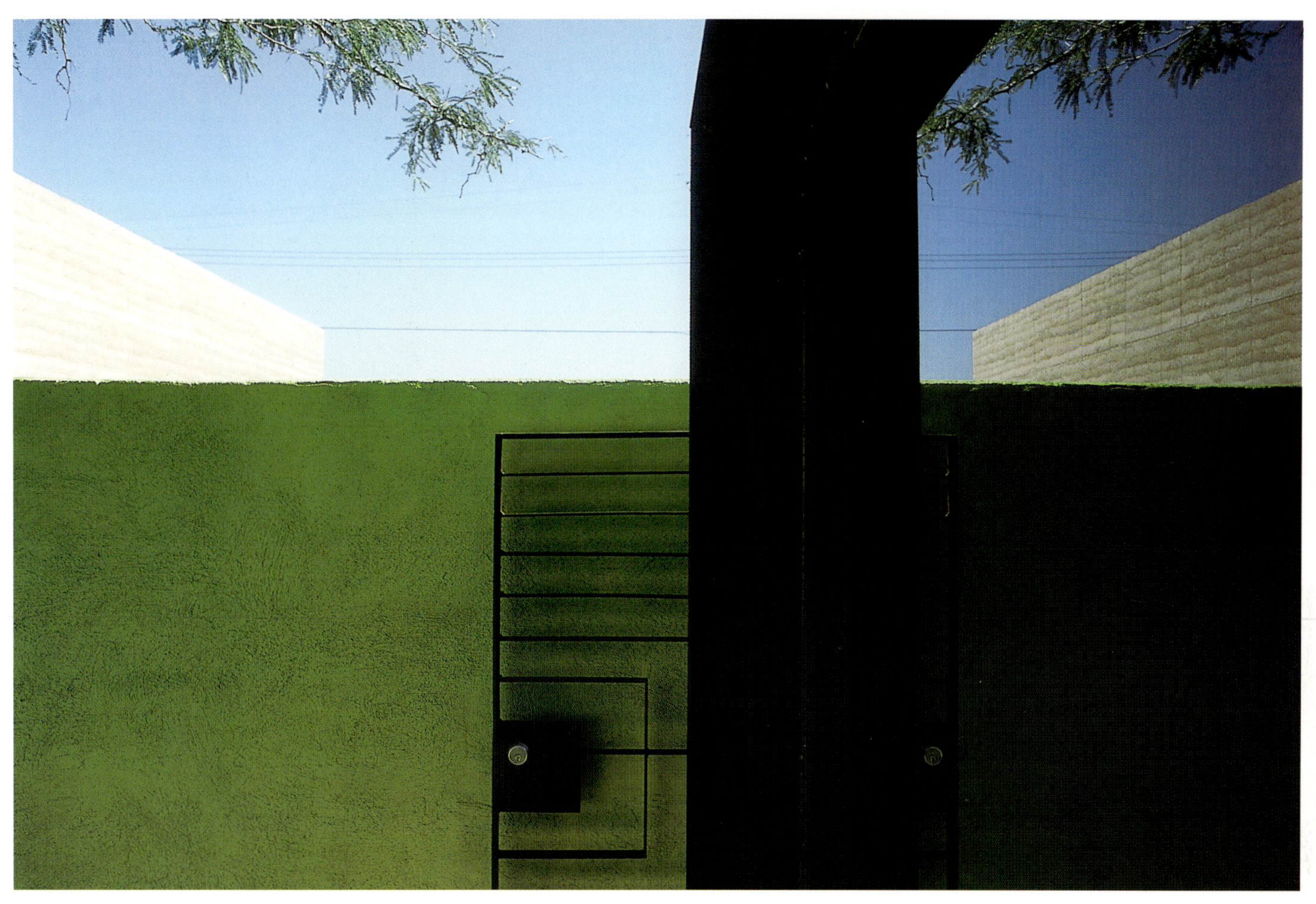

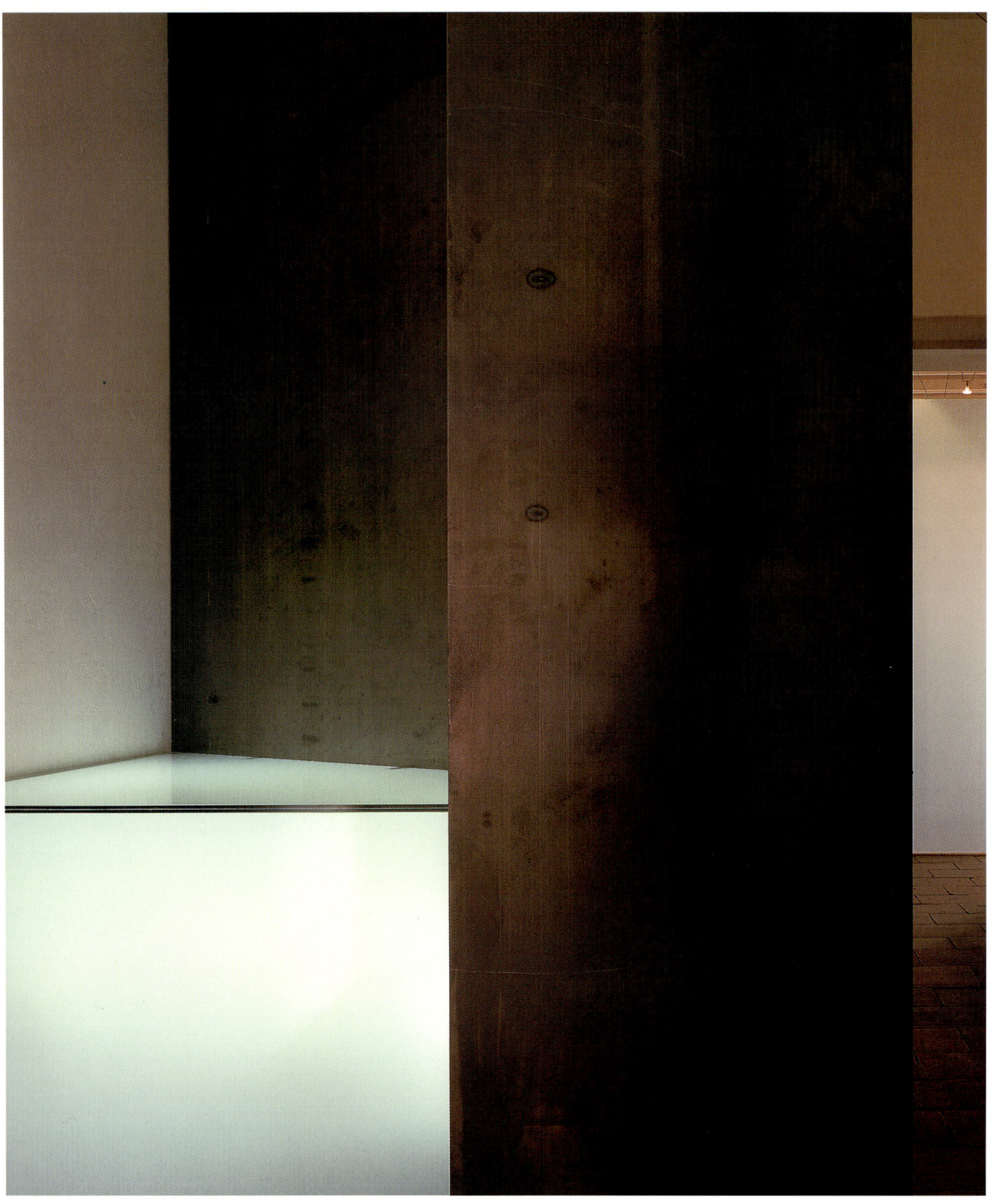

GODAT DESIGN STUDIO

This project involved building a graphic design firm's offices into a leased historic adobe. To start, the interior white plaster surfaces of the existing walls and the terra-cotta floors were refinished and most of the doors removed. The building owner prohibited any other alterations or significant attachments to the building and we were only given two-and-a-half months to complete the project from conception to finish. These conditions fundamentally determined the direction of our work.

Two principal materials, plate steel and translucent glass, were employed for the new elements. Chosen for their availability and the quality of their factory finish, these materials eliminated the arduous and time-consuming process of fabricating and finishing more common case goods.

We organized the interior by positioning a series of freestanding veils in each of the open passageways. While serving multiple functions, these elements screen spaces from one another and simultaneously allow for fluid movement. All other furnishings were designed as stand-alone pieces as well.

On occasion, a drywall form was simply leaned against the existing walls to display work. Square openings were cut in these walls to fine-tune the light quality from the larger windows behind the drywall.

The Godat Design Studio is located in the same neighborhood as the Convent Avenue Studios and my offices at 400 Rubio Avenue. It is a pleasure for me to visit it on occasion and see how well-loved and maintained the place remains.

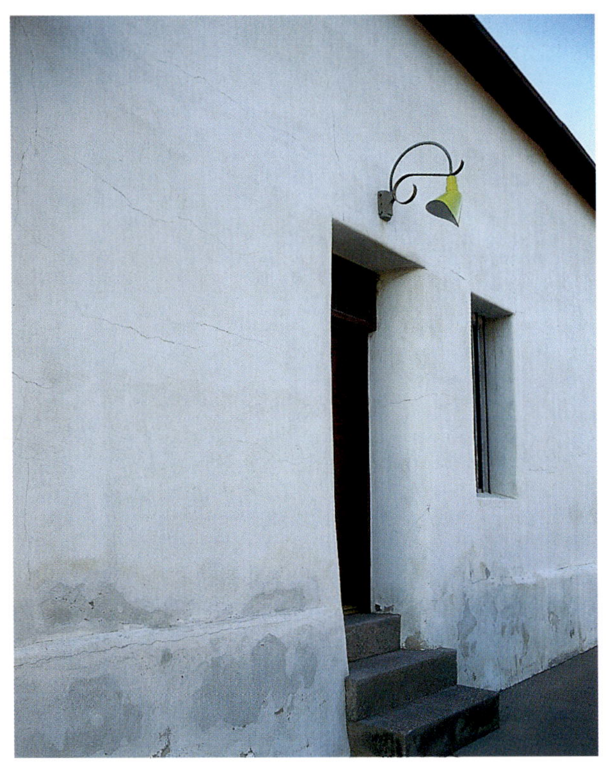

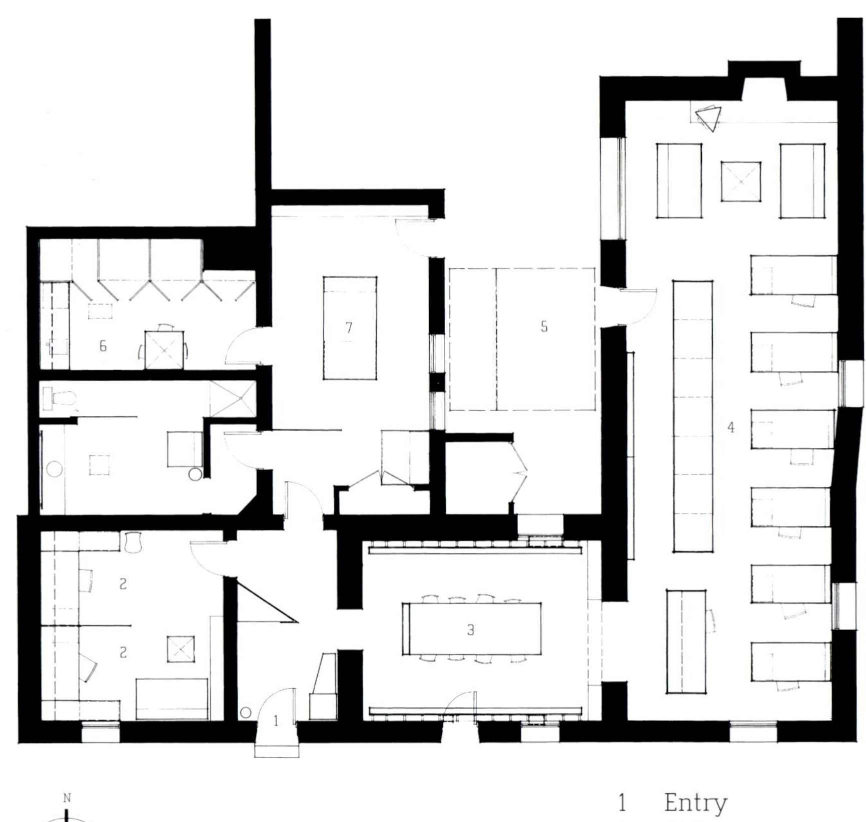

1 Entry
2 Office
3 Conference
4 Design Studio
5 Courtyard
6 Kitchen
7 Workroom

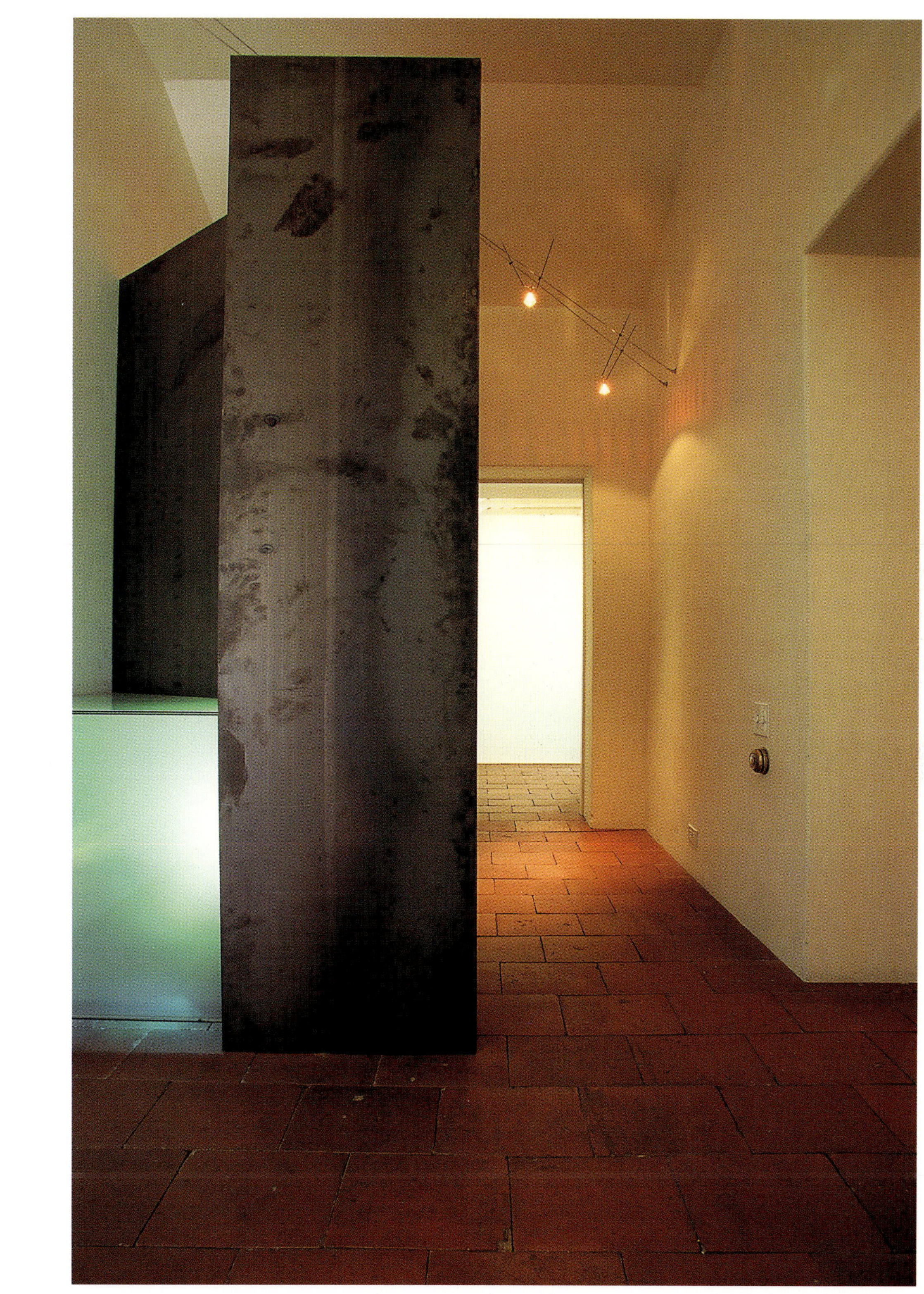

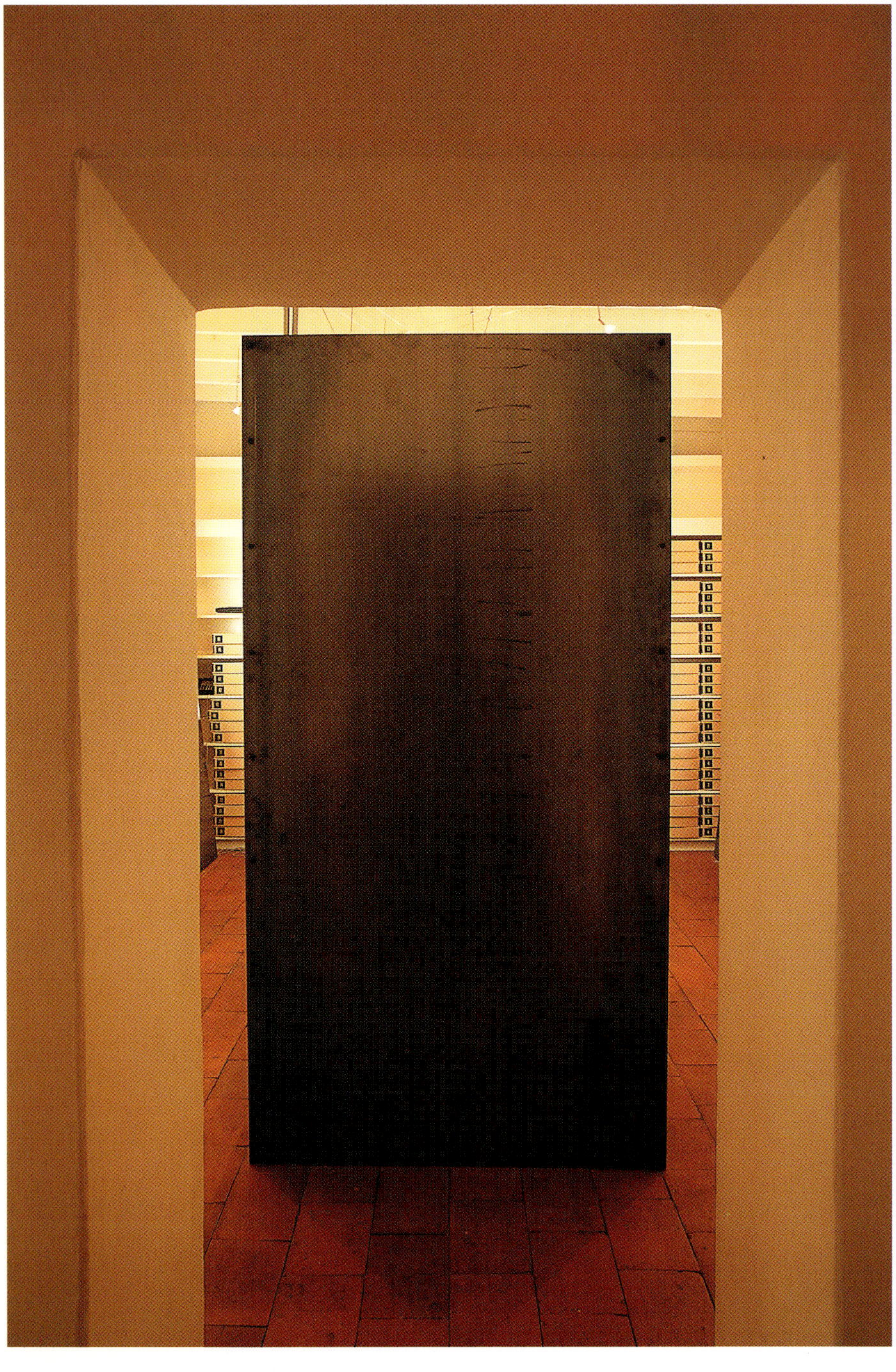

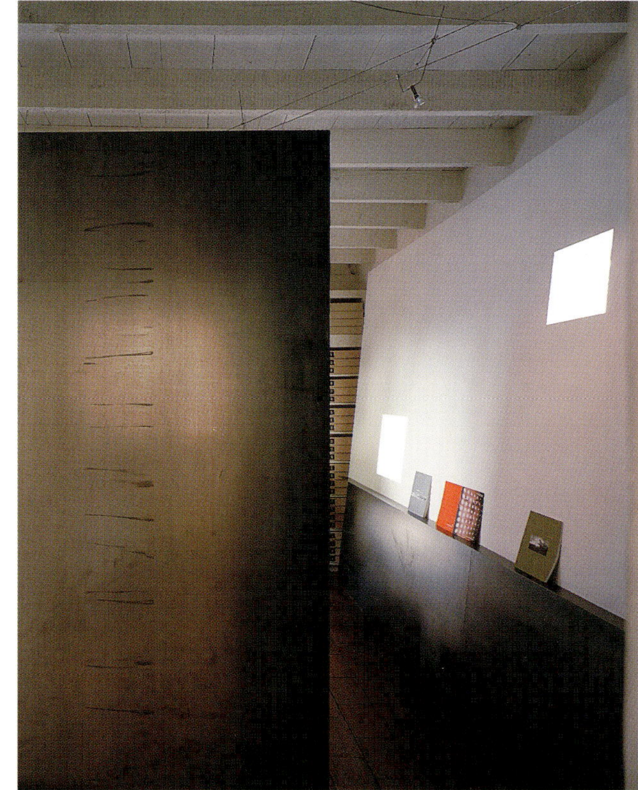

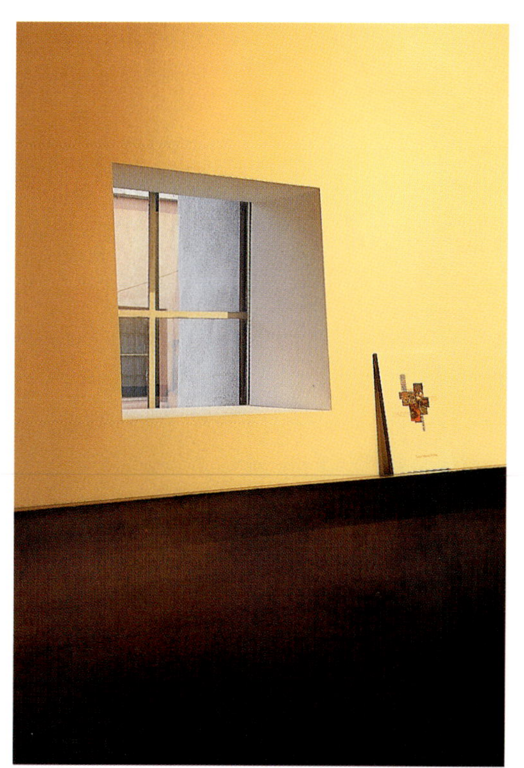

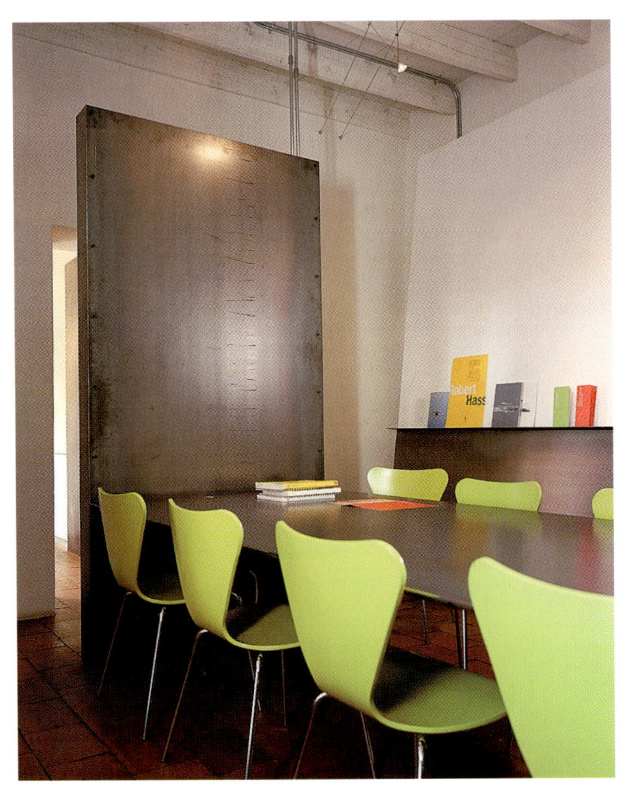
Hass

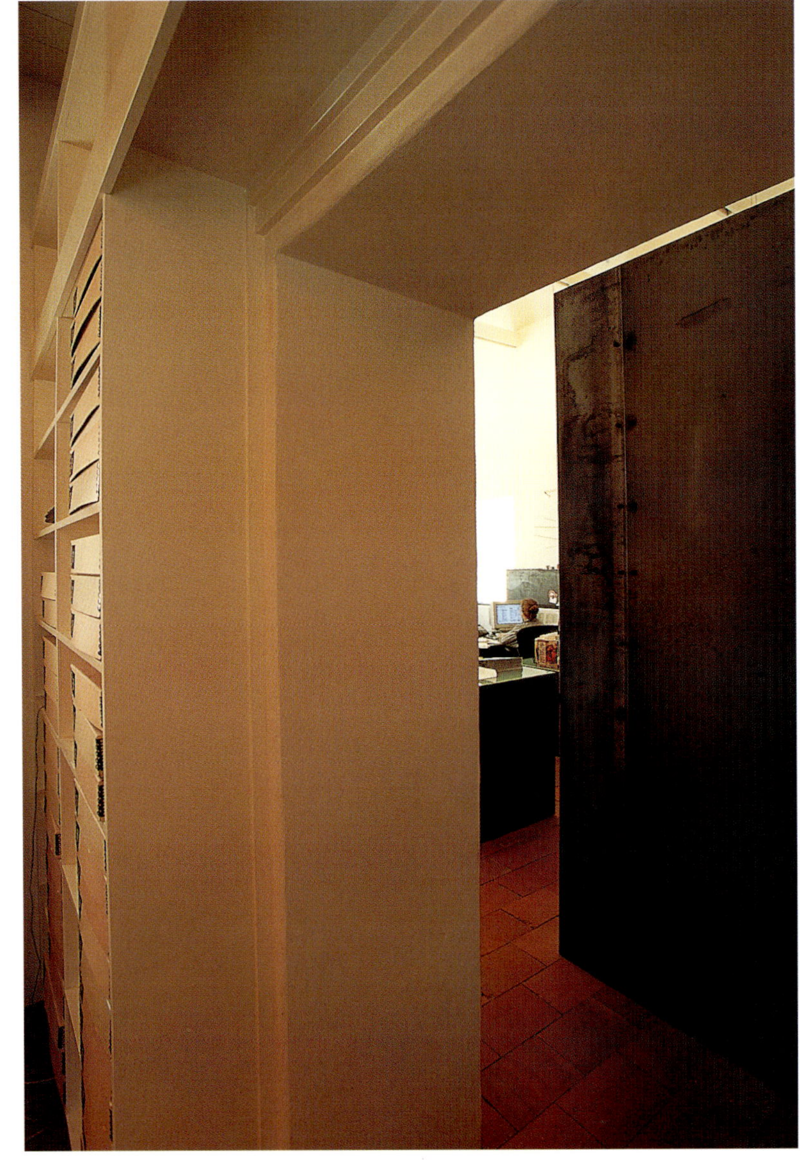

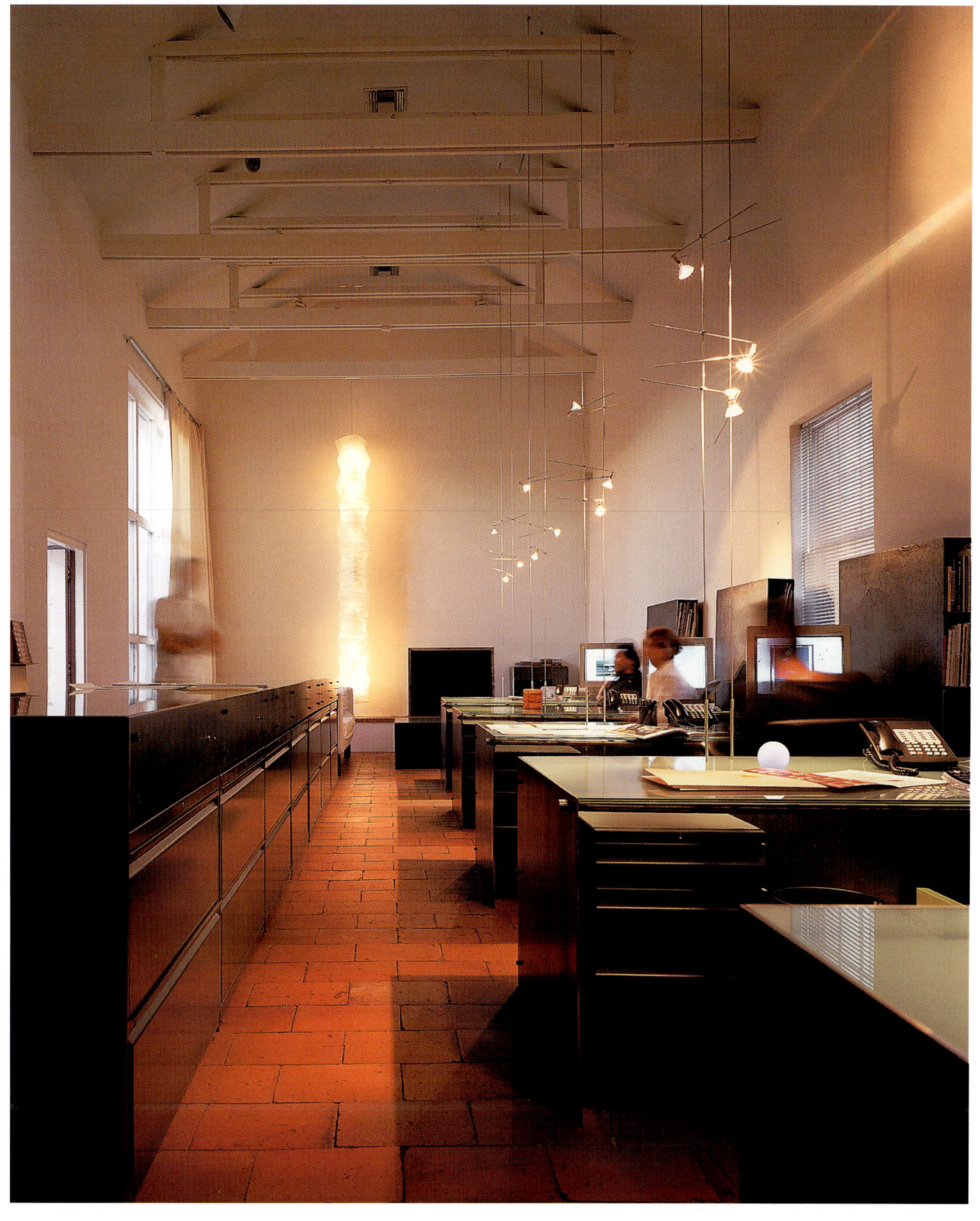

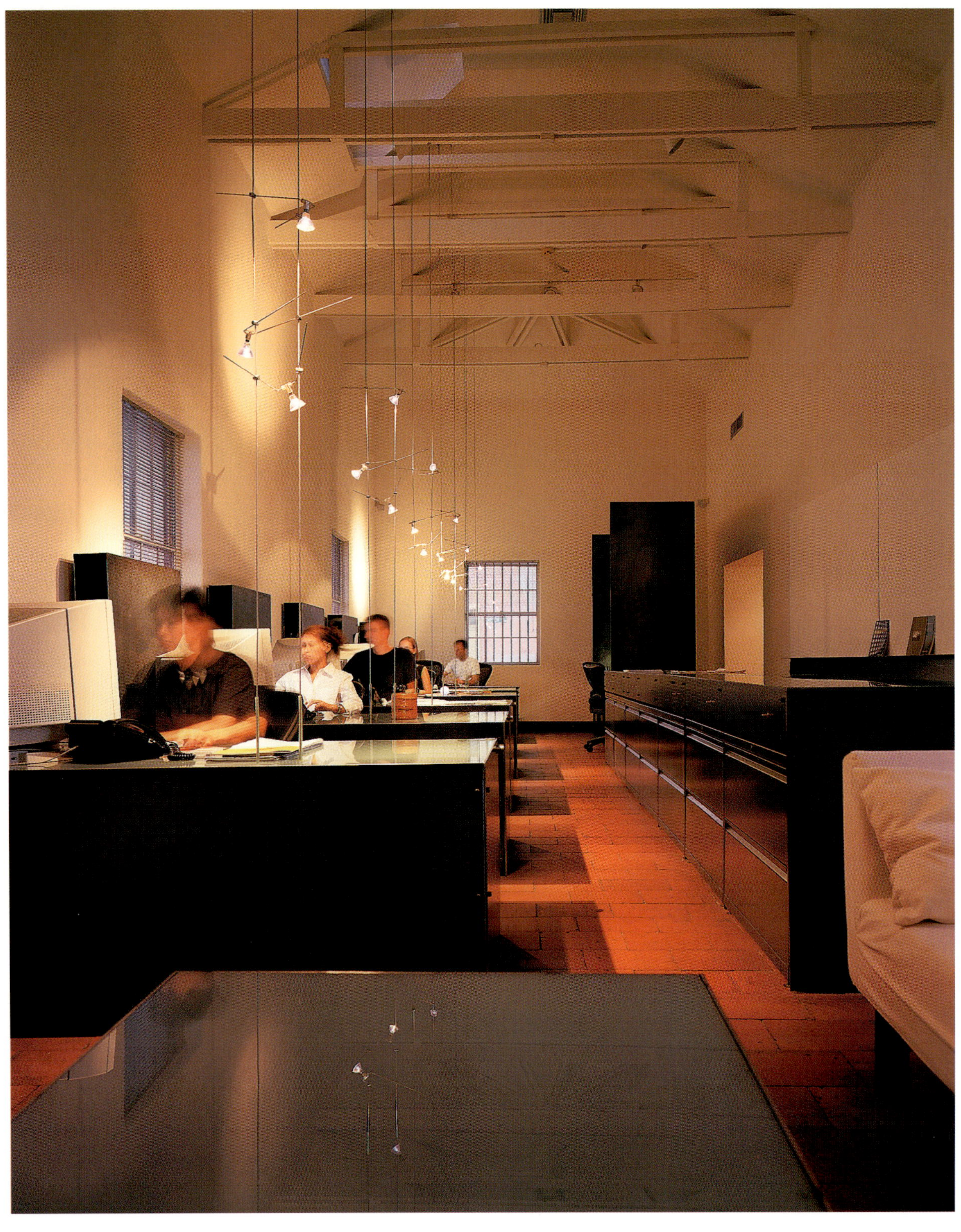

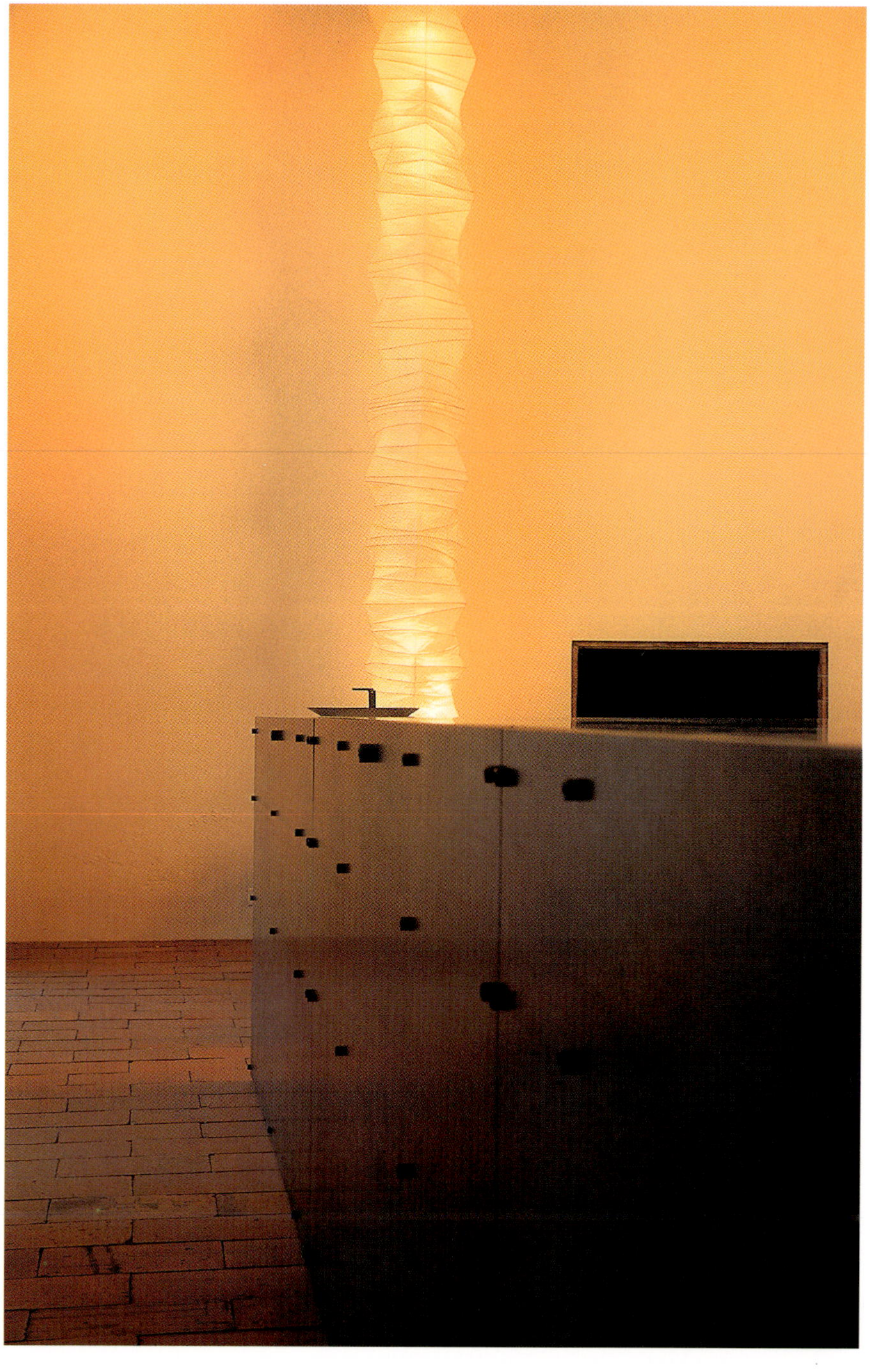

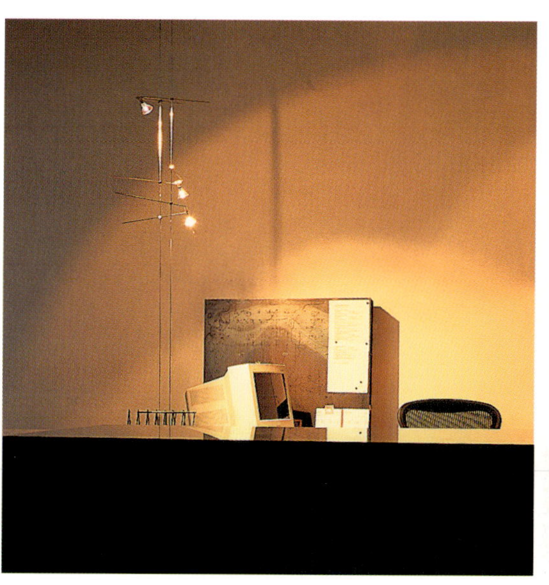

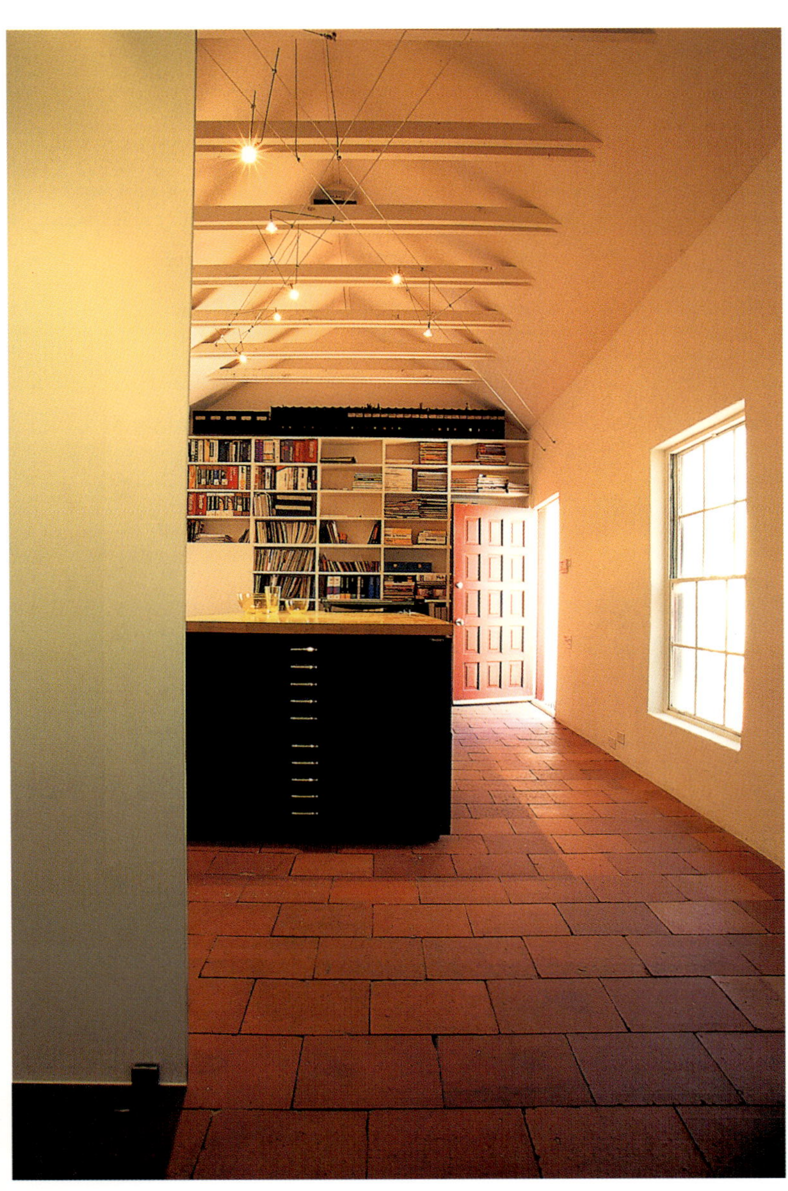

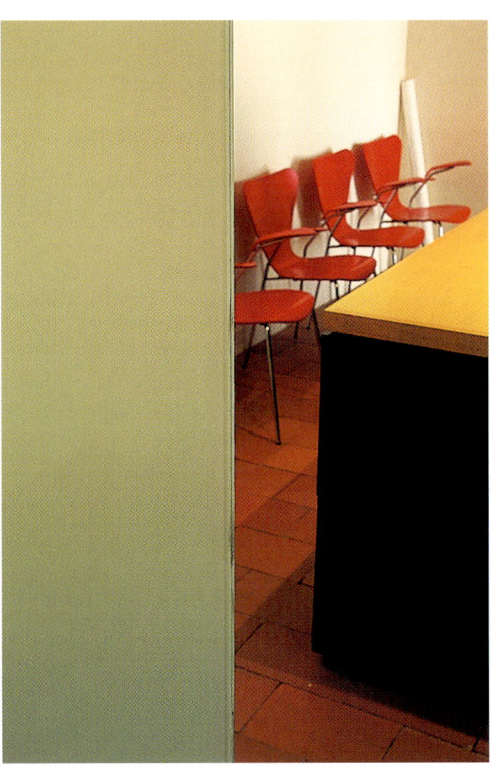

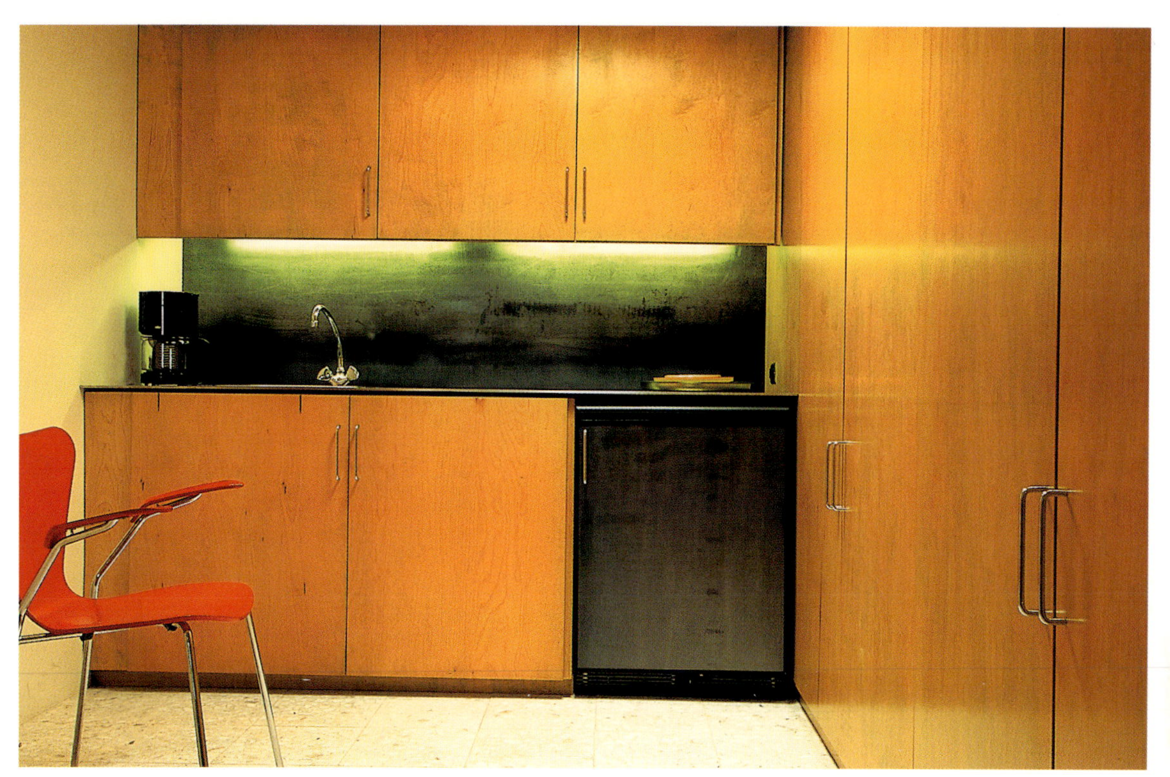

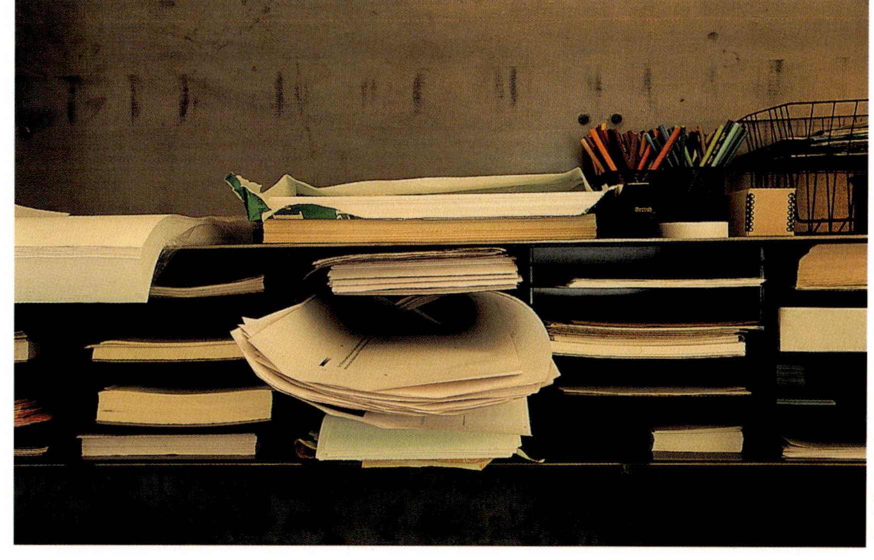

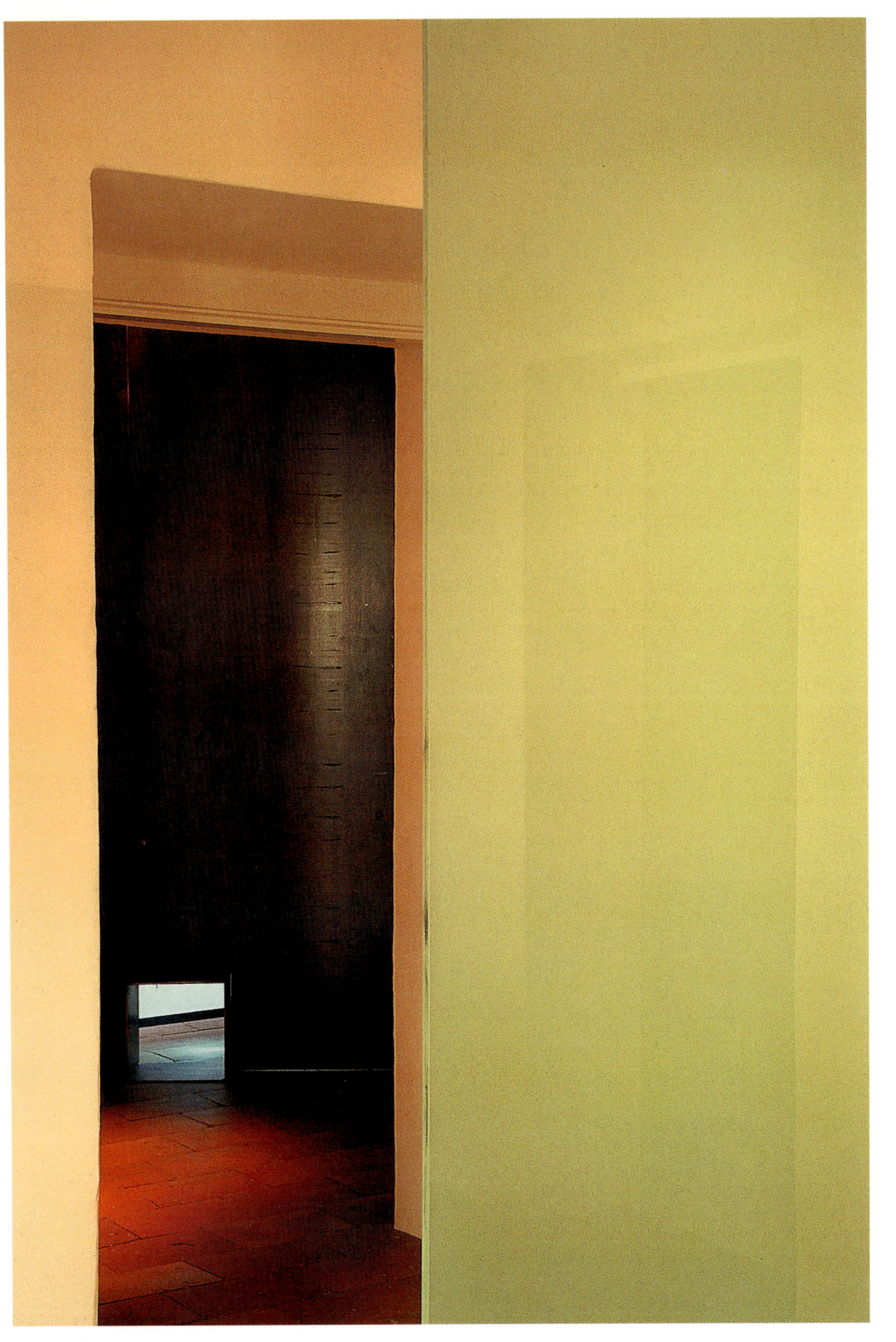

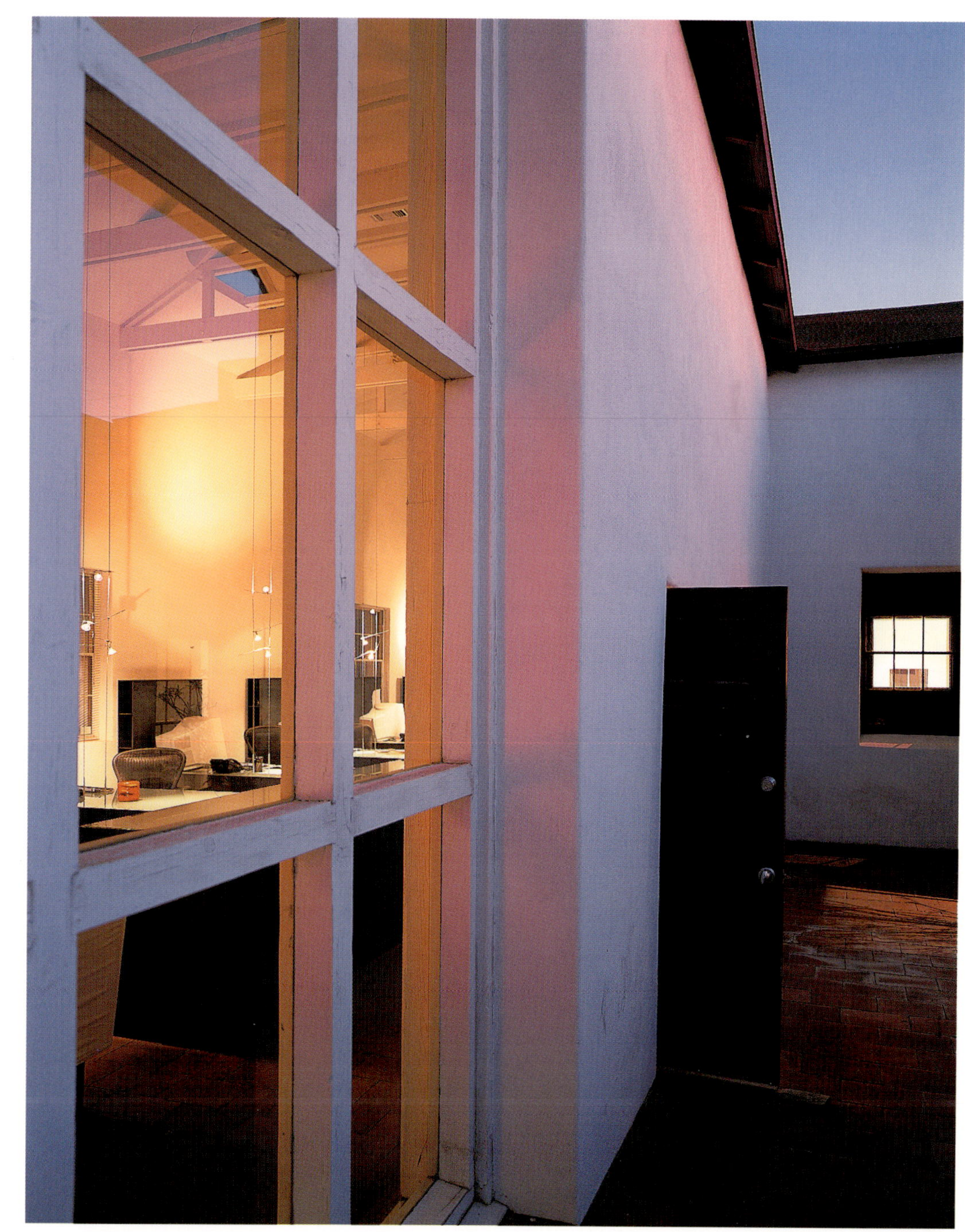

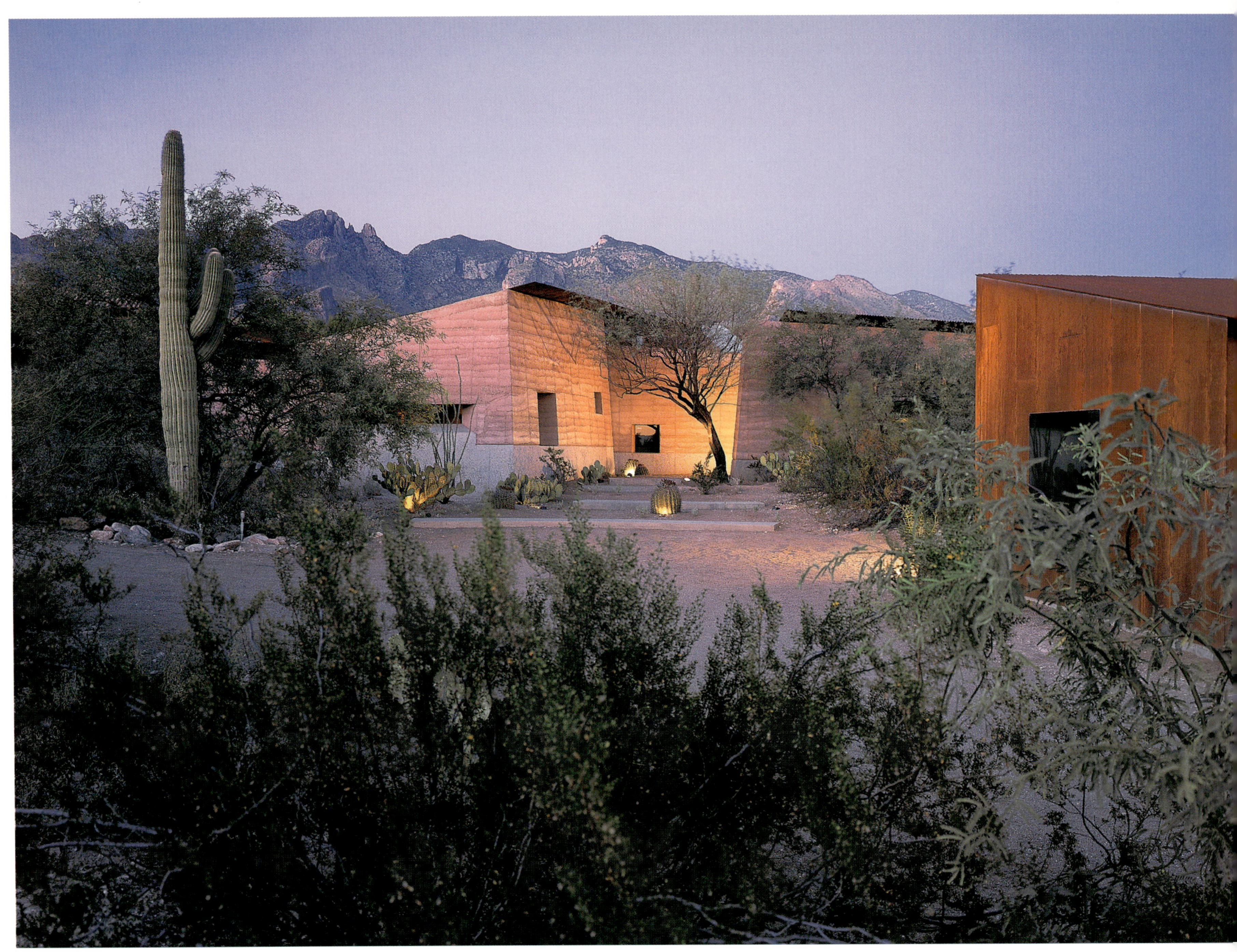

CATALINA HOUSE

The house's gaze is transfixed on the view of the dramatic Catalina Mountain Range to the northeast—a given.

Three forms, arranged in a defiant stance like a wagon train, camp around a fragile complex of saguaro cactuses, mesquite trees, and burrowing fauna.

The main house is divided into two clearly defined "wings." The general living and entertaining areas to the east are open and airy indoor-outdoor spaces. The private zone to the west is turned slightly to capture early morning sun and generally assumes the posture of a cave. The resulting geometries are translated three-dimensionally by battered rammed-earth wall planes and reversed gable roof forms. The various slopes are positioned for their effect on the house's spatial experiences. A coarse exterior shell presents itself to the harsh environment of the desert, while soft sensual cherry wood is used for interior elements.

The garage, a framed form with weathered steel cladding, was built after the main house. Its site was used as the staging area for the construction of the rammed-earth walls. As a result, no trees or cacti were destroyed on the site and only one additional tree was planted.

My first house.

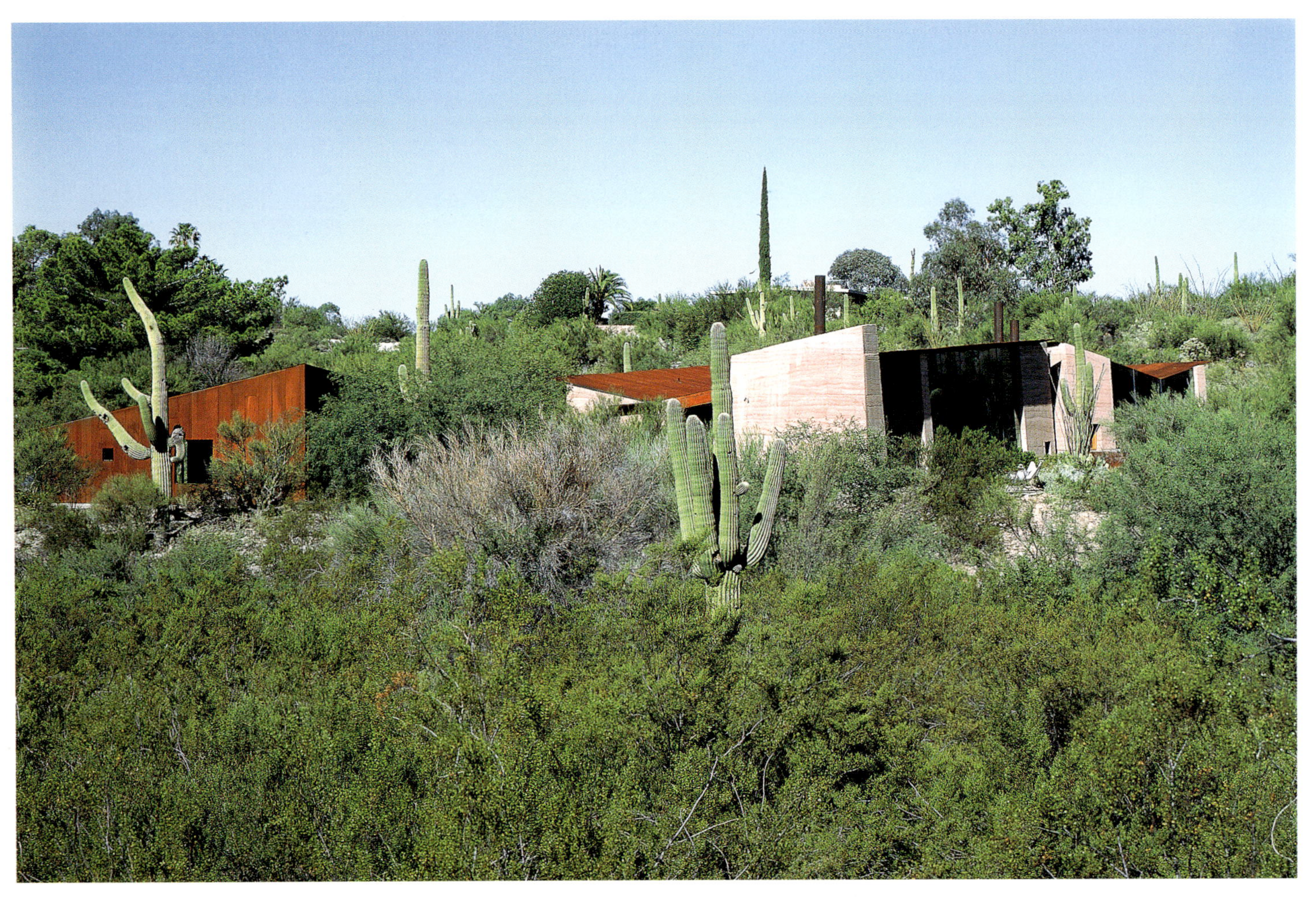

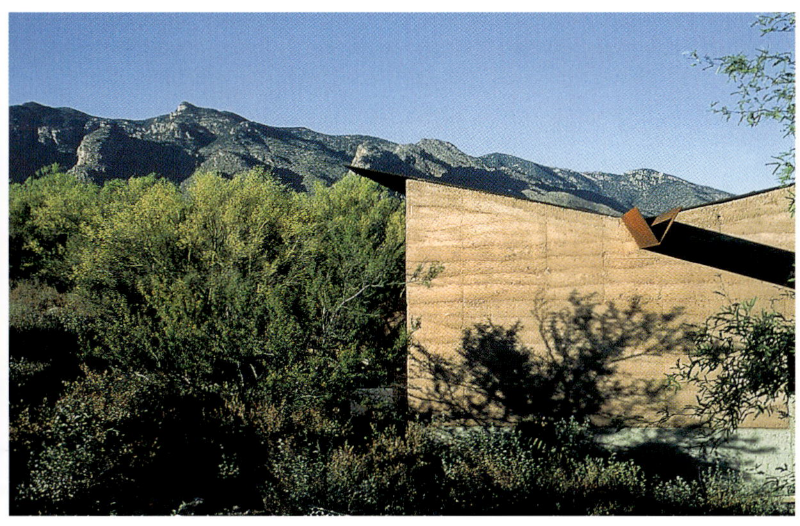

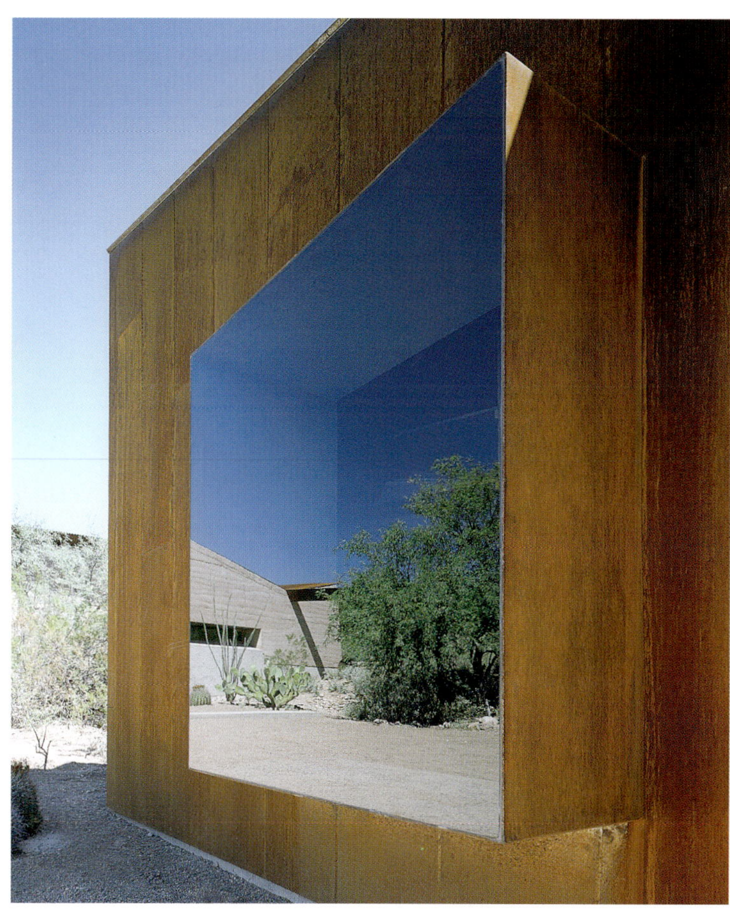

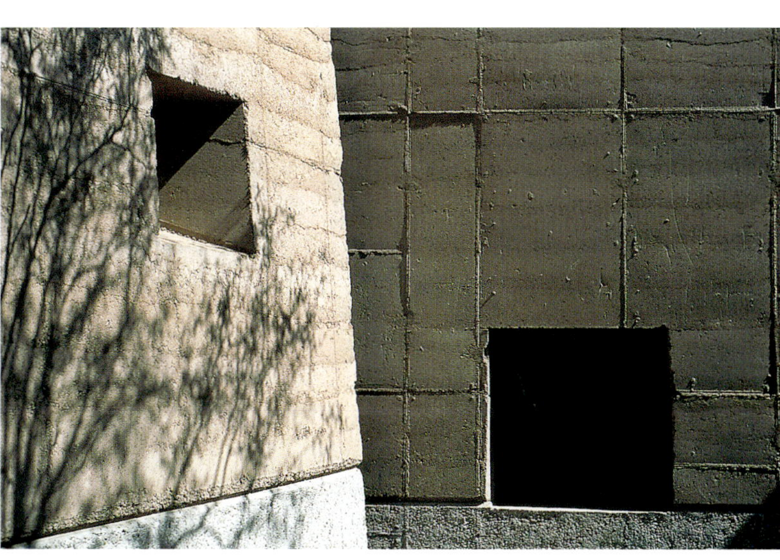

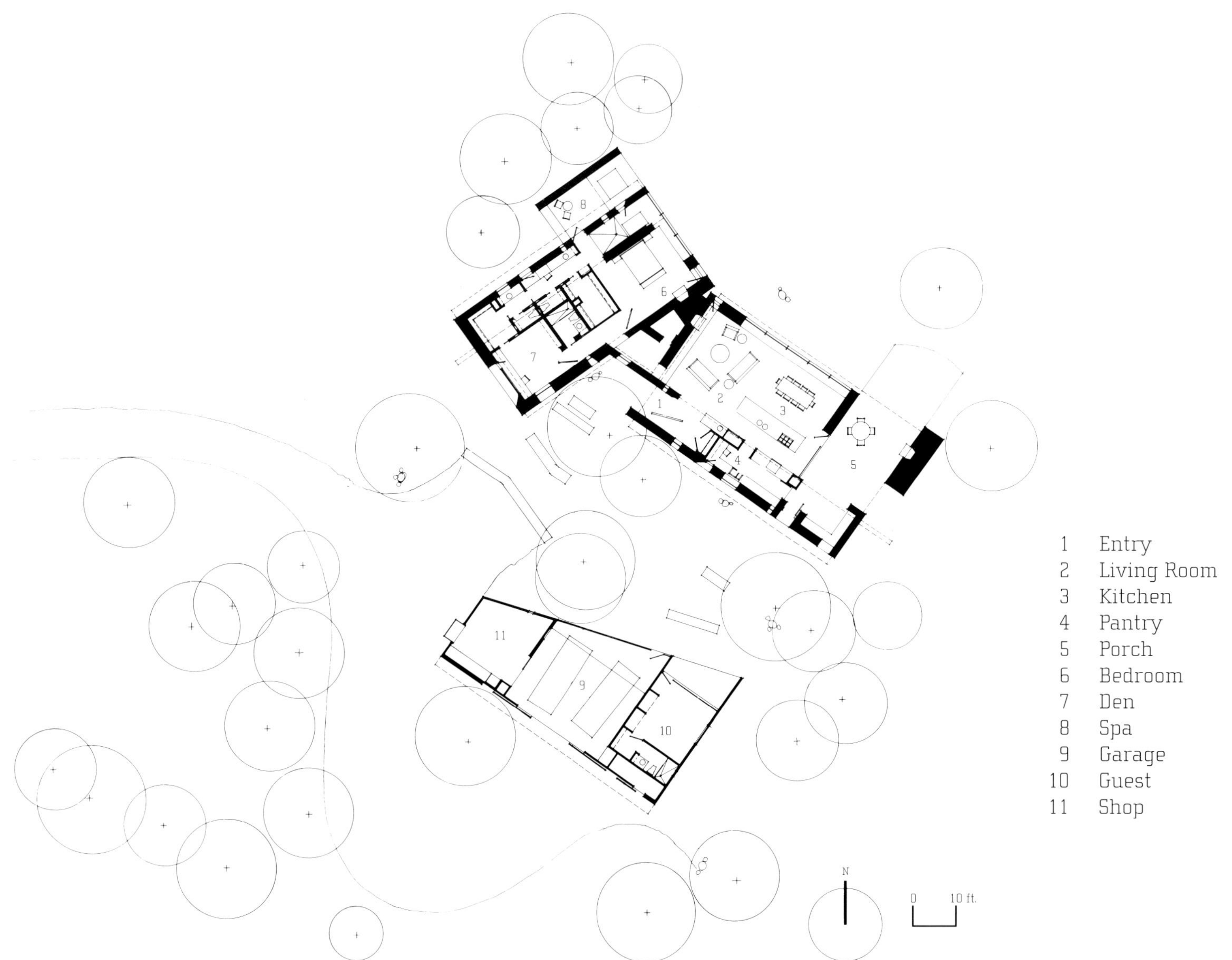

1 Entry
2 Living Room
3 Kitchen
4 Pantry
5 Porch
6 Bedroom
7 Den
8 Spa
9 Garage
10 Guest
11 Shop

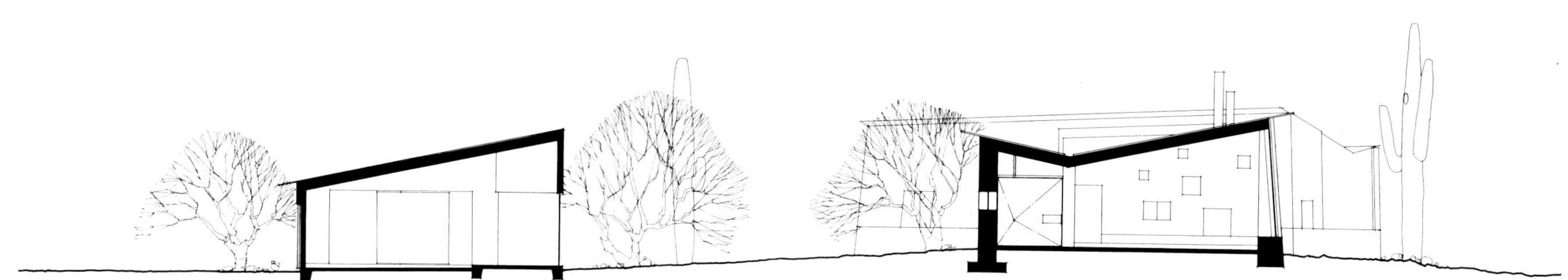

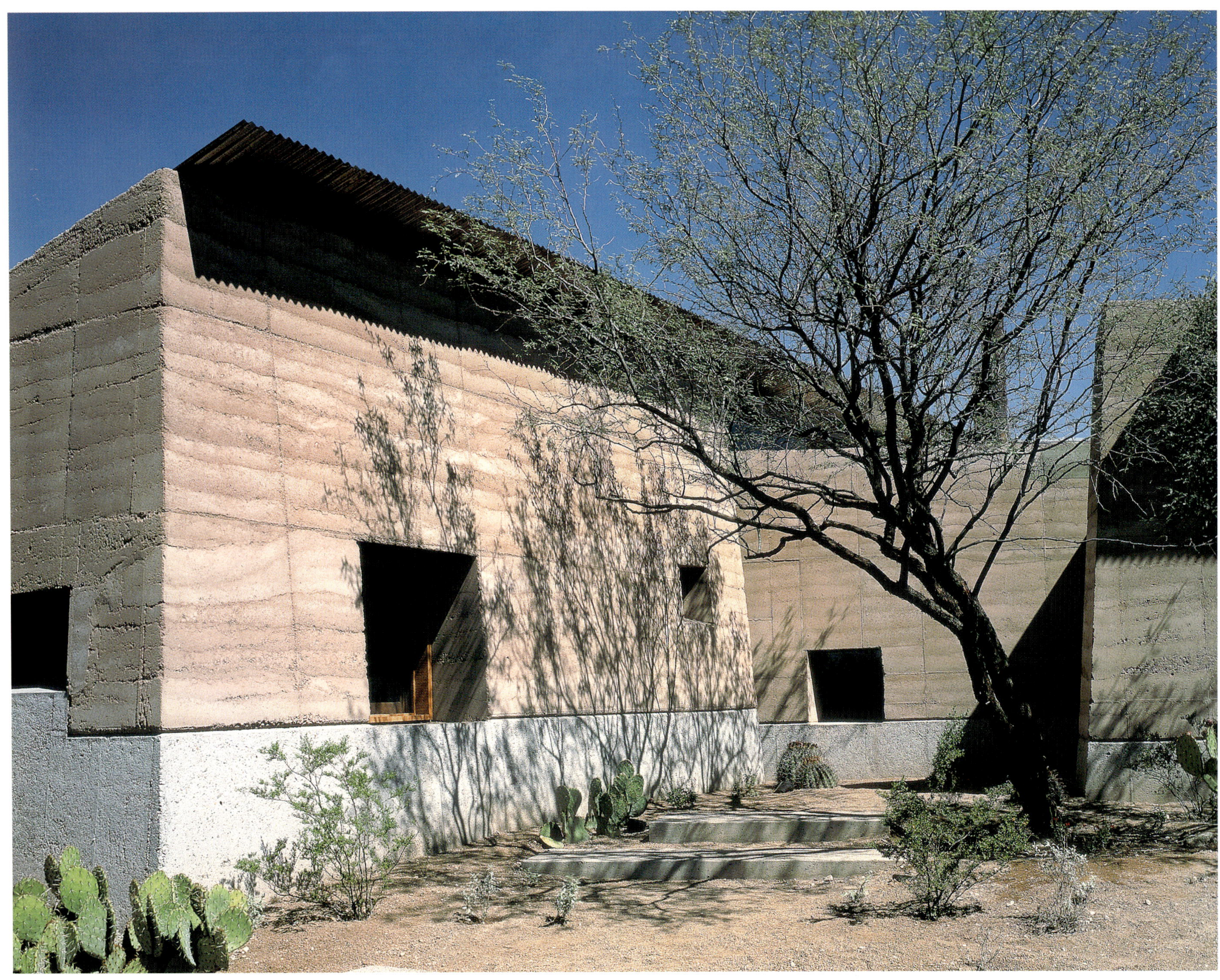

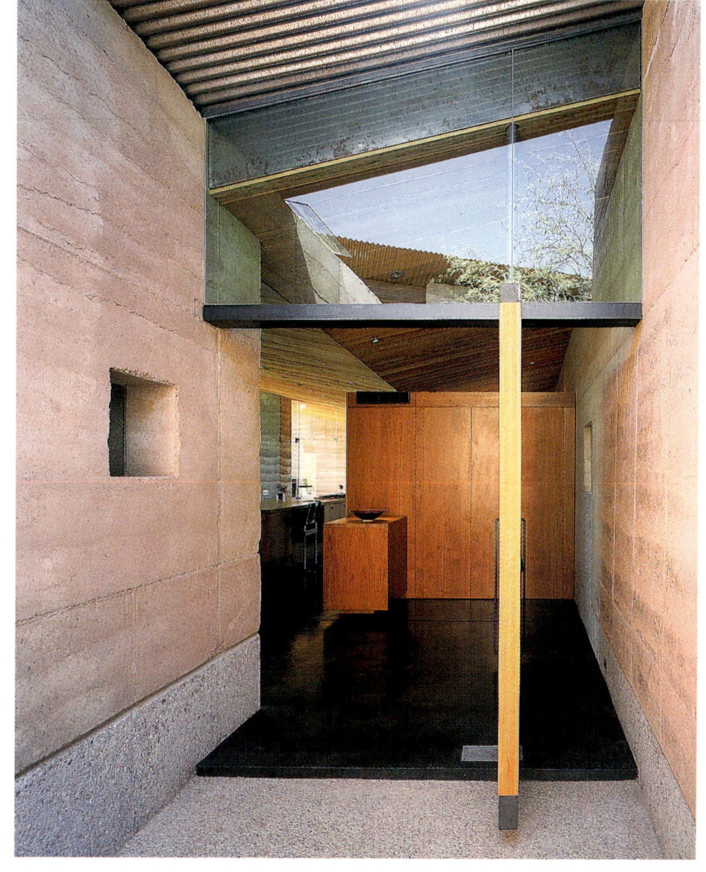

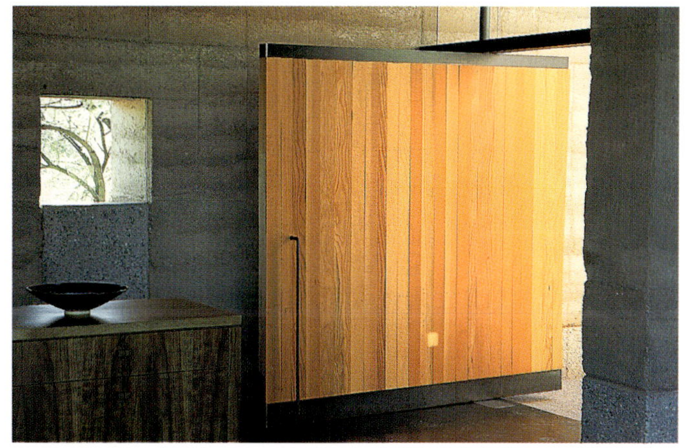

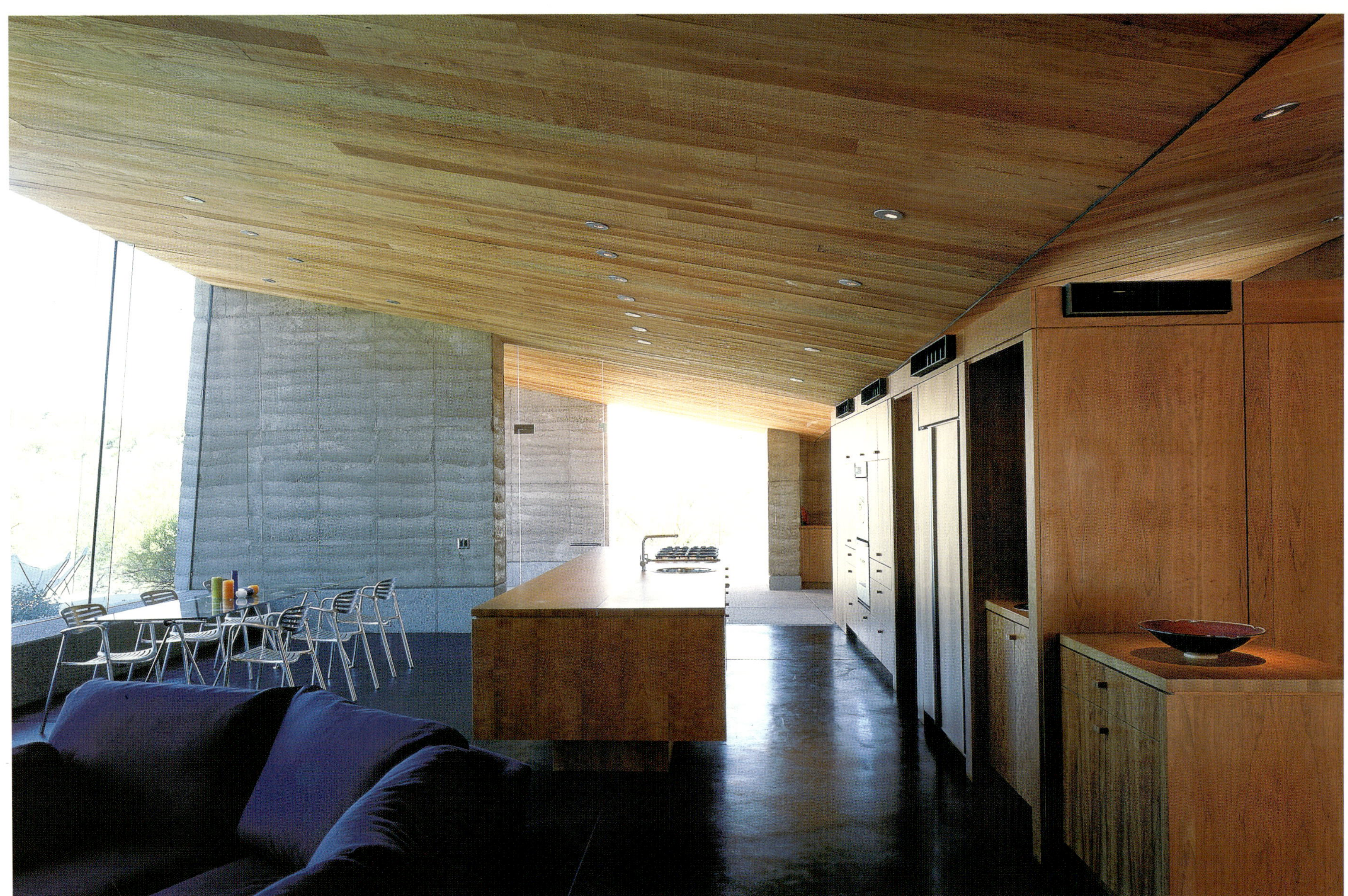

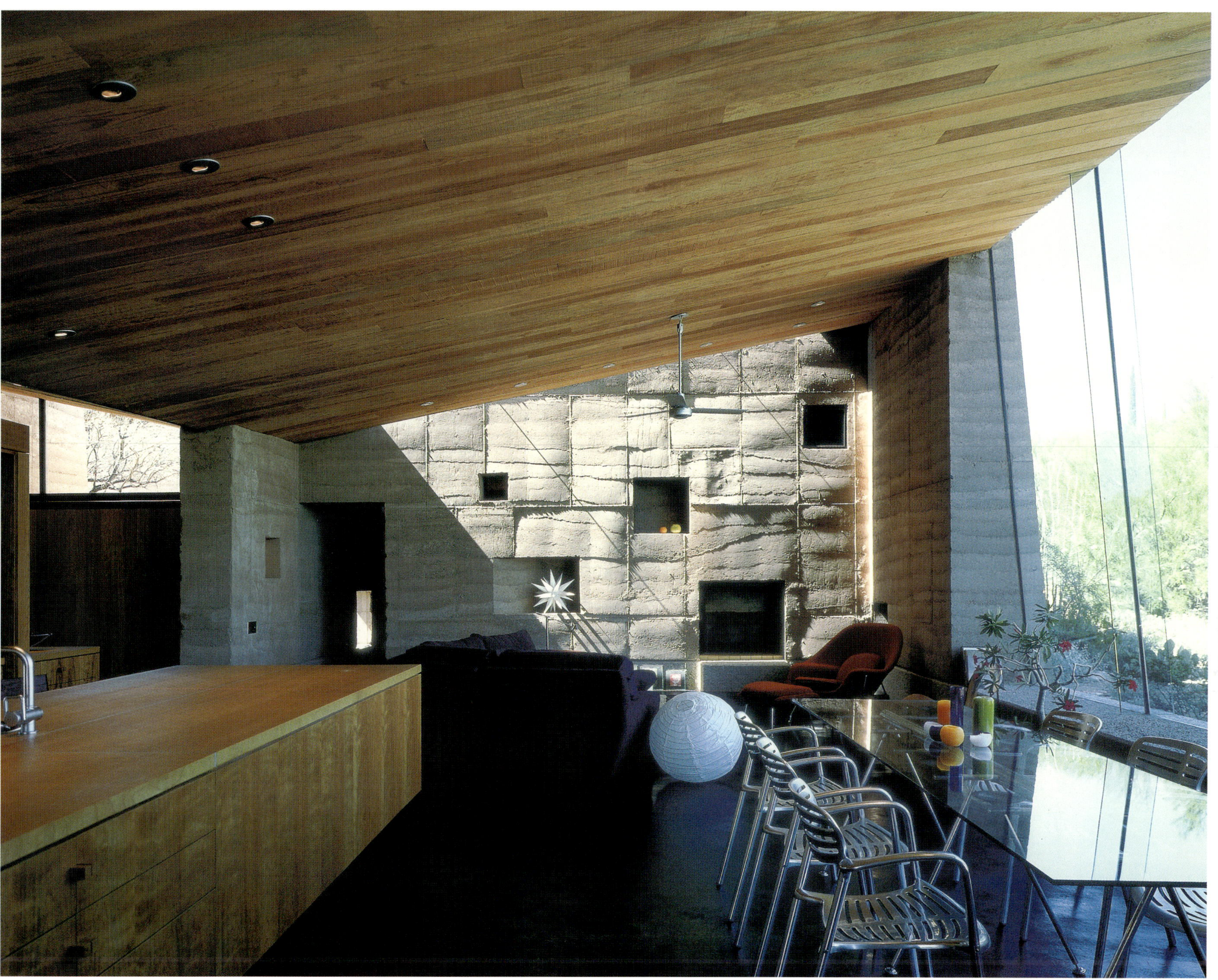

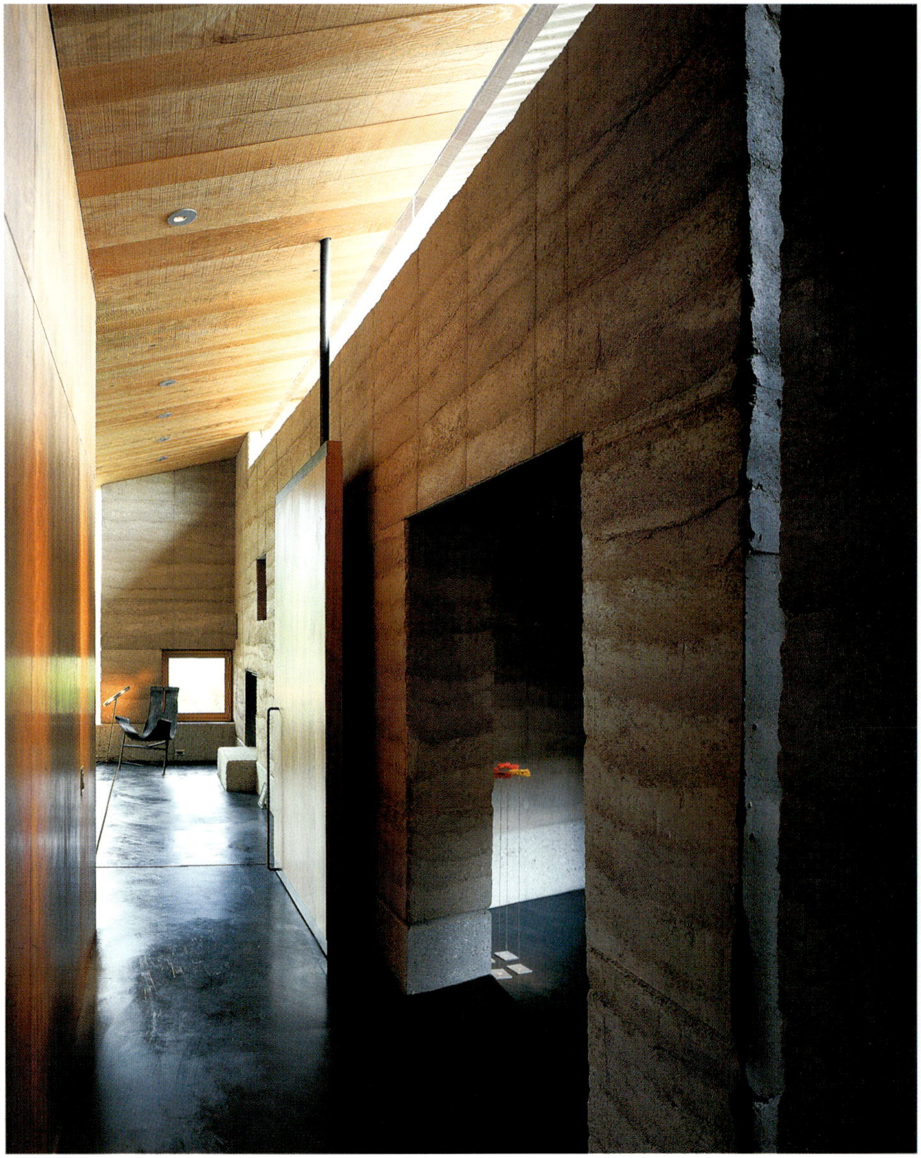

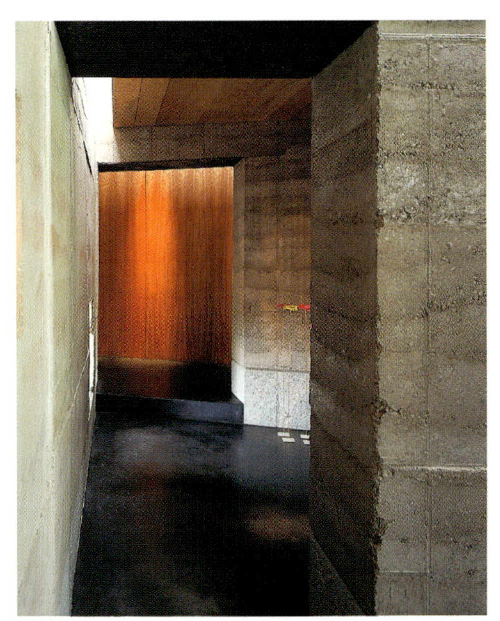

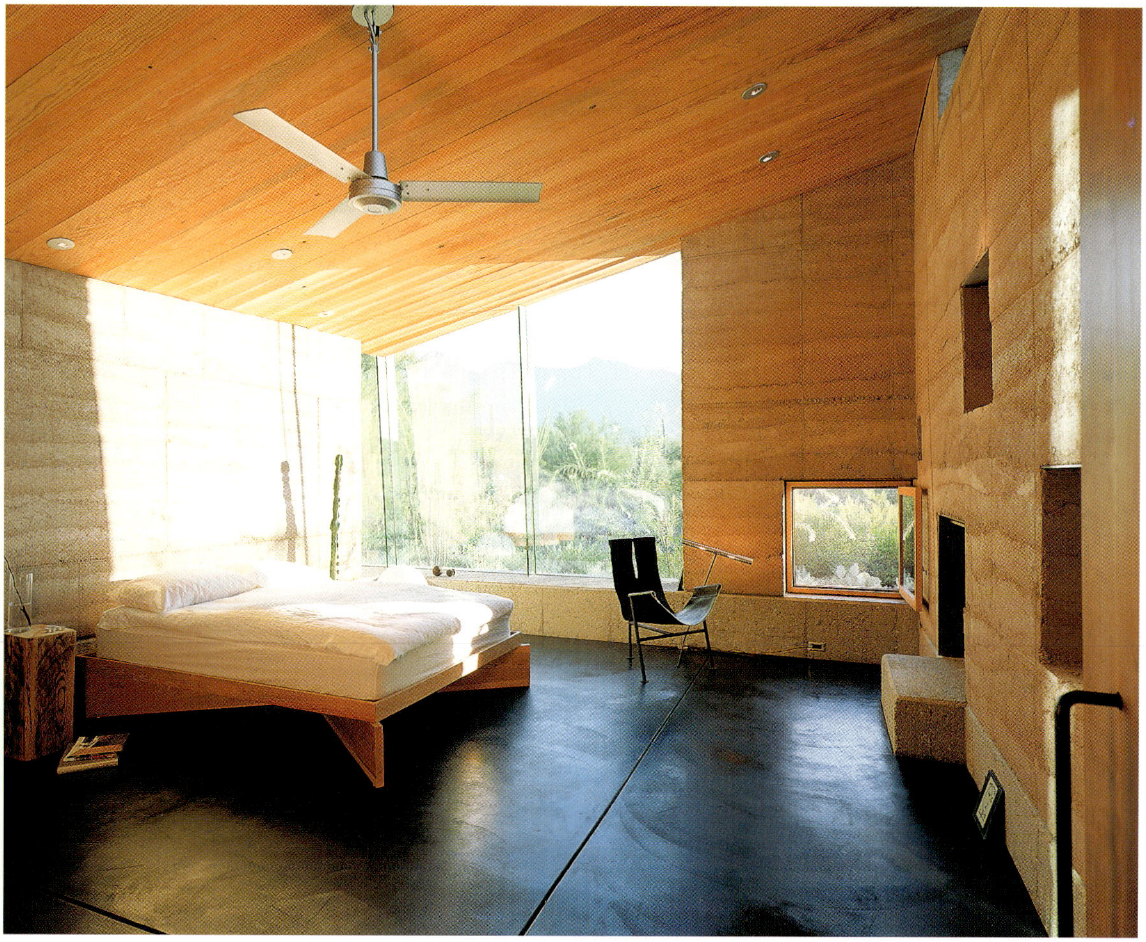

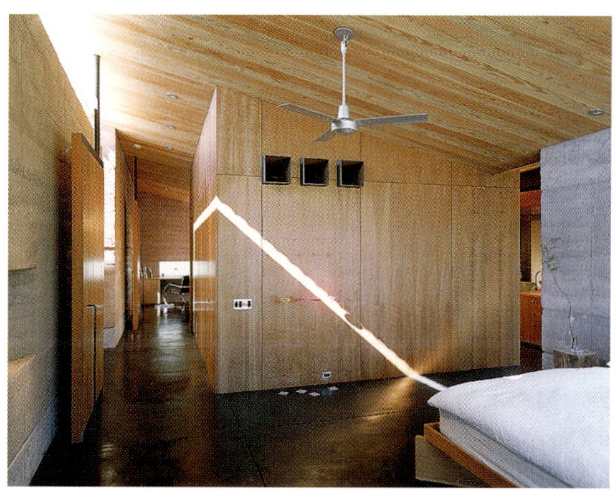

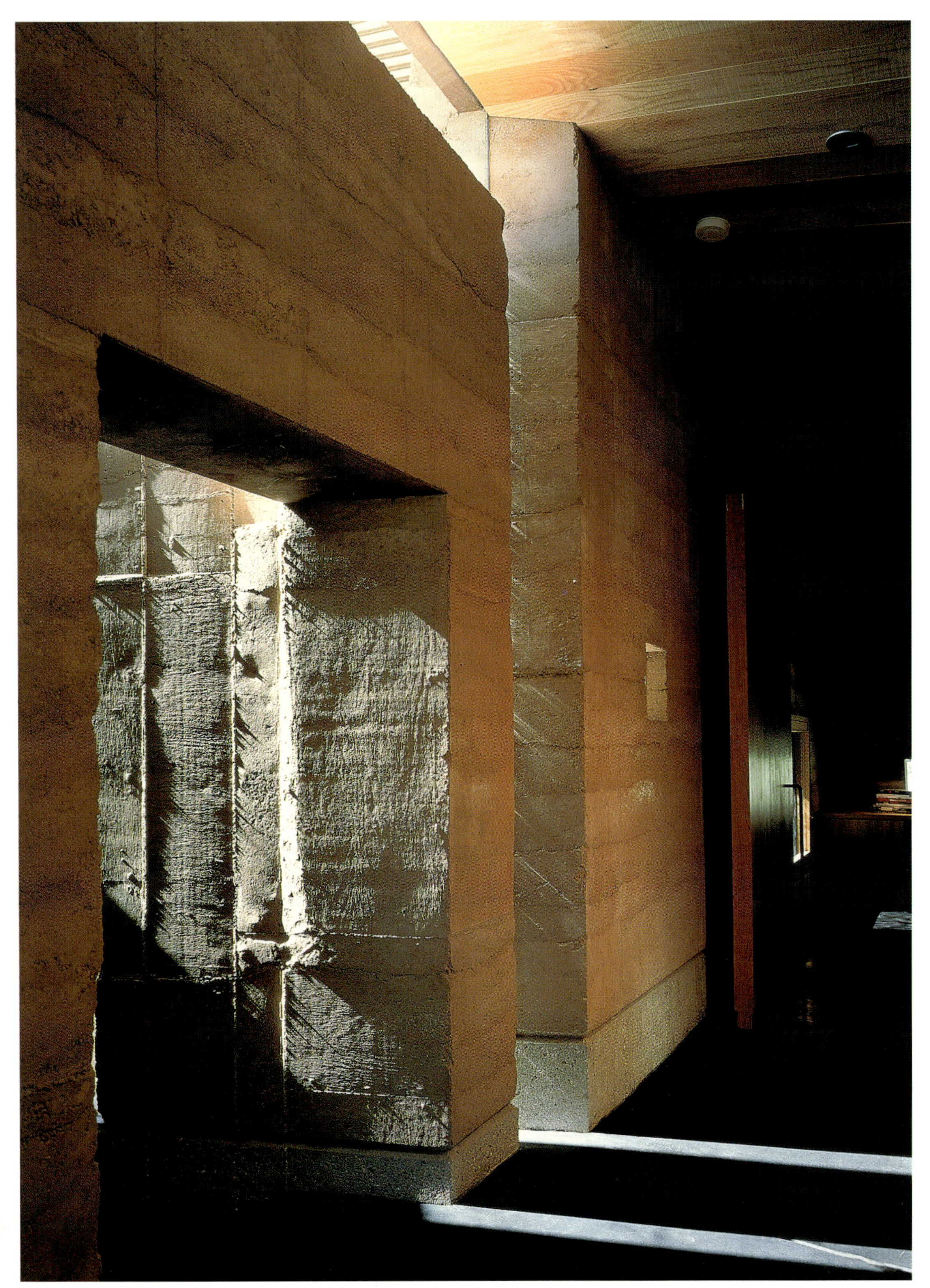

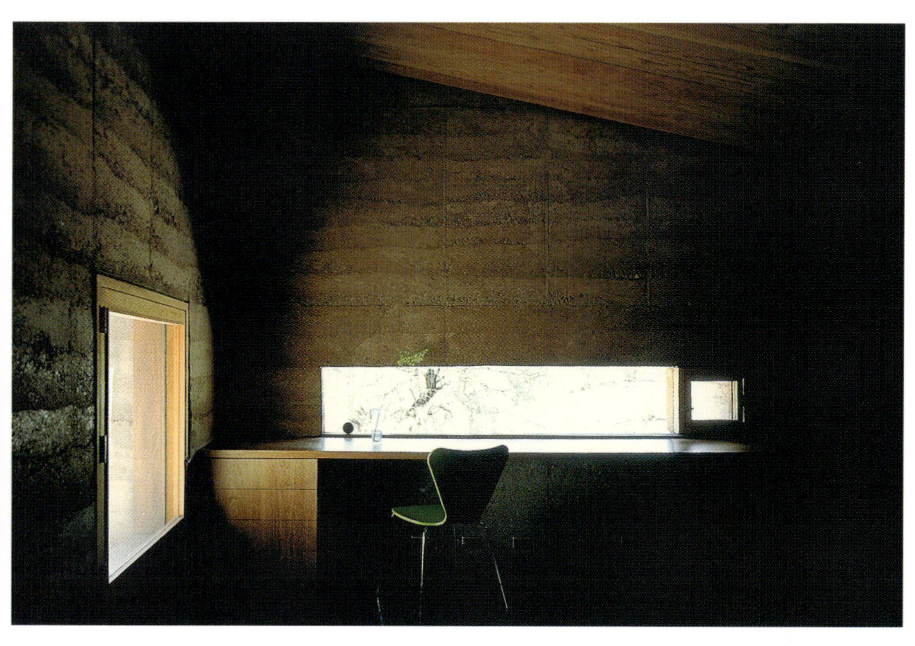

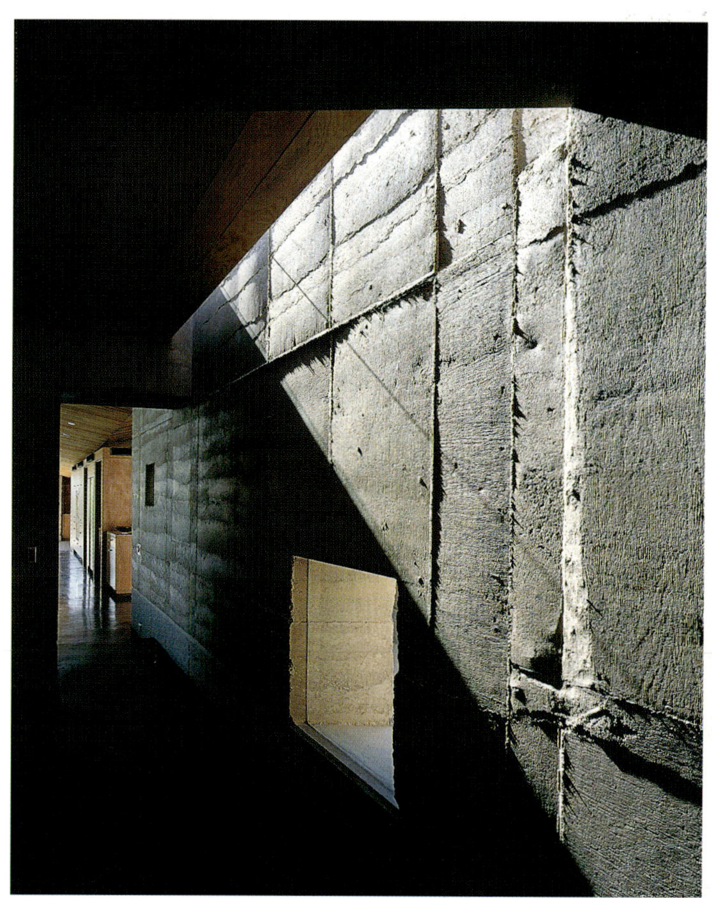

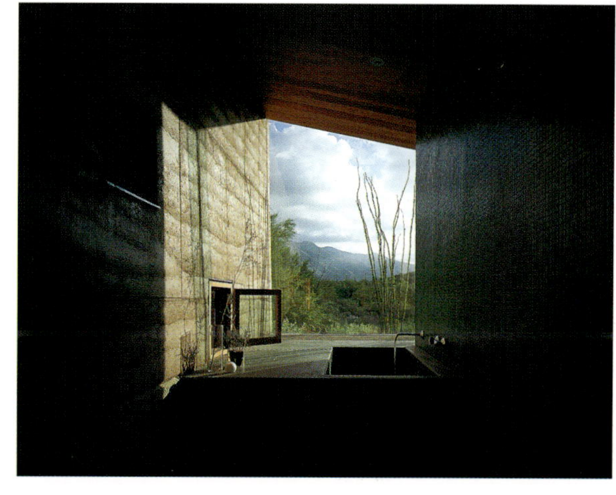

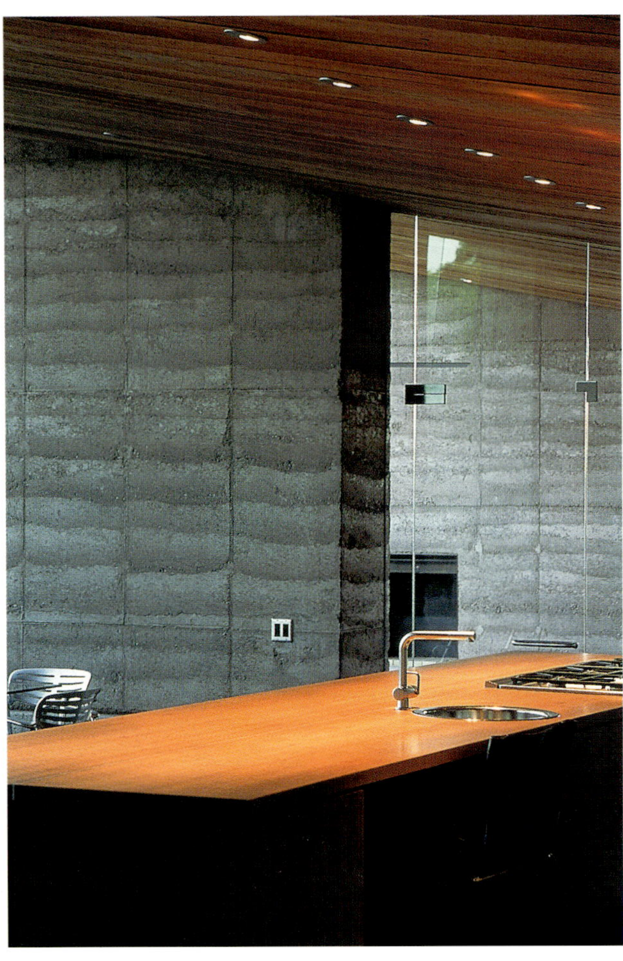

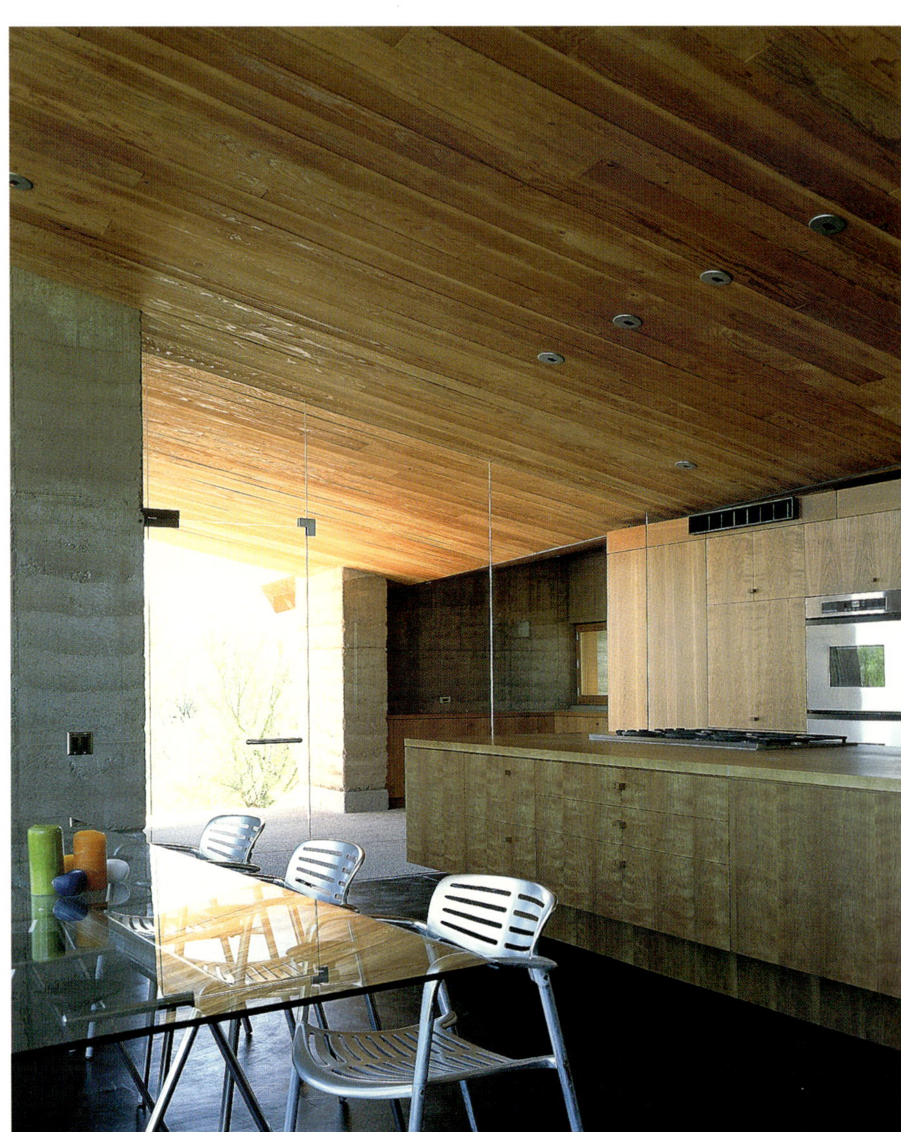

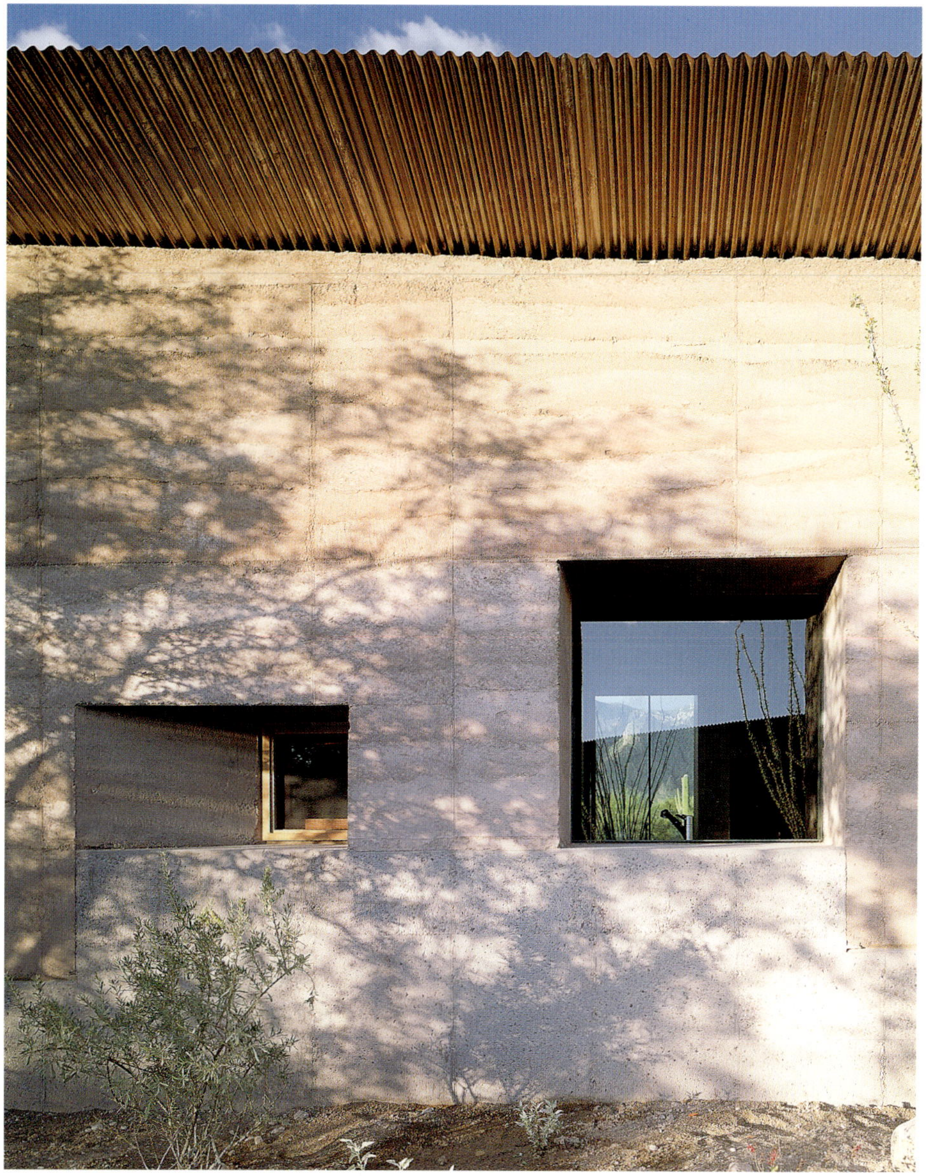

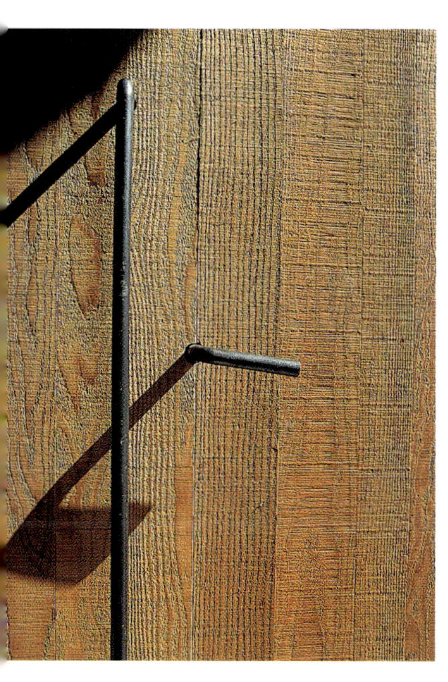

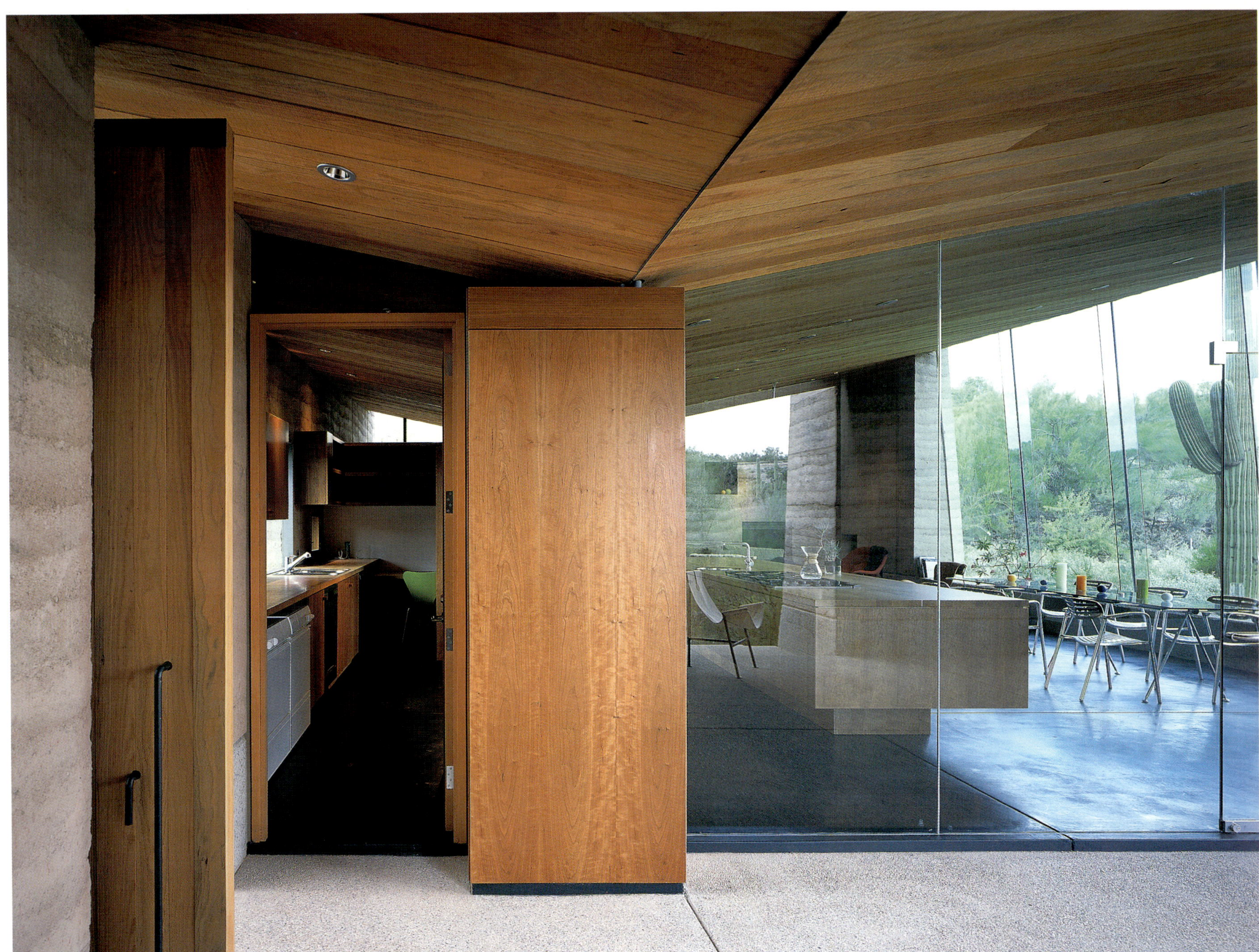

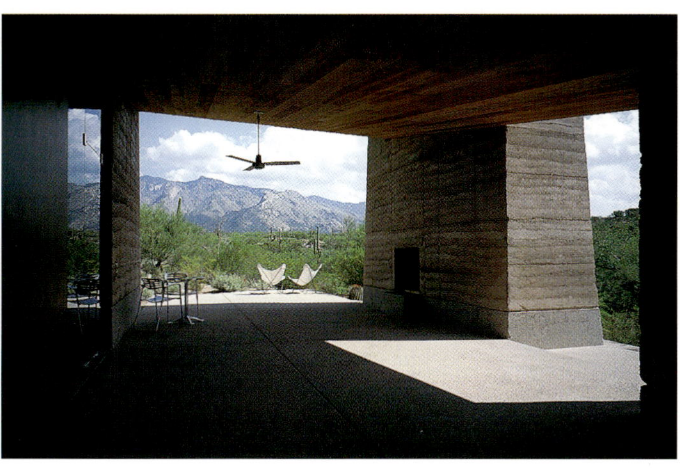

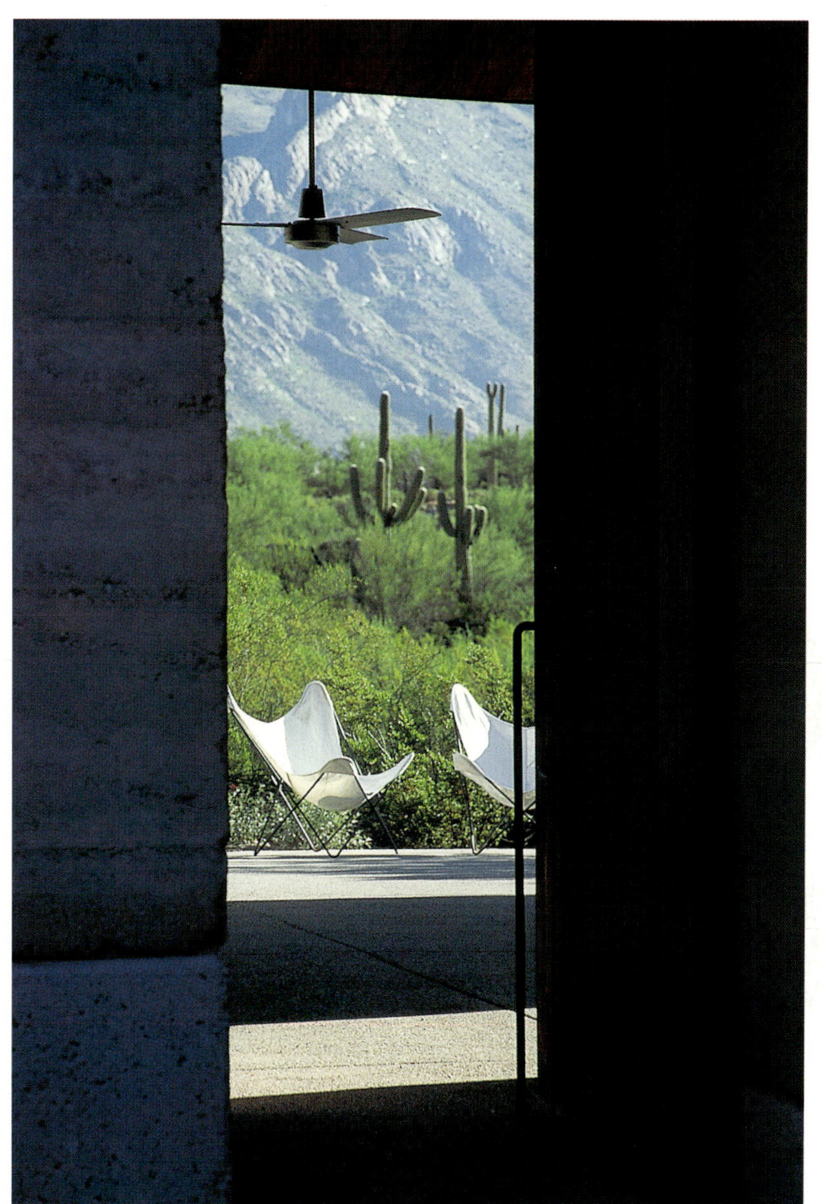

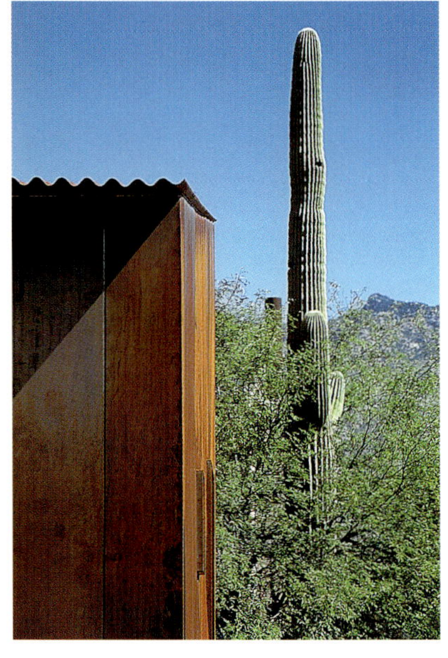

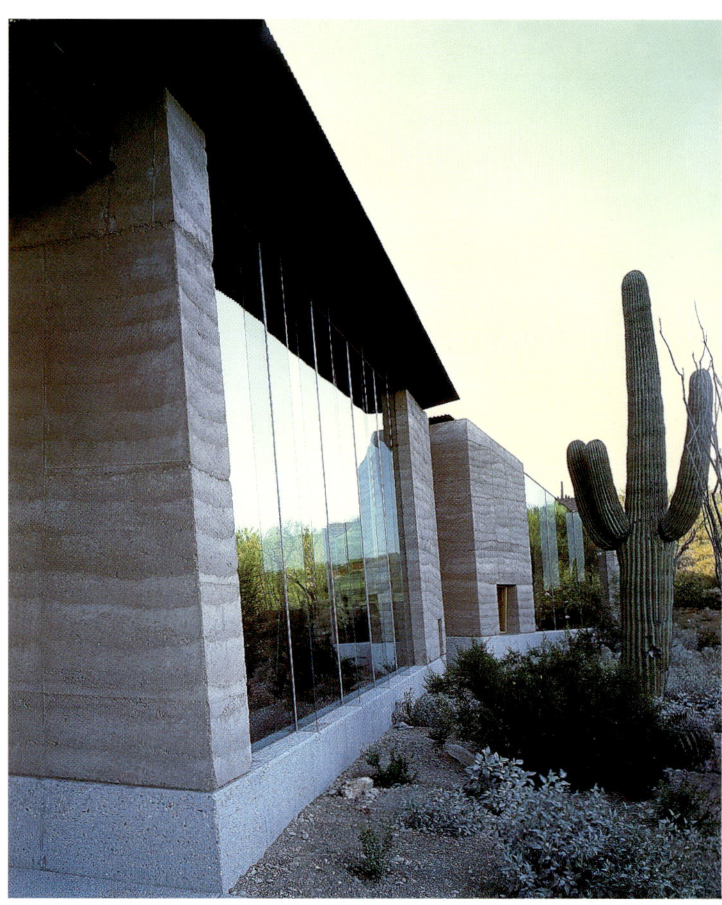

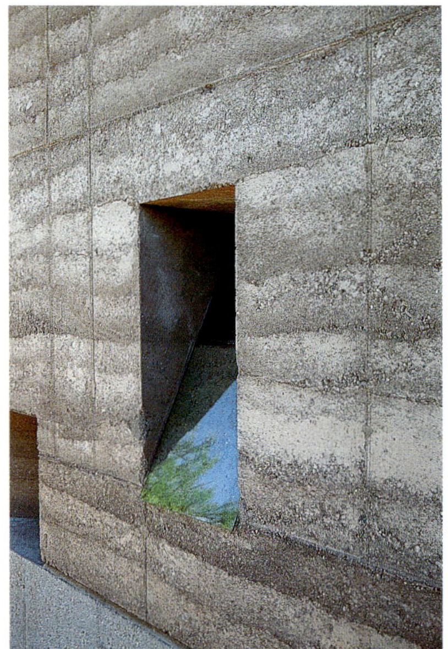

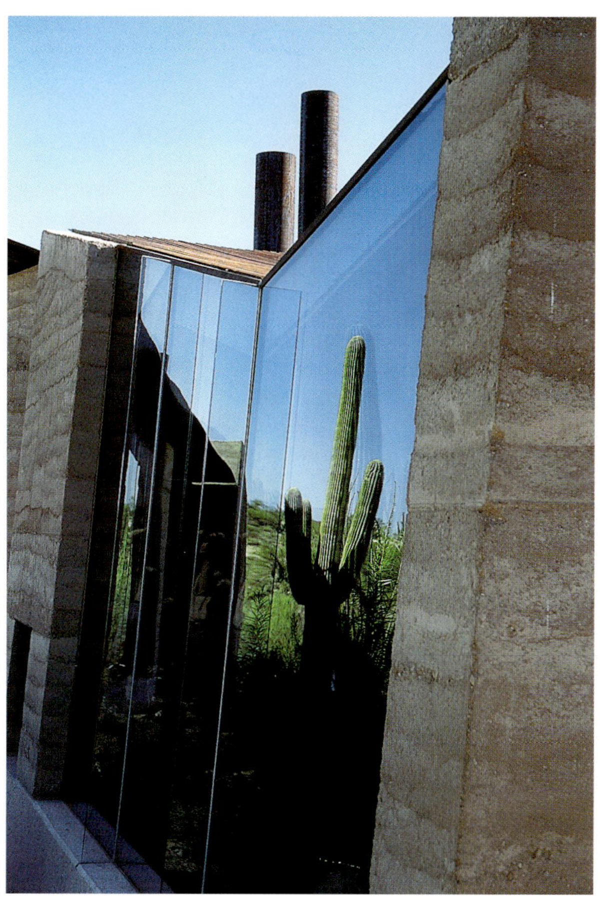
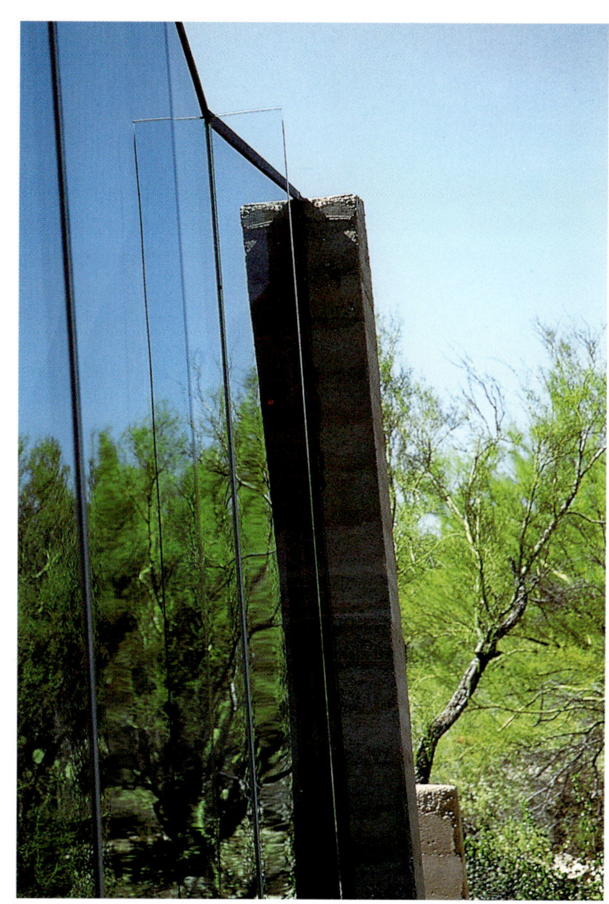

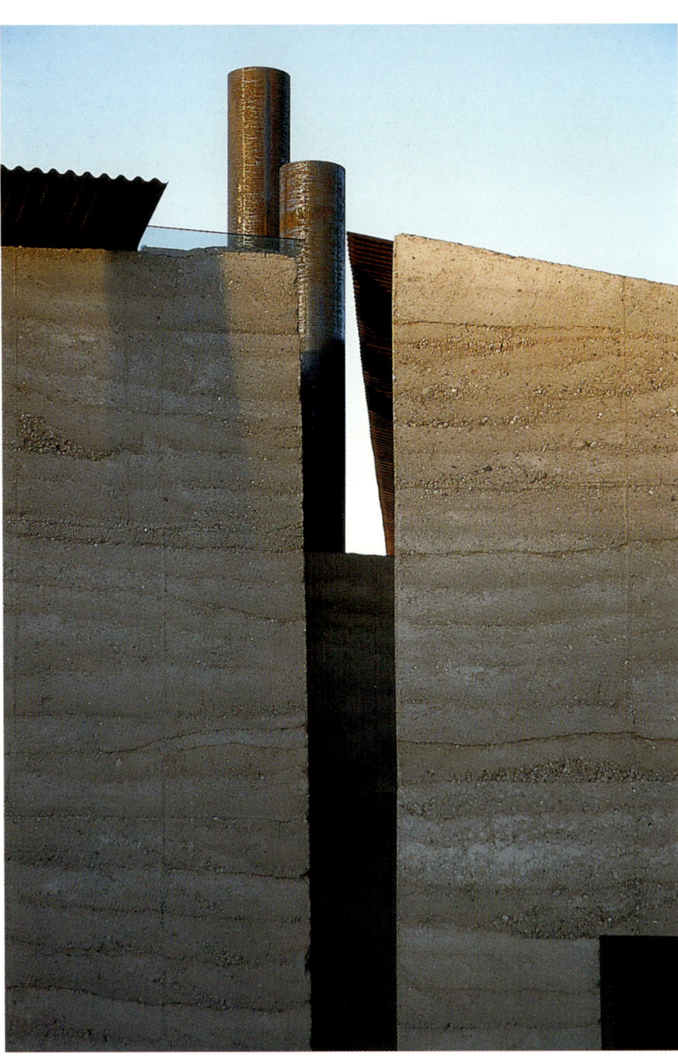

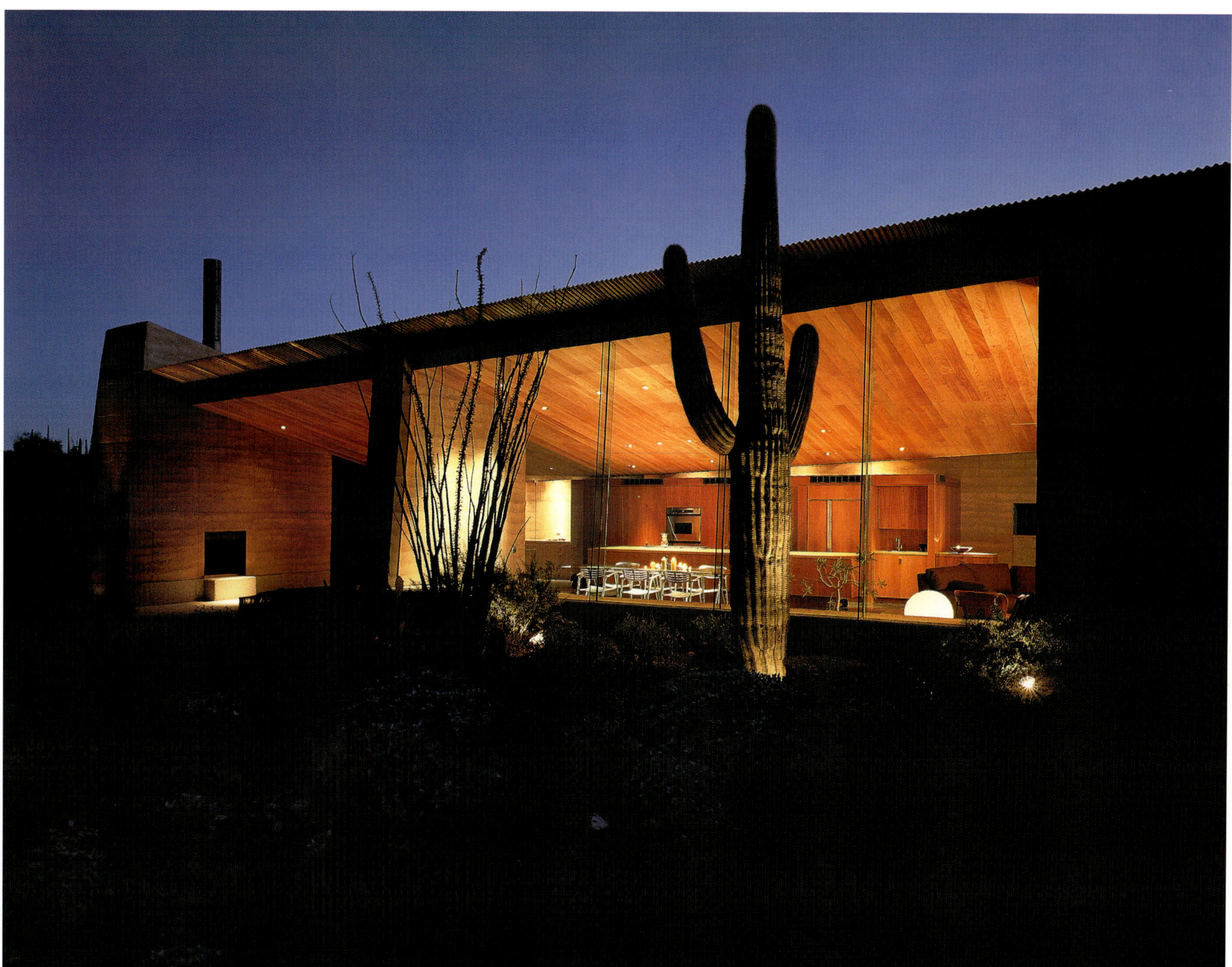

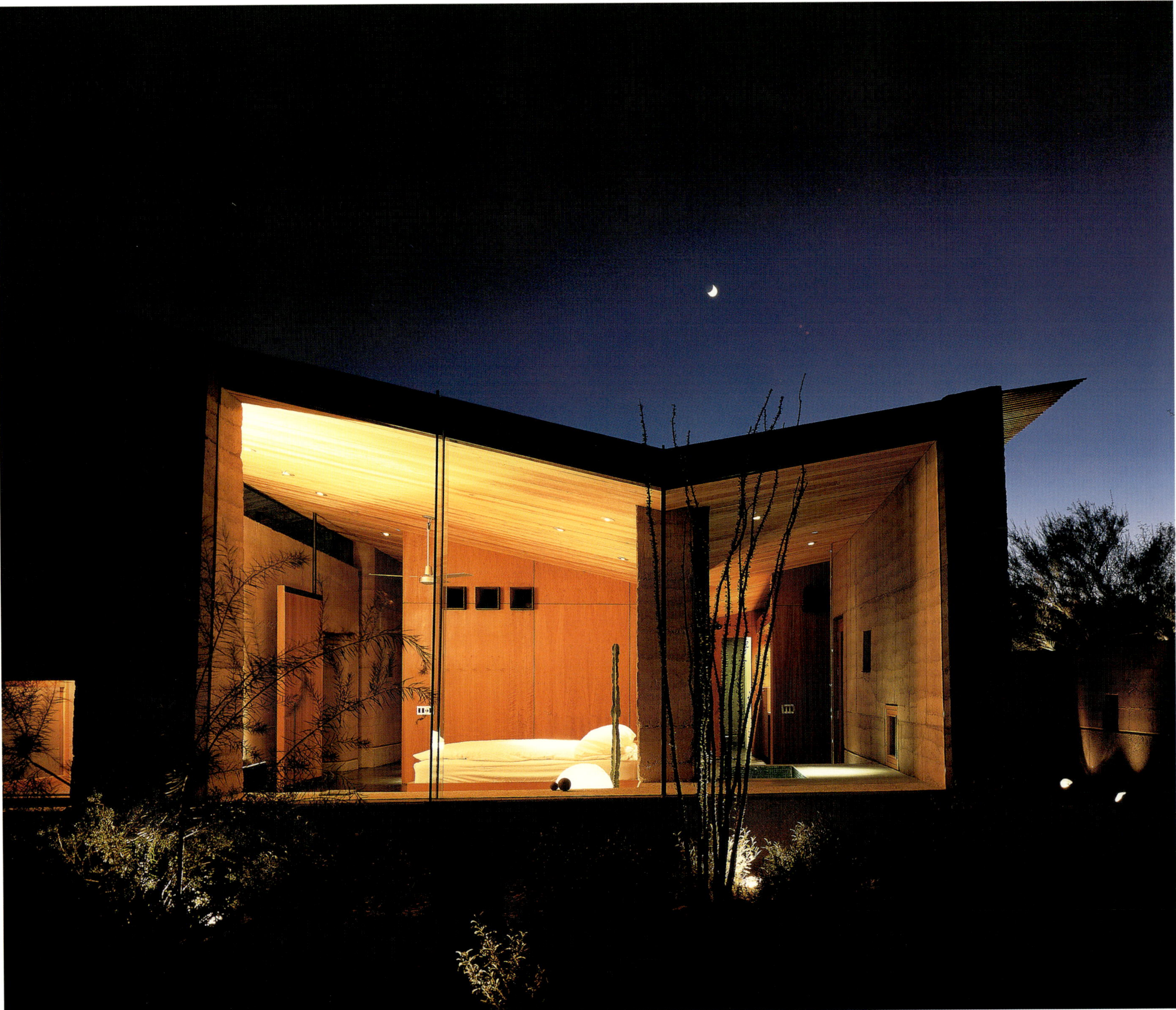

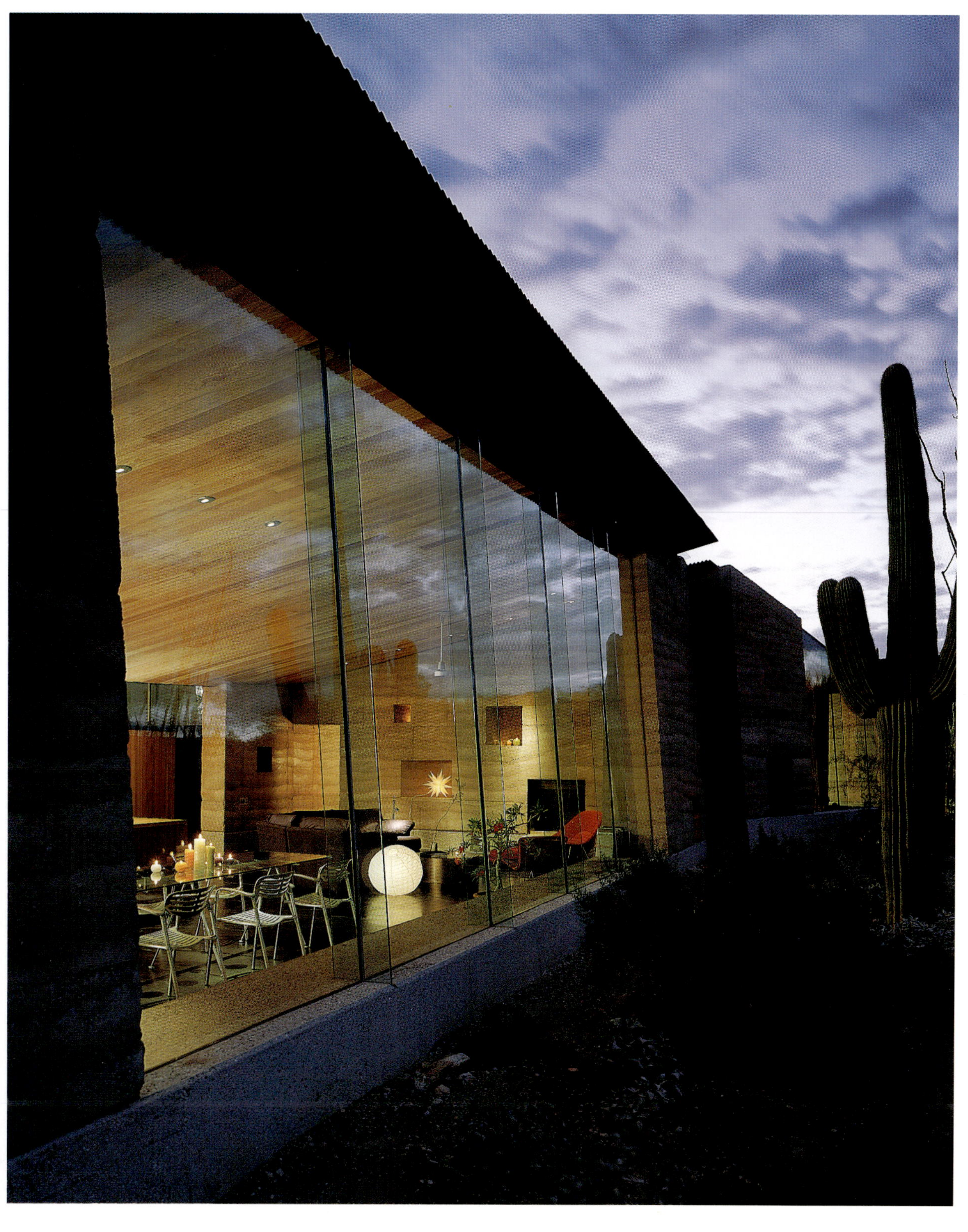

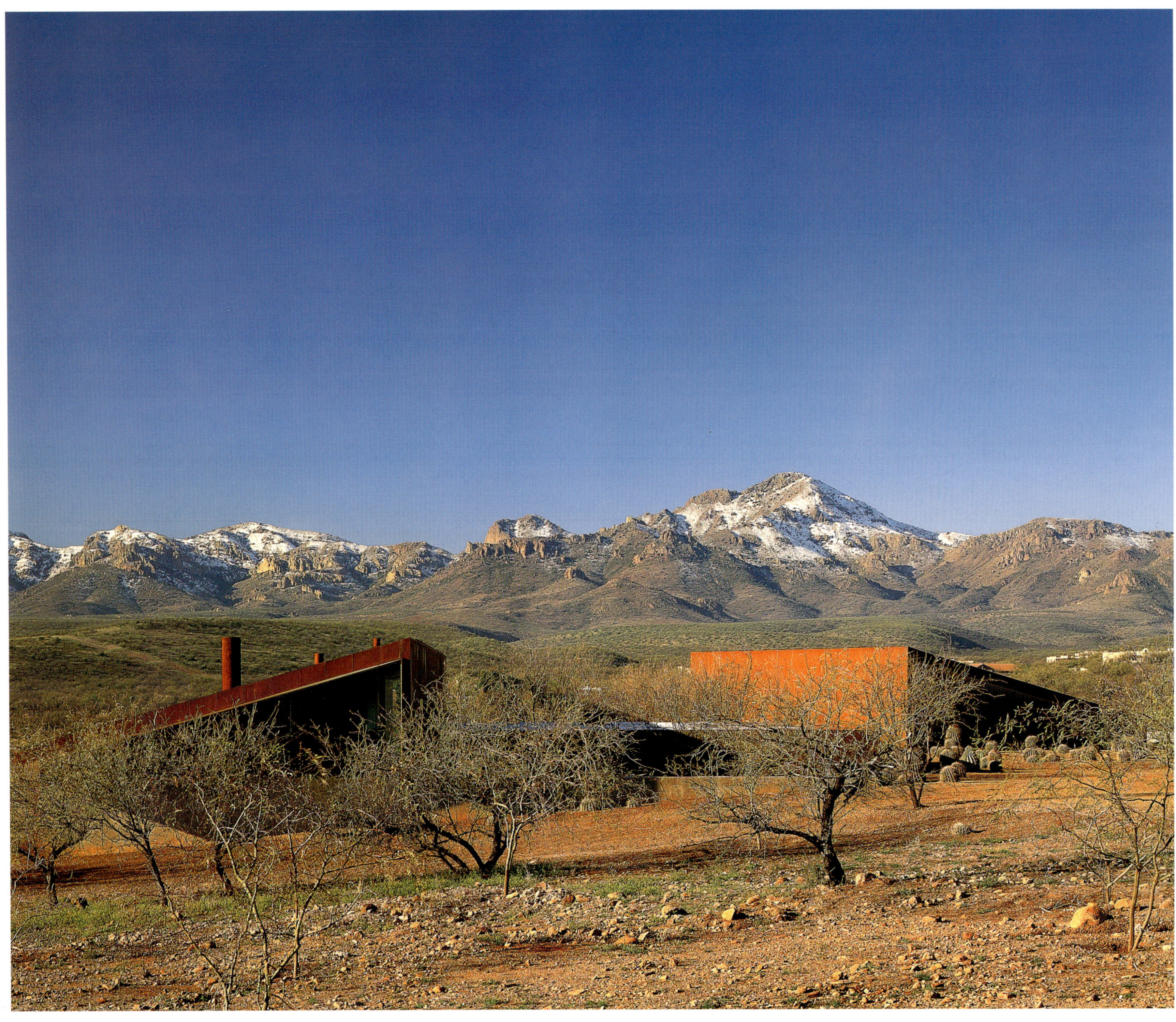

TUBAC HOUSE

From the gravel drive only the glazed ends of the above-grade forms can be seen, hovering. At night they appear as abstract glowing forms. From this view the building's concept is revealed. A level shelf was cut into the hill and defined by two U-shaped concrete retaining walls. Two simple shed forms frame a large linear courtyard below.

The gravel path to the house crunches beneath your feet. Through the garden of barrel cactuses that appear to be standing guard, one descends into a courtyard by way of a stair wedged between the two retaining walls. From here, an oasis unfolds: cool dark shaded areas, the sound of water trickling, humming birds, the smell of sage and flowers, reflections. Planting arrangements and detailing assert a refined man-made character. The courtyard provides relief from the overwhelmingly expansive setting while the two buildings frame a cropped view of Tumacacaori Peak—the client's favorite. A negative edge pool located at the west end of the courtyard extends the experience to this view.

The house's weathered steel forms, like some rusted artifacts from a cowboy camp, are oriented to frame prime views. The coarseness of the rough steel exterior contrasts with the refinement of the interior palette of white plaster, stainless steel, maple, and translucent glass. Protruding steel box window forms penetrate the building in apparently random but carefully selected locations to frame specific views of lightning storms and distant mountain ranges.

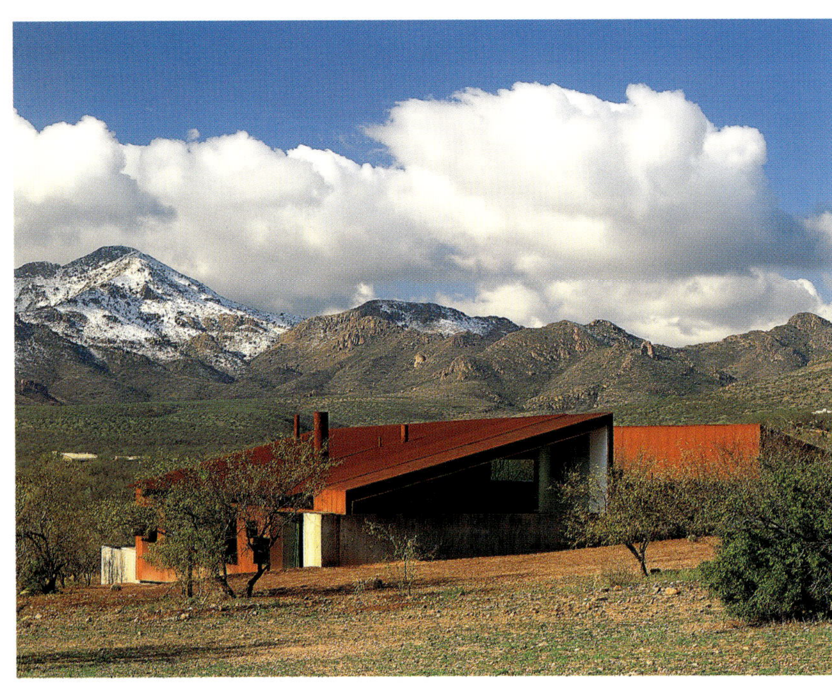

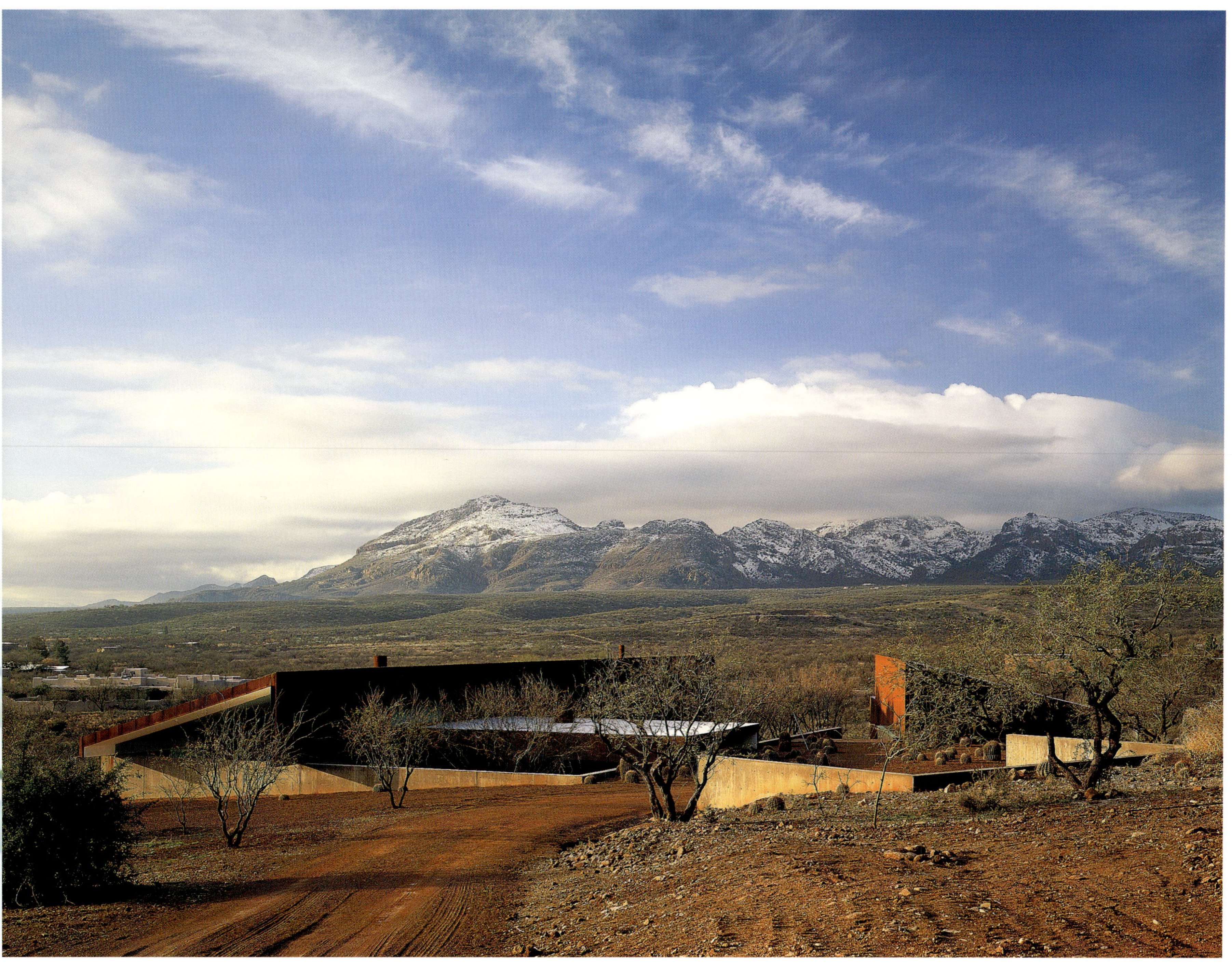

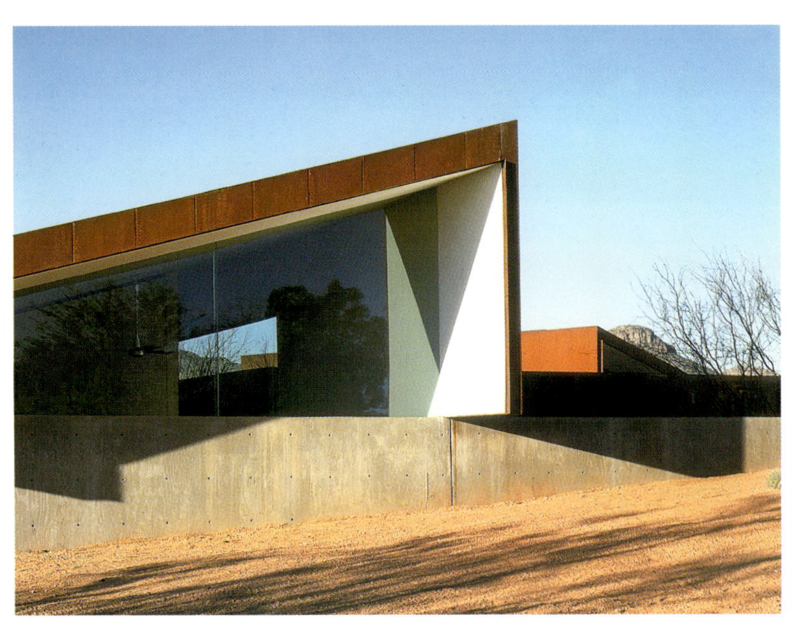

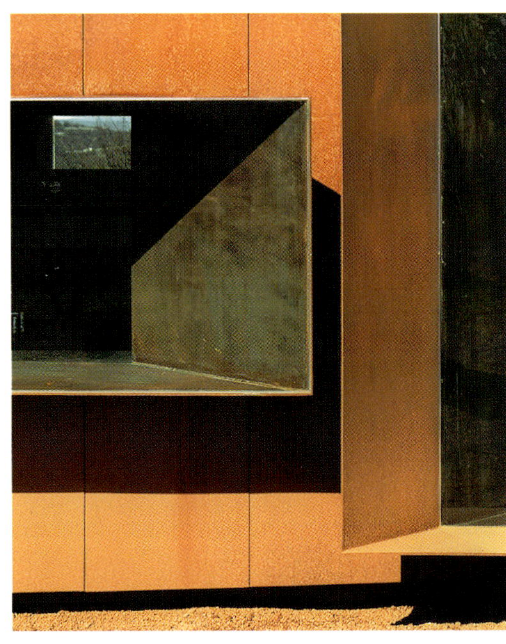

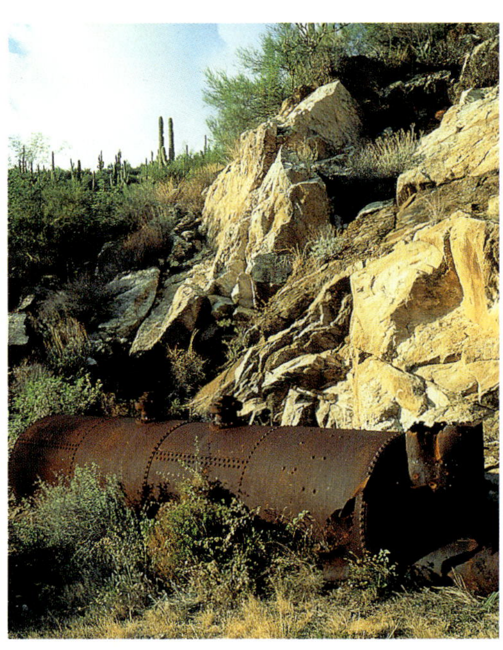

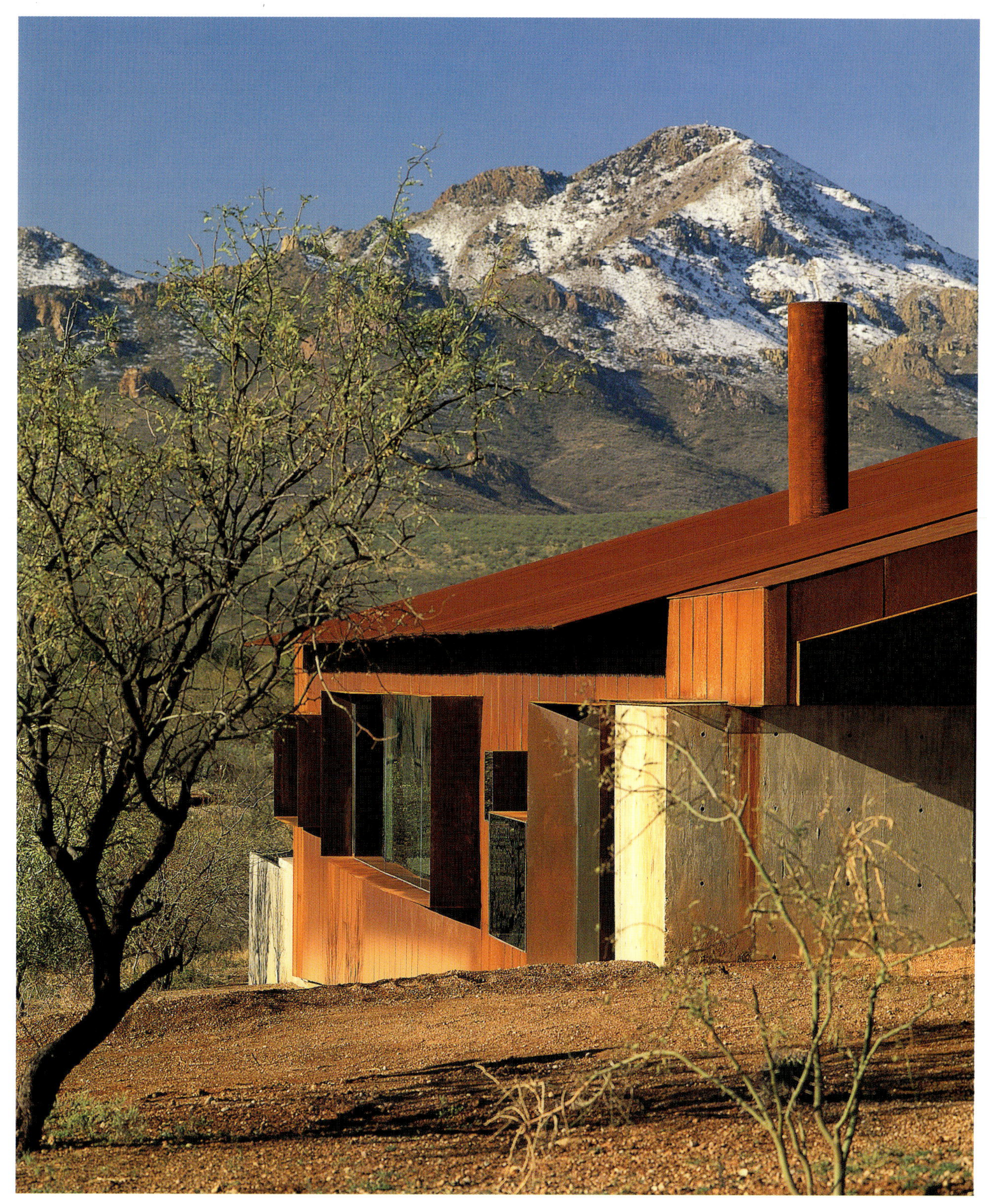

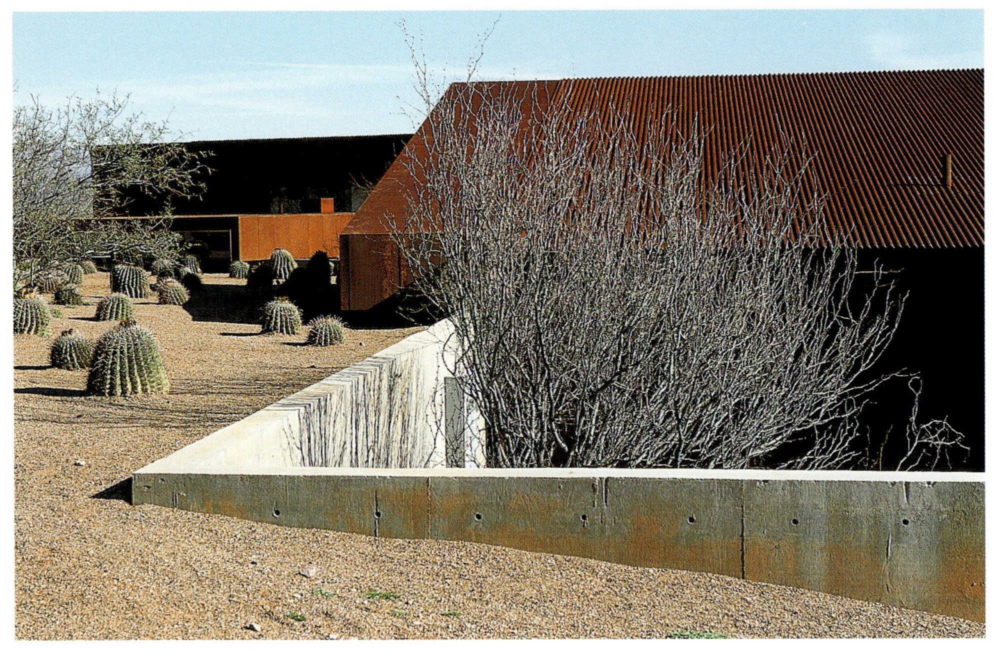

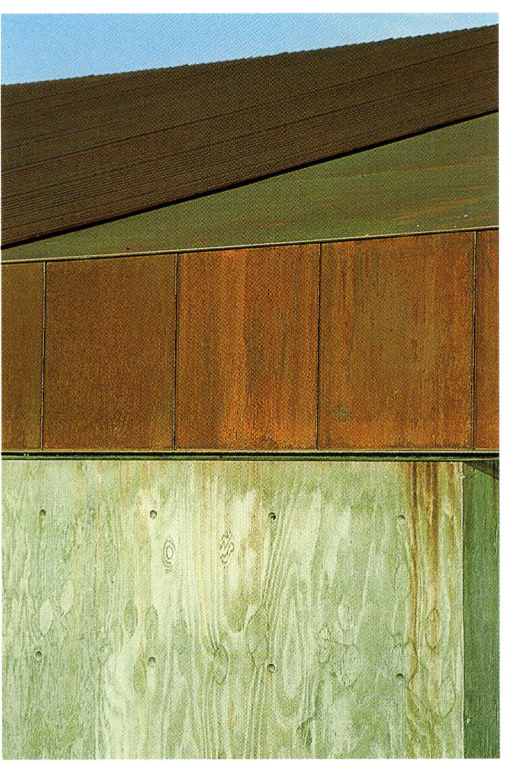

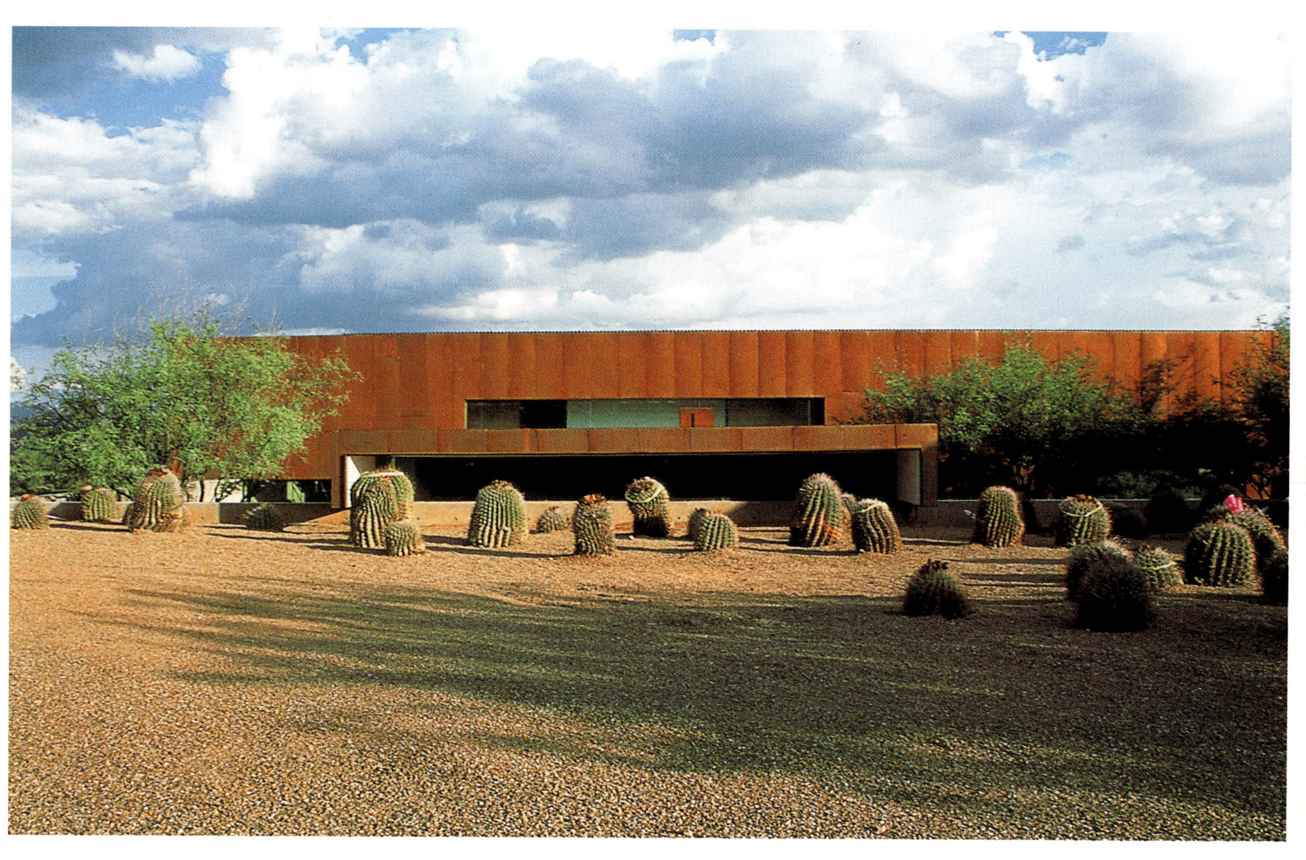

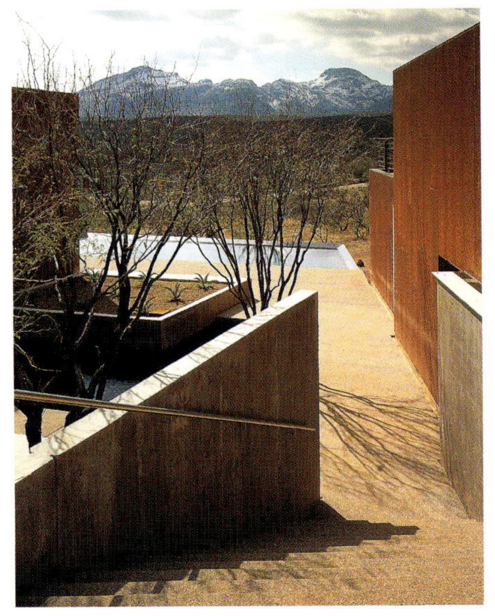

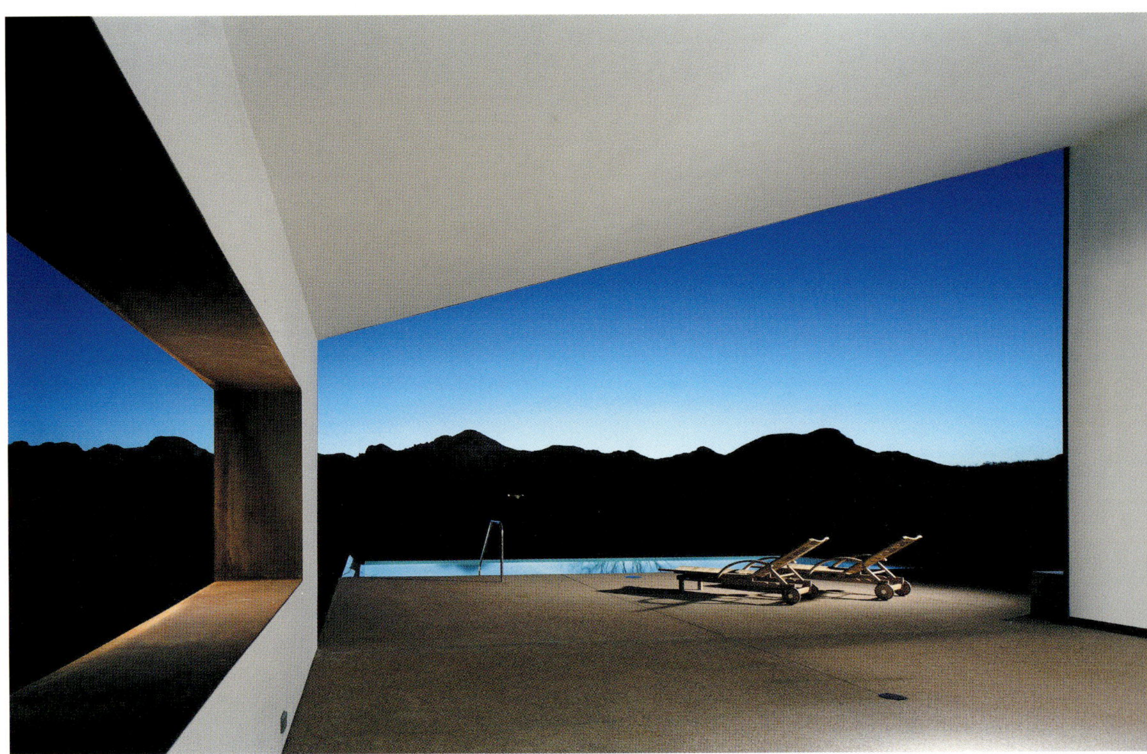

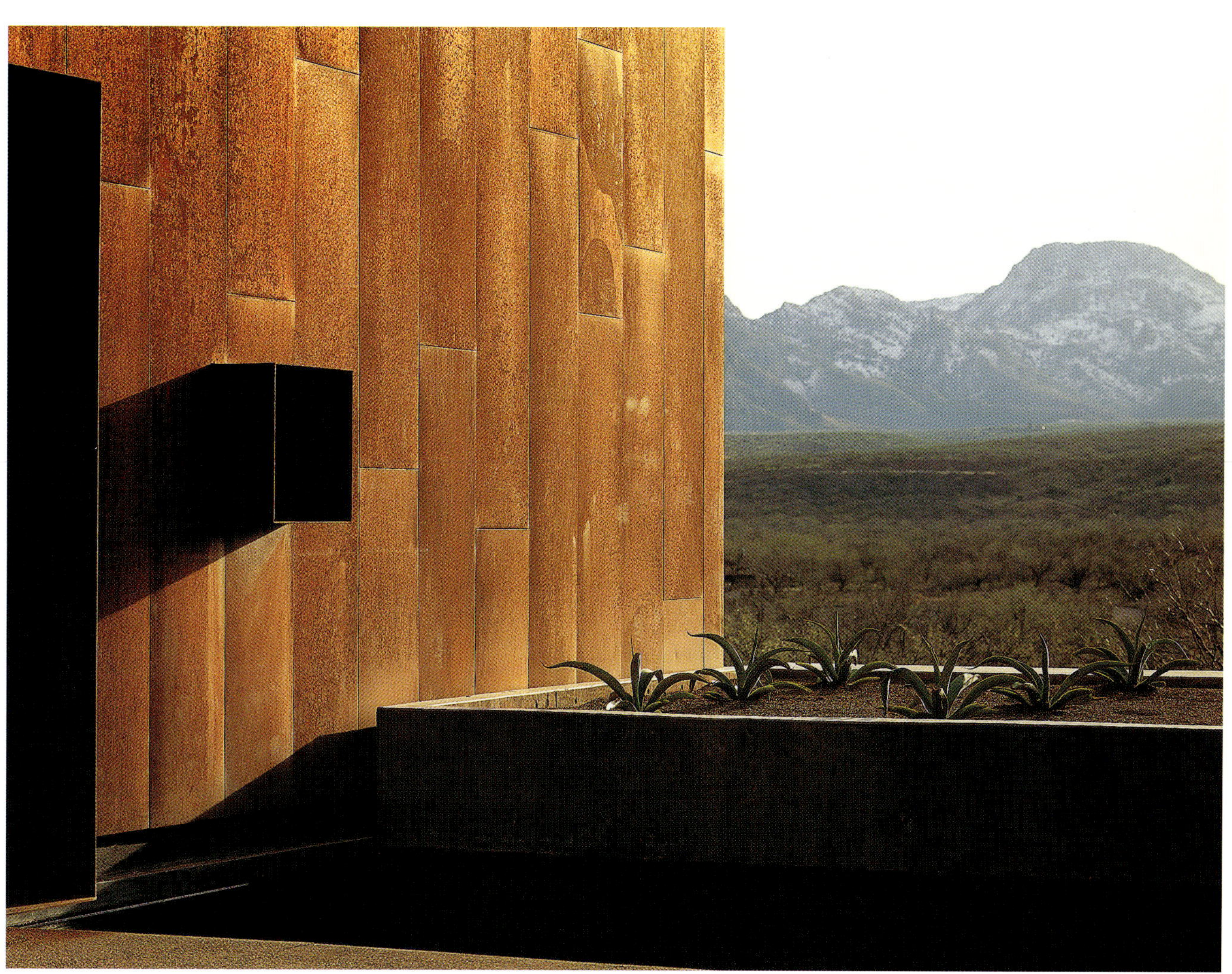

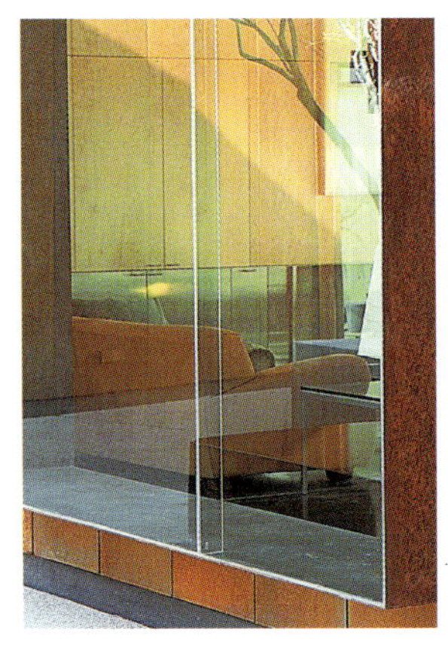

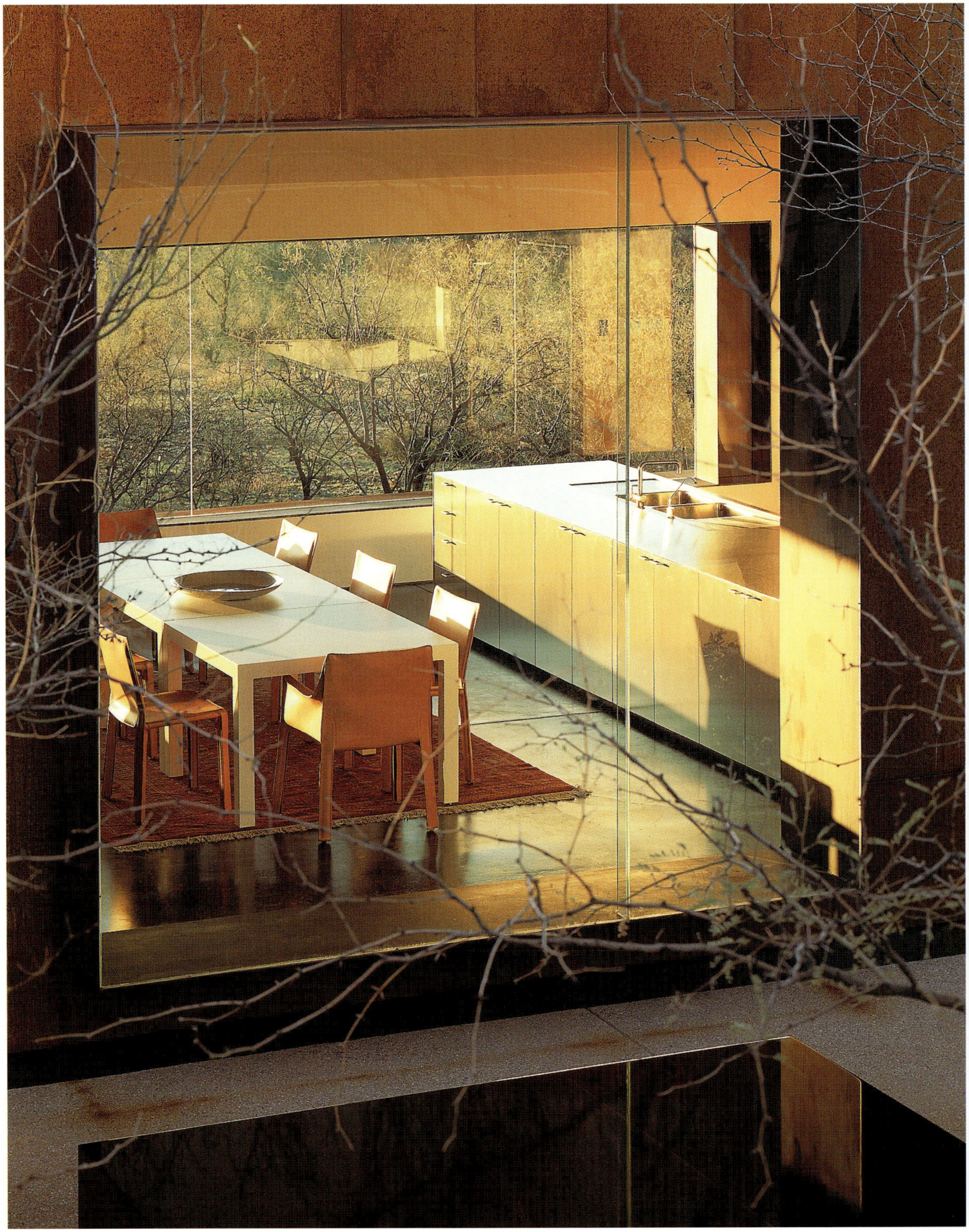

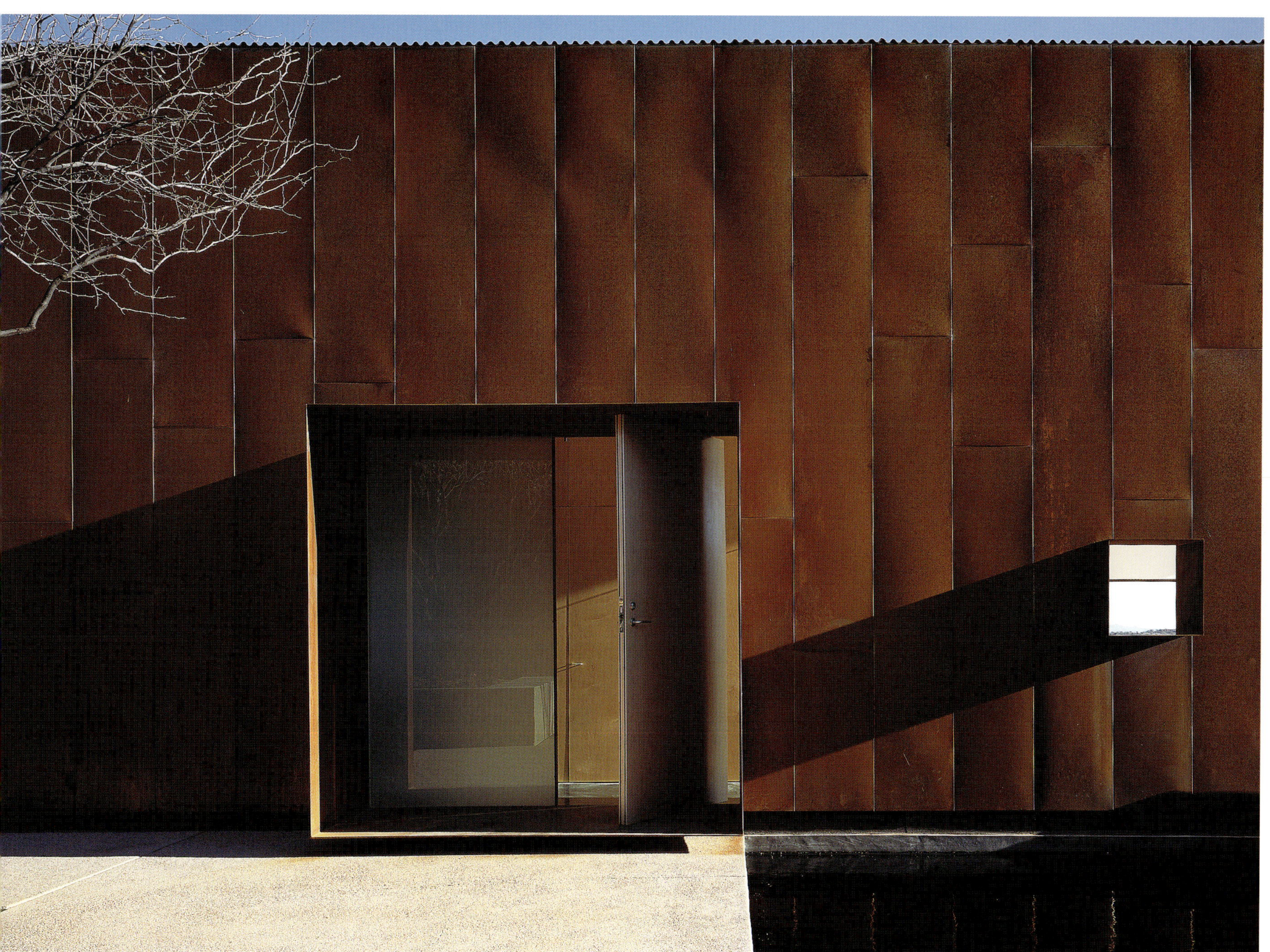

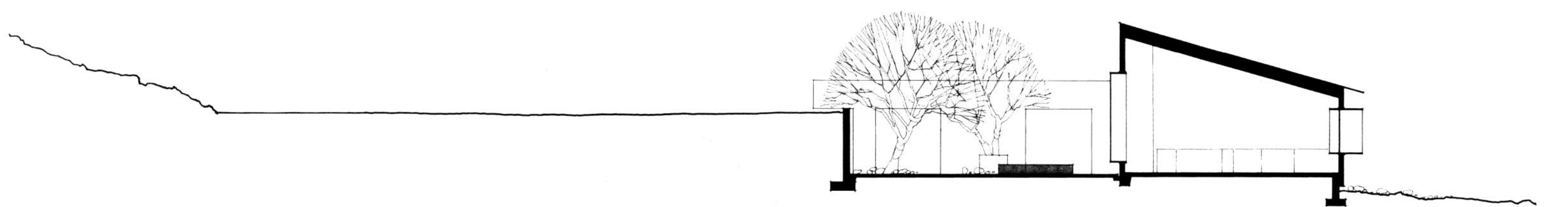

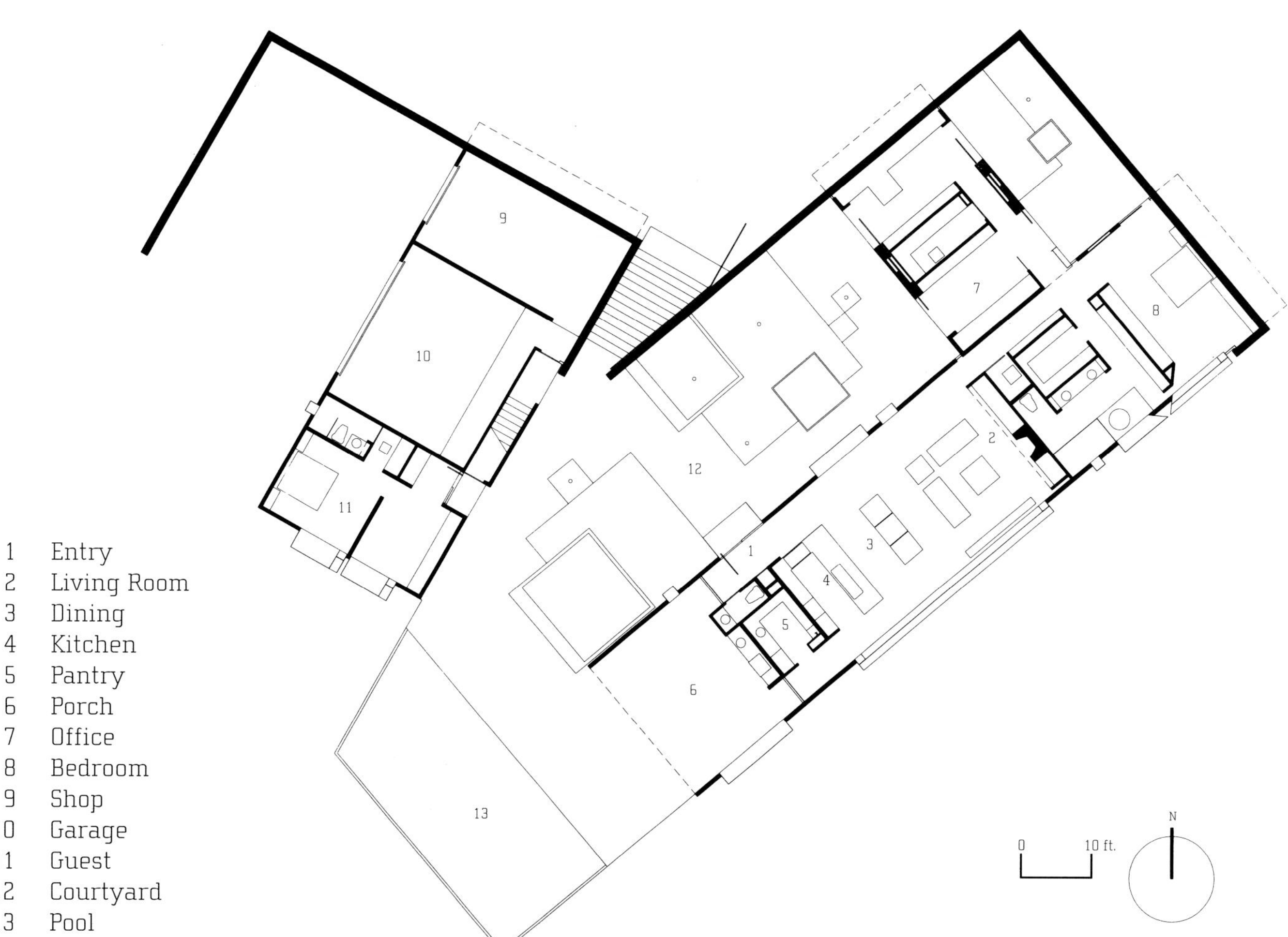
1 Entry
2 Living Room
3 Dining
4 Kitchen
5 Pantry
6 Porch
7 Office
8 Bedroom
9 Shop
10 Garage
11 Guest
12 Courtyard
13 Pool
0
10 ft.
N

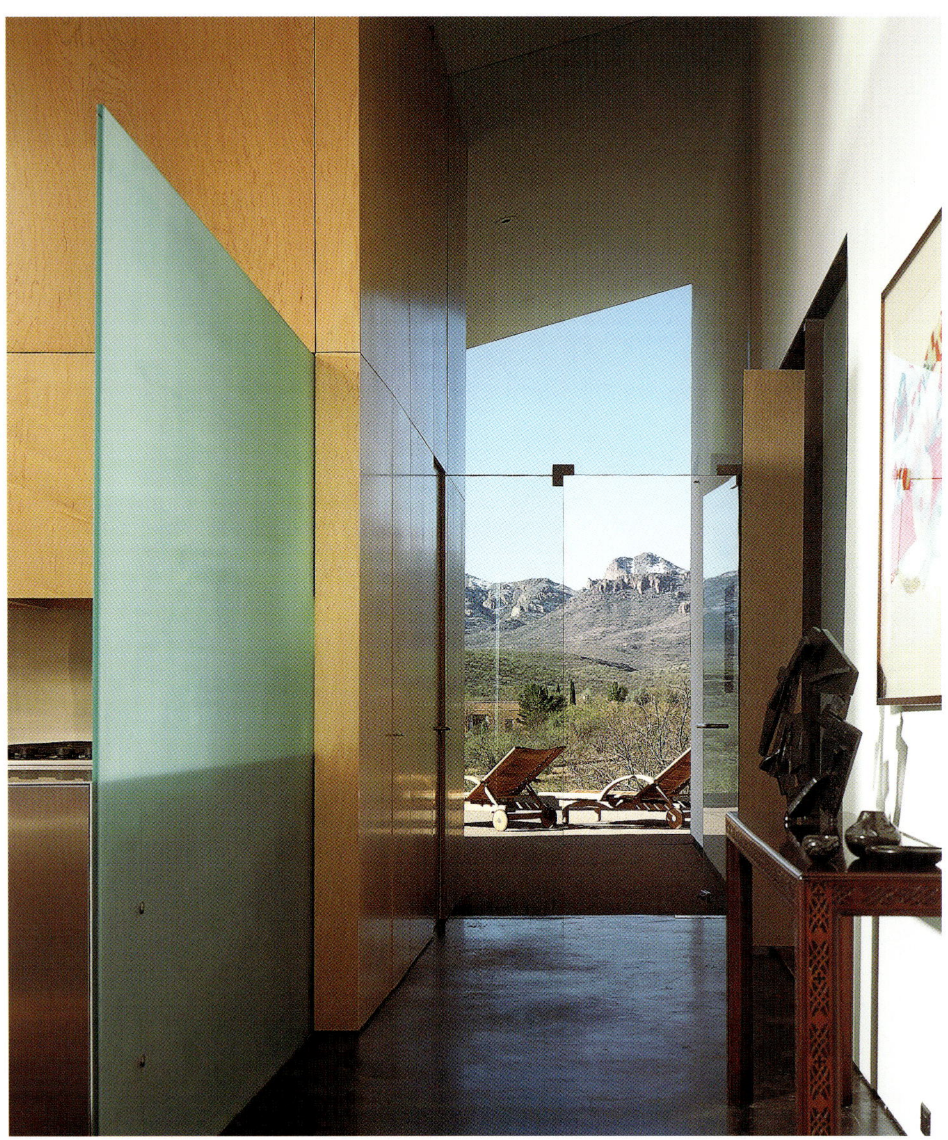

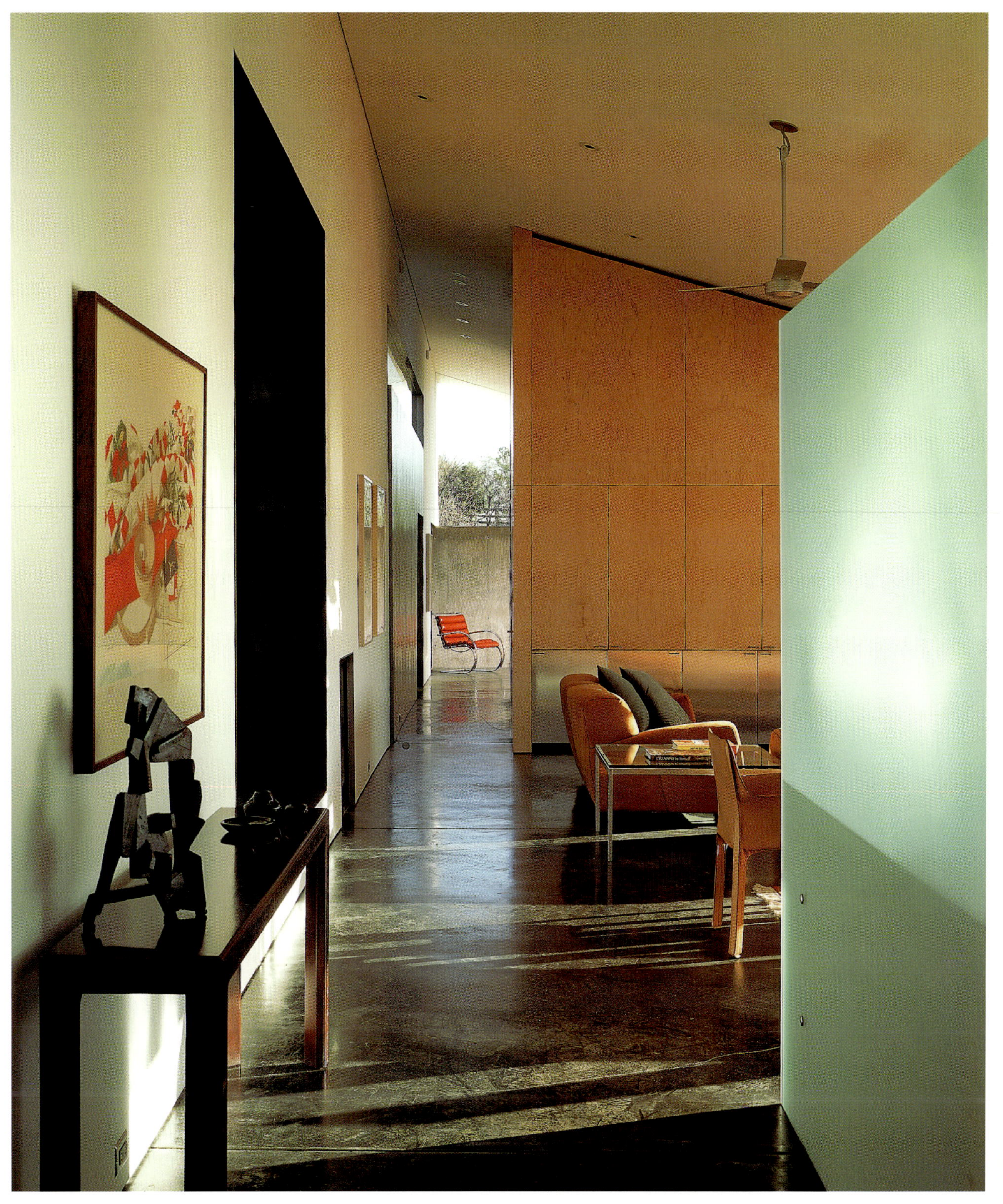

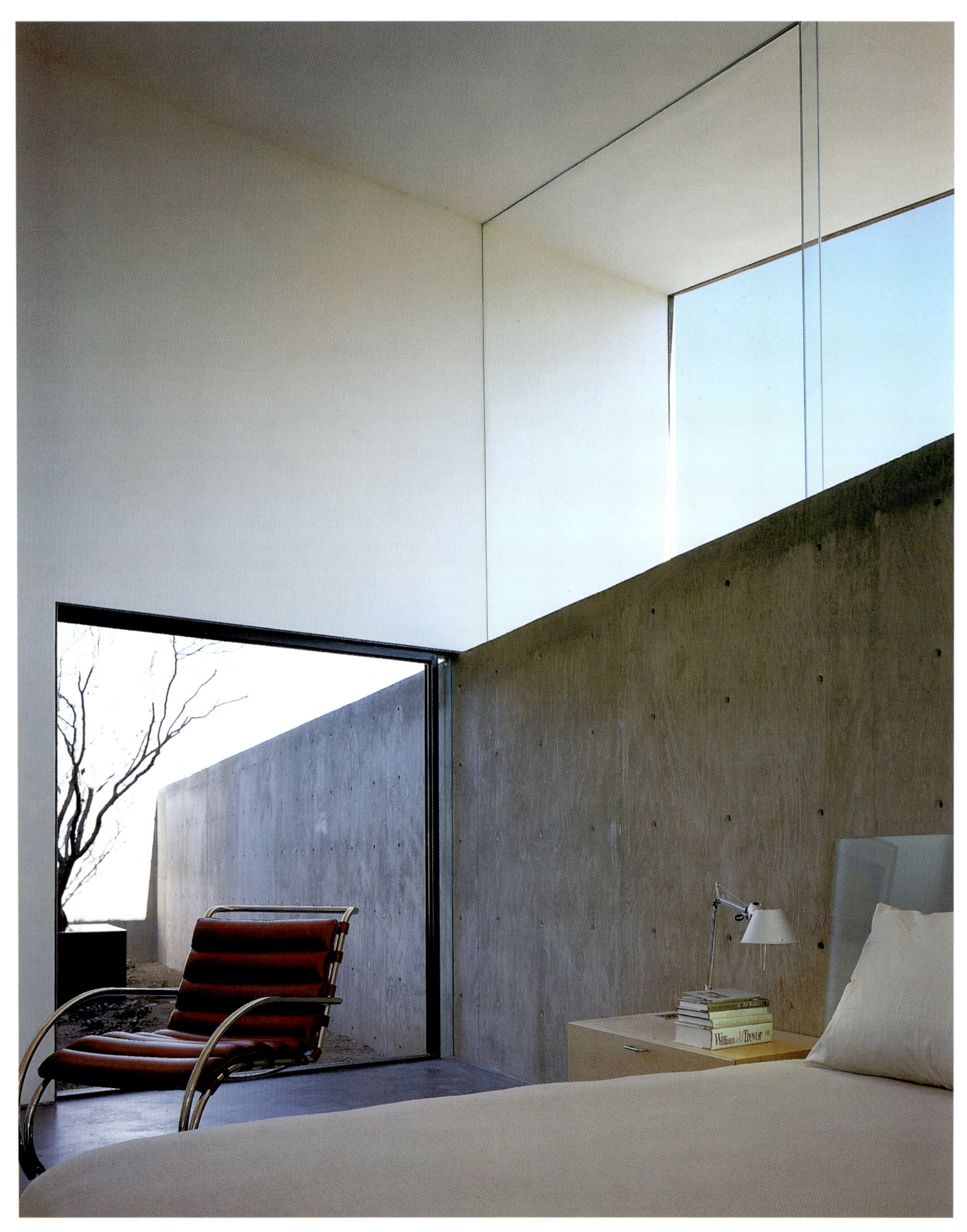

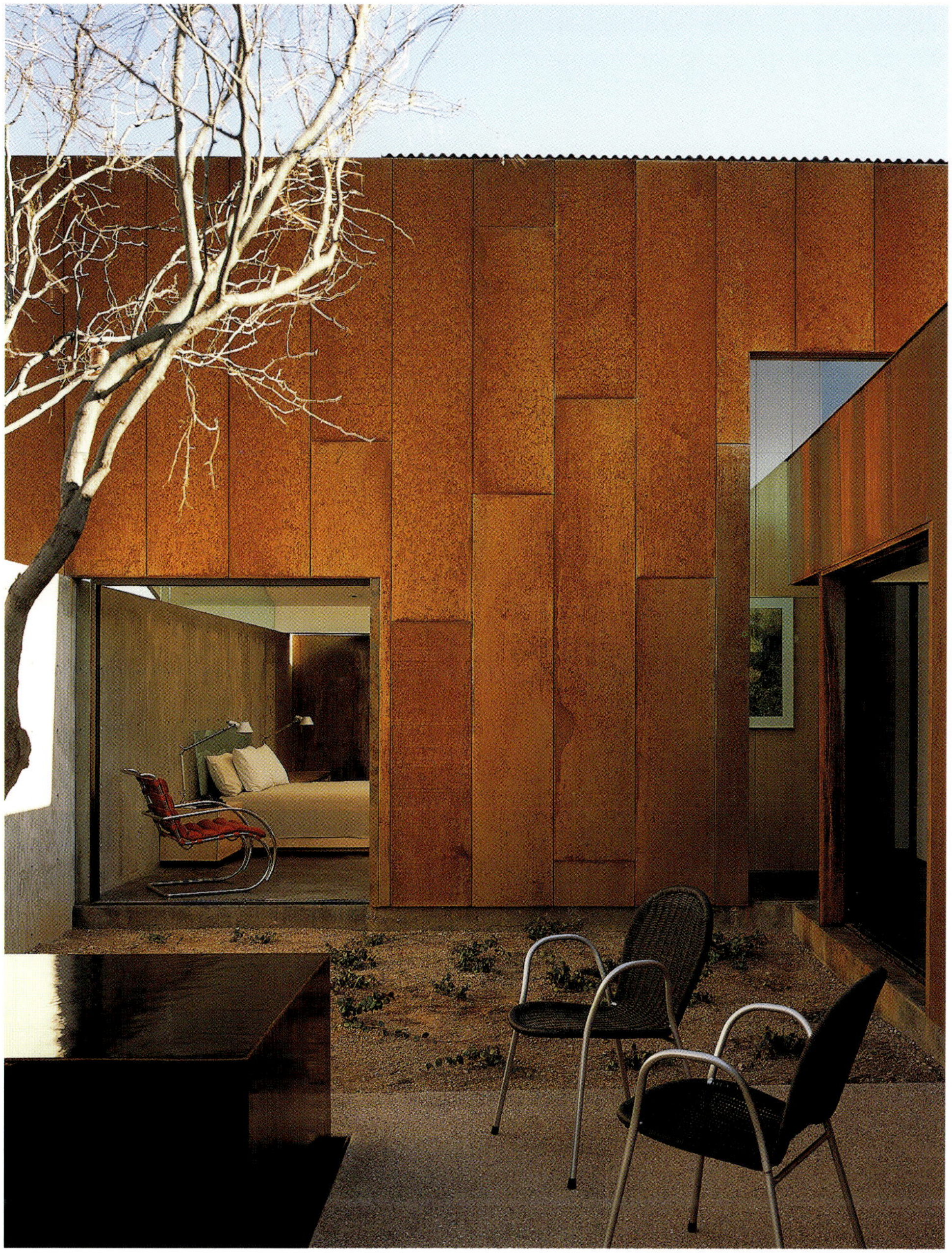

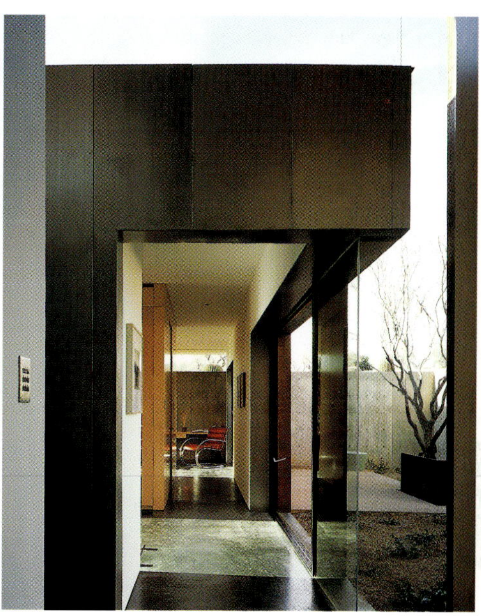

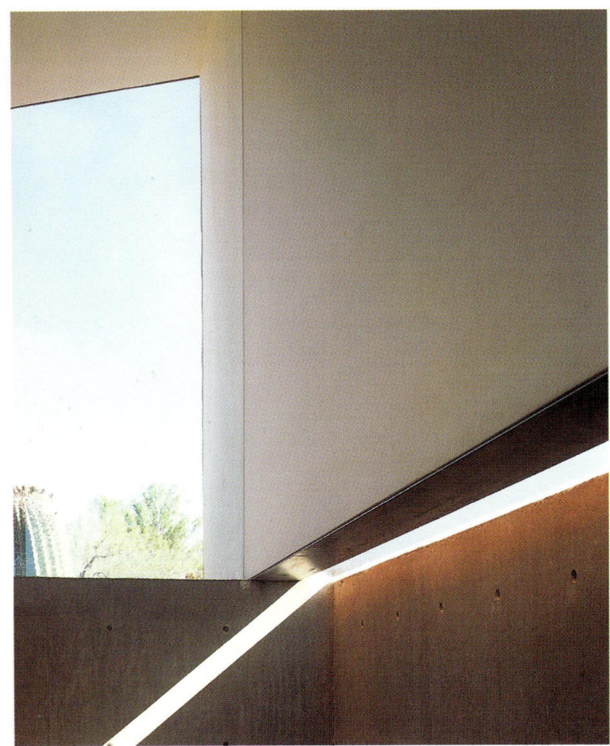

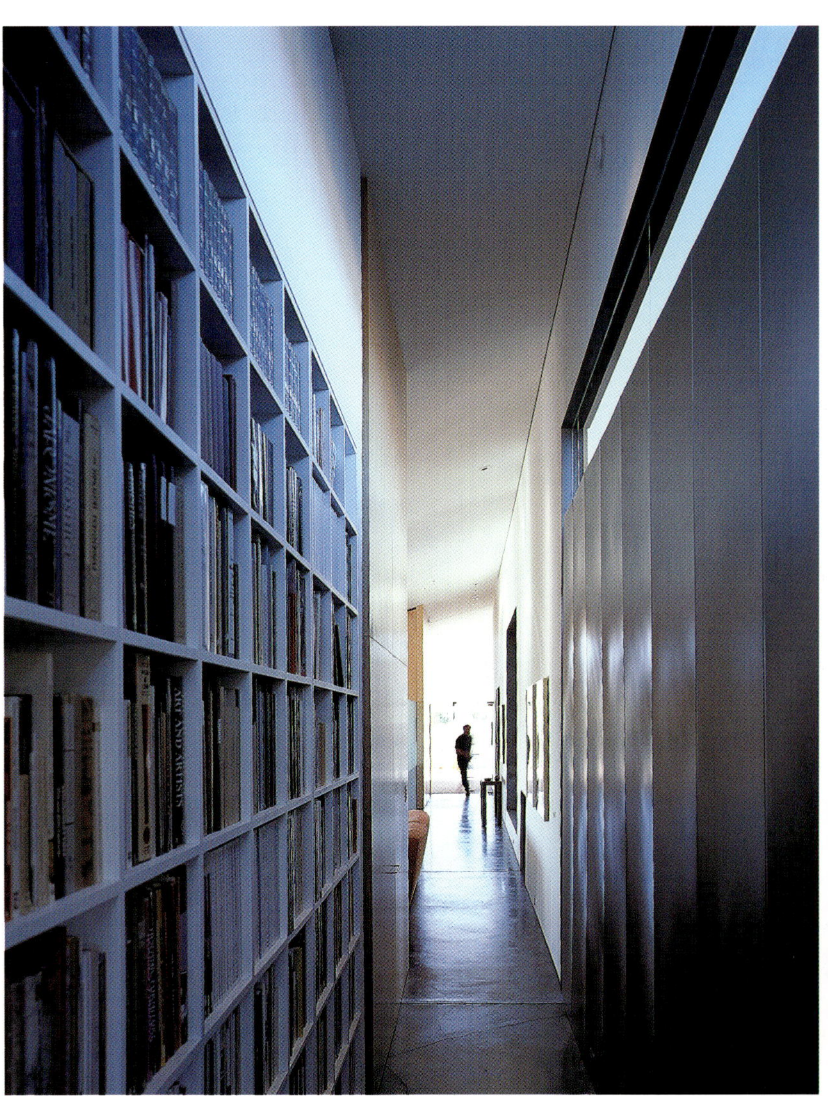

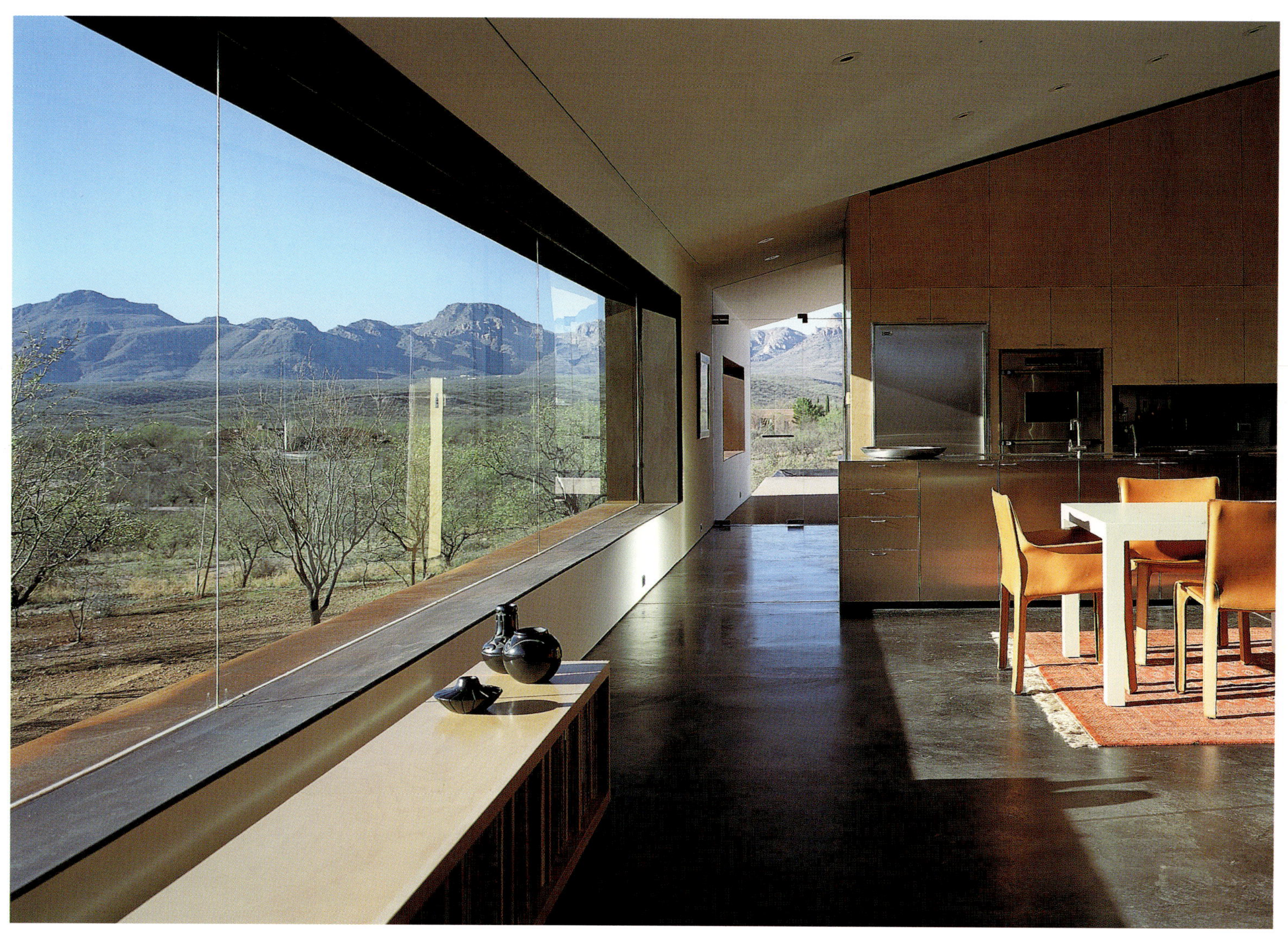

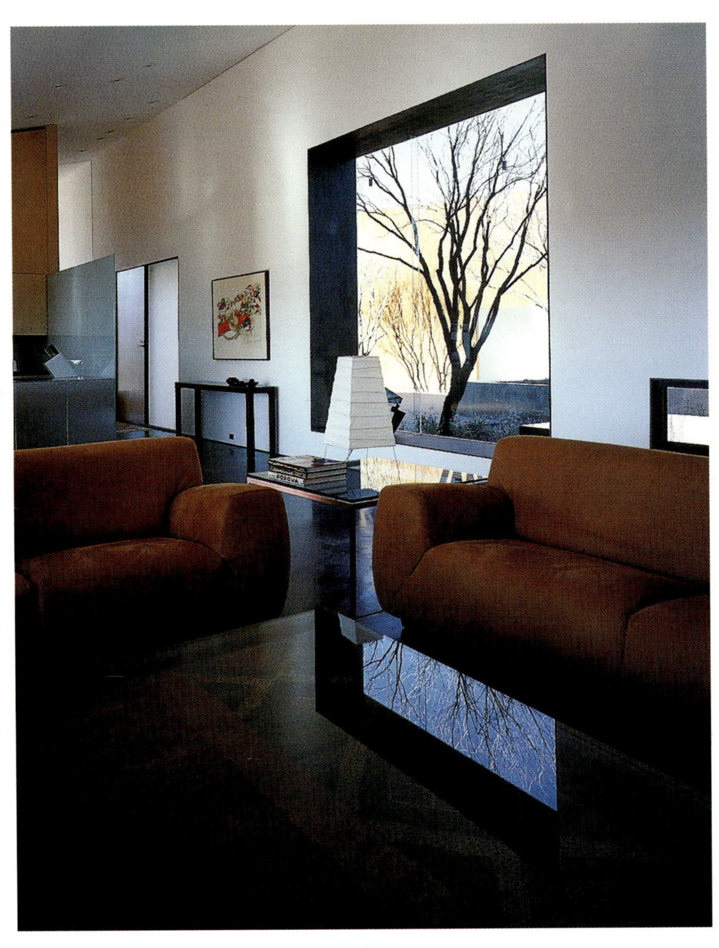

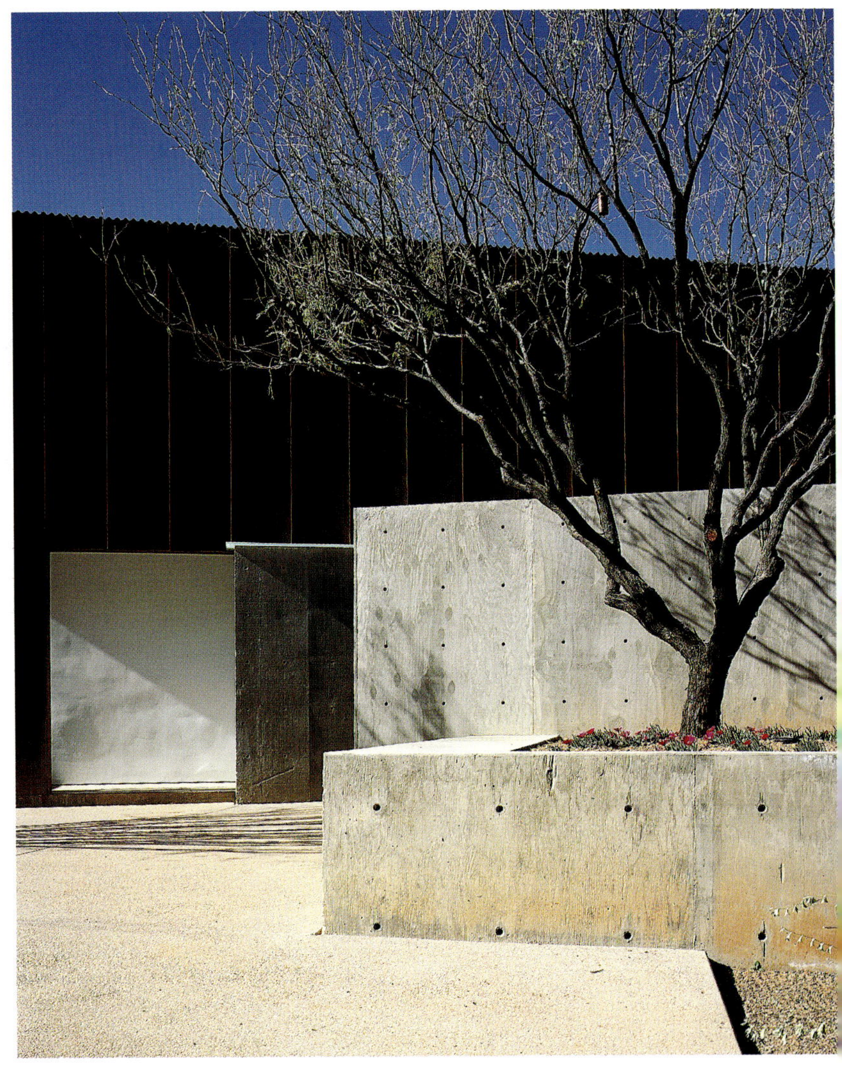

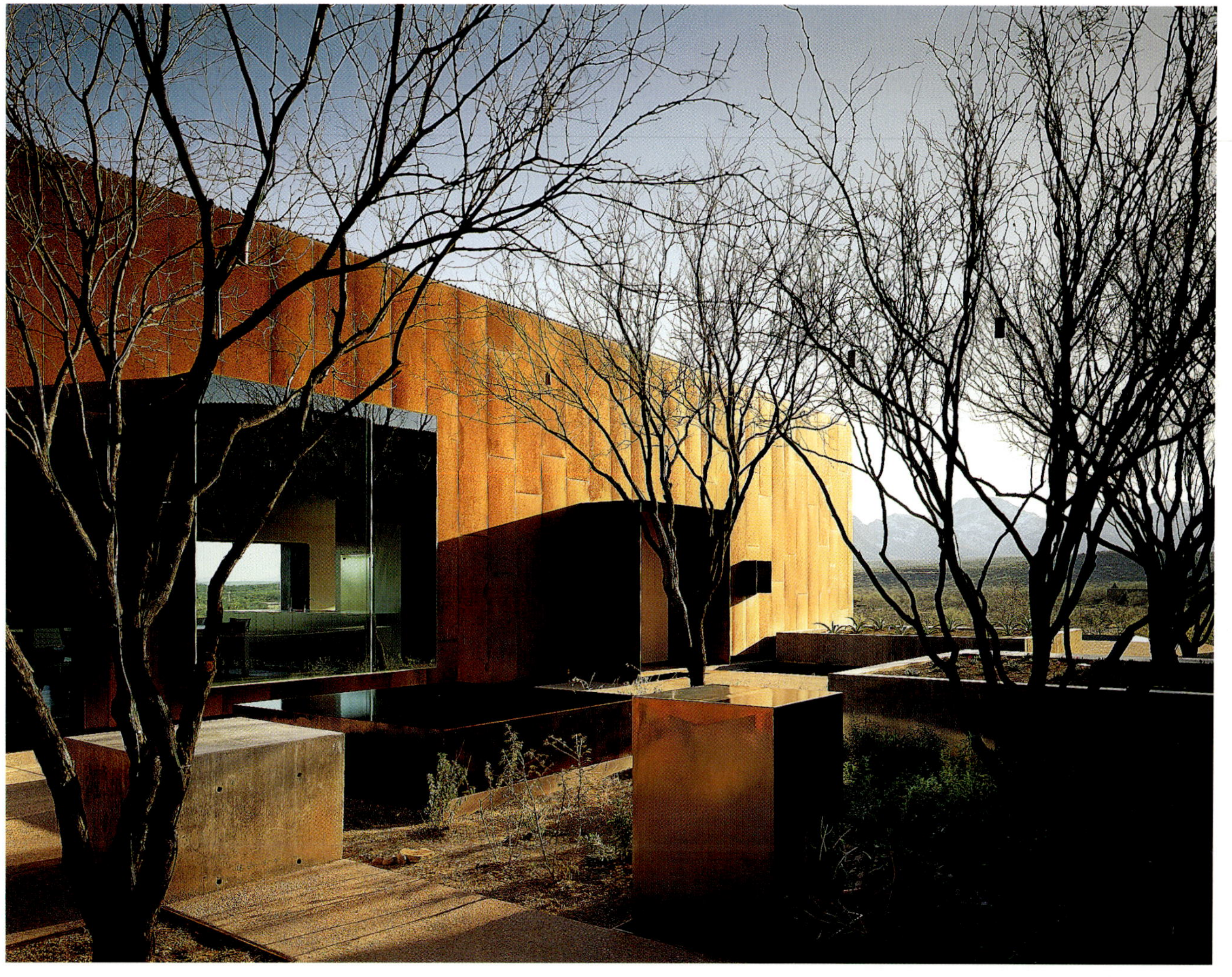

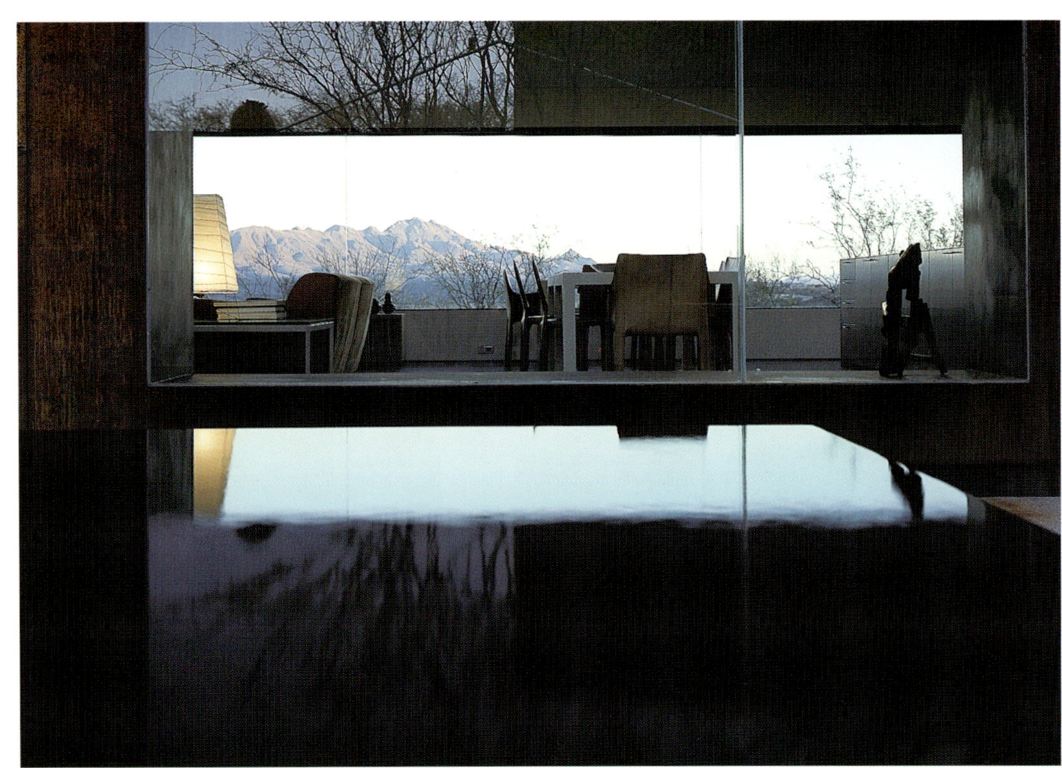

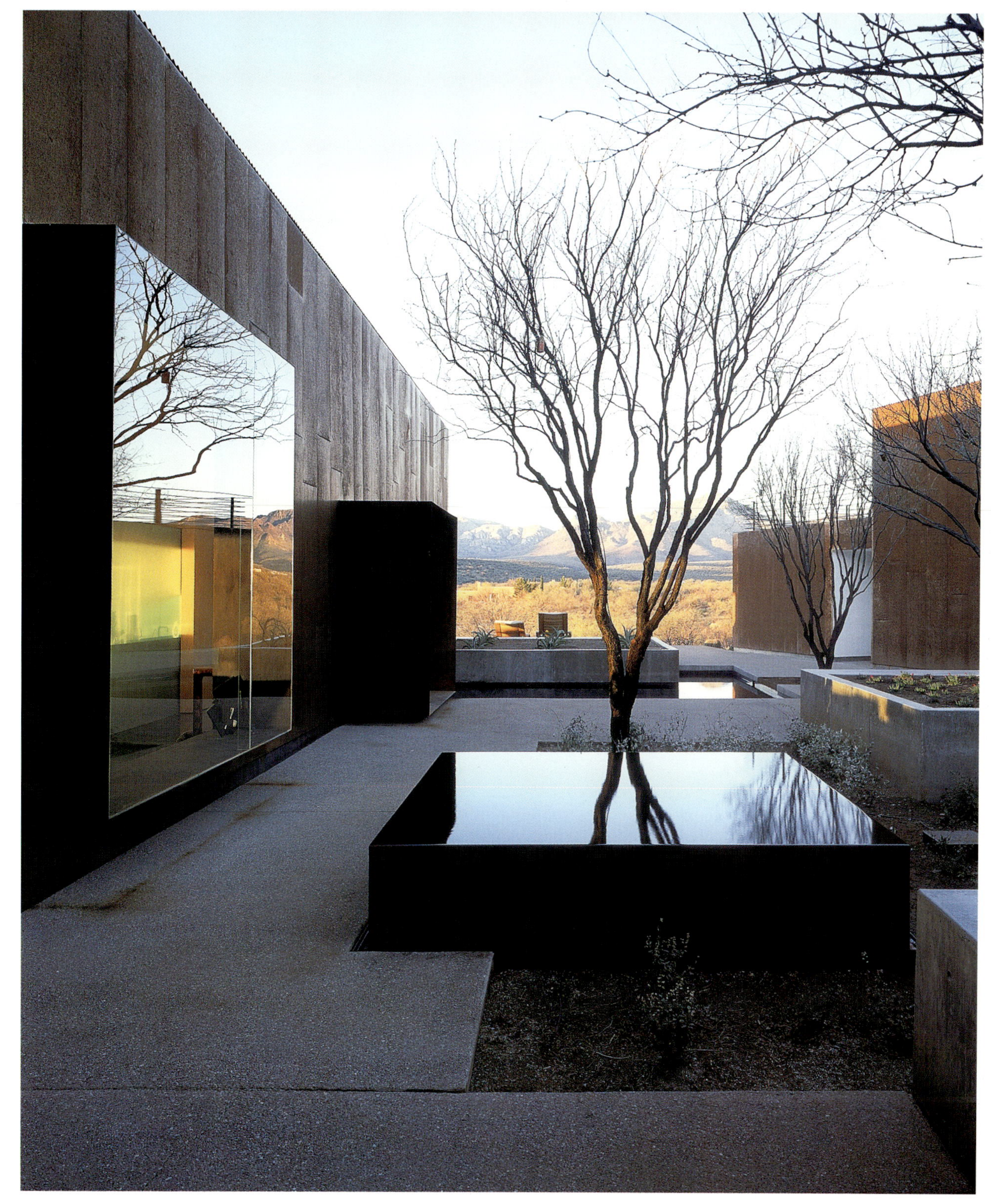

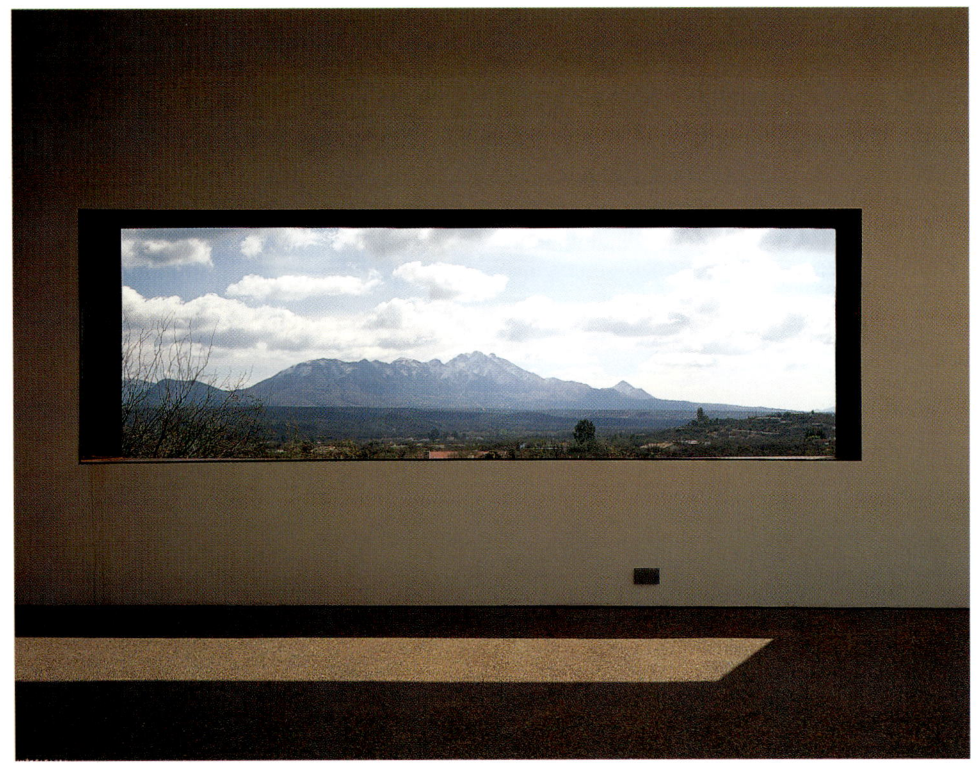

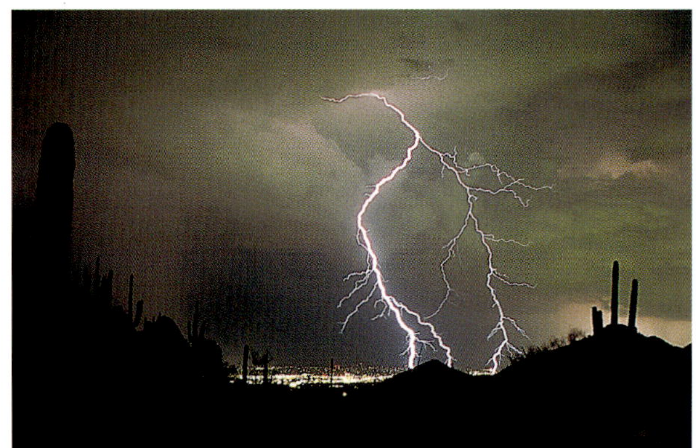

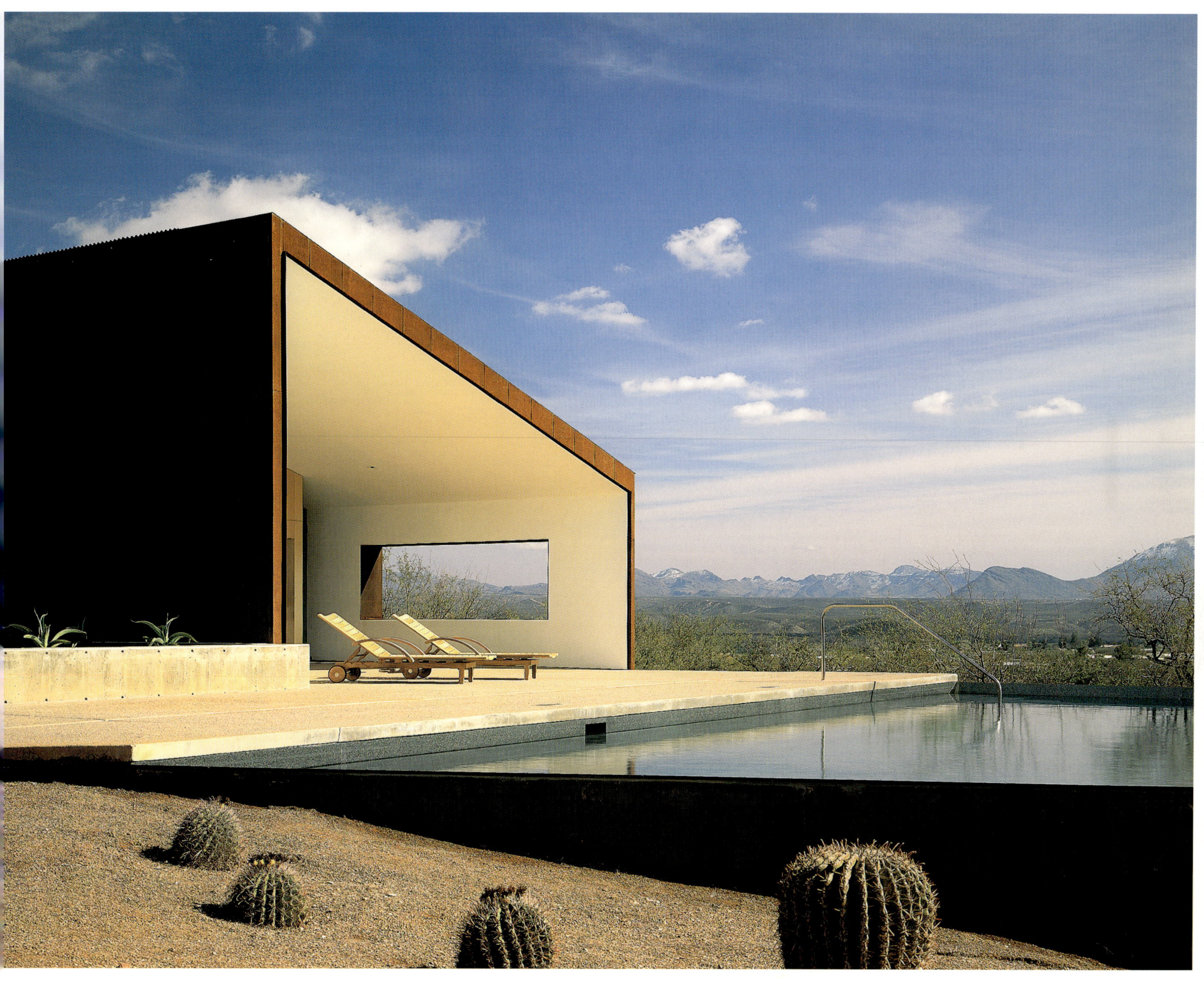

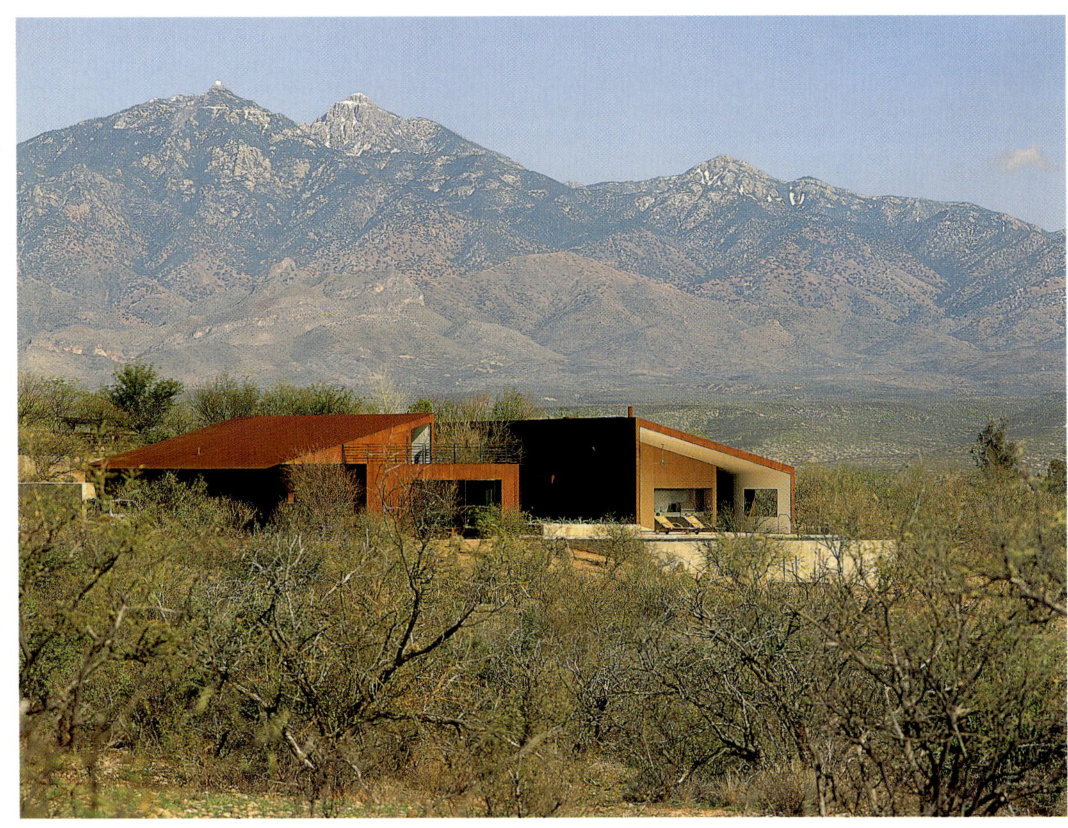

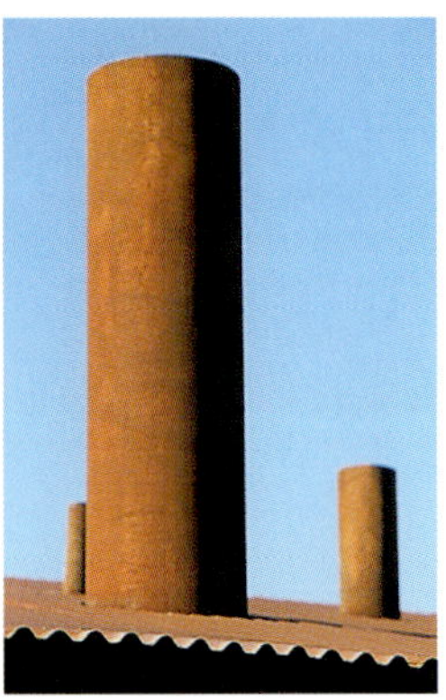

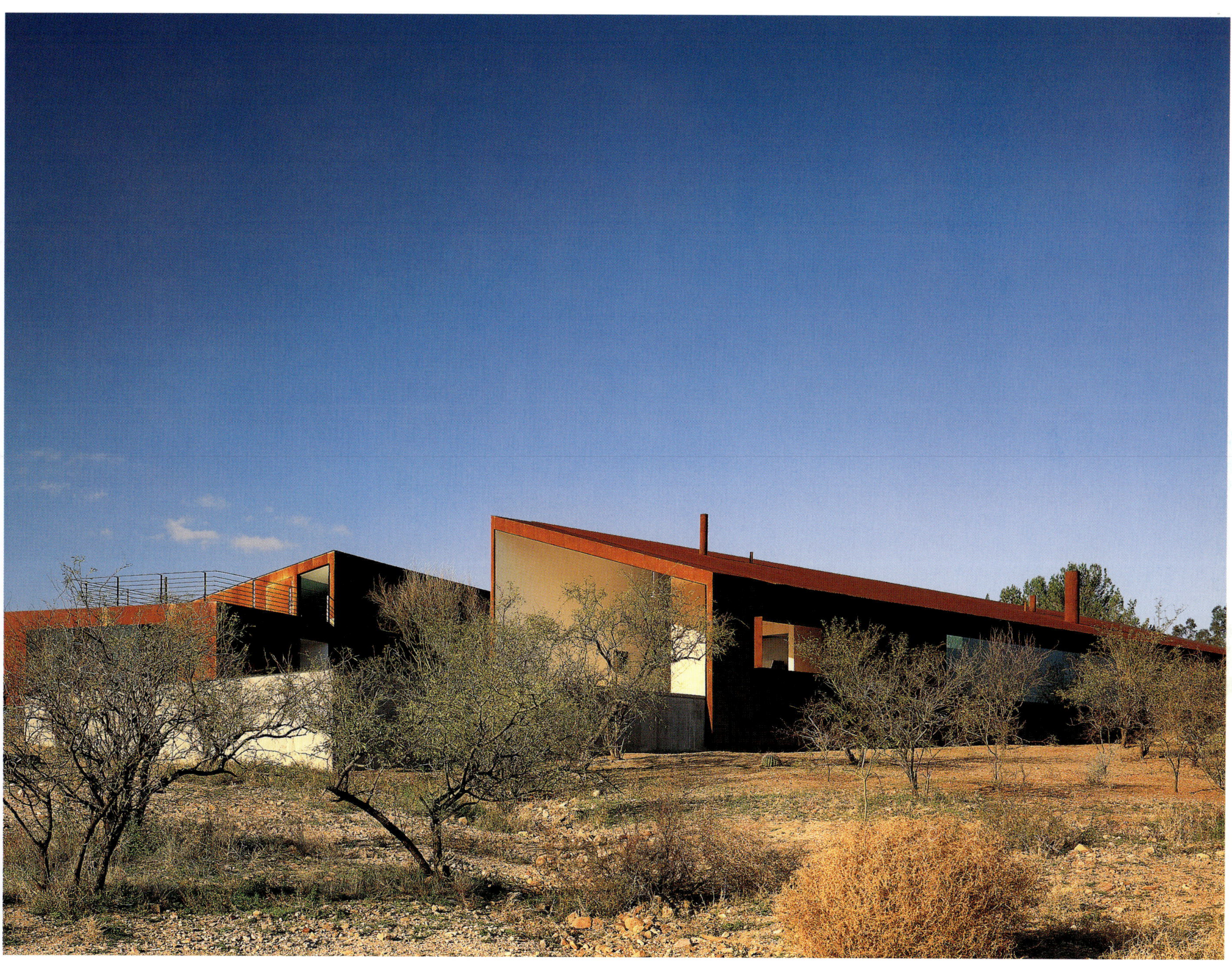

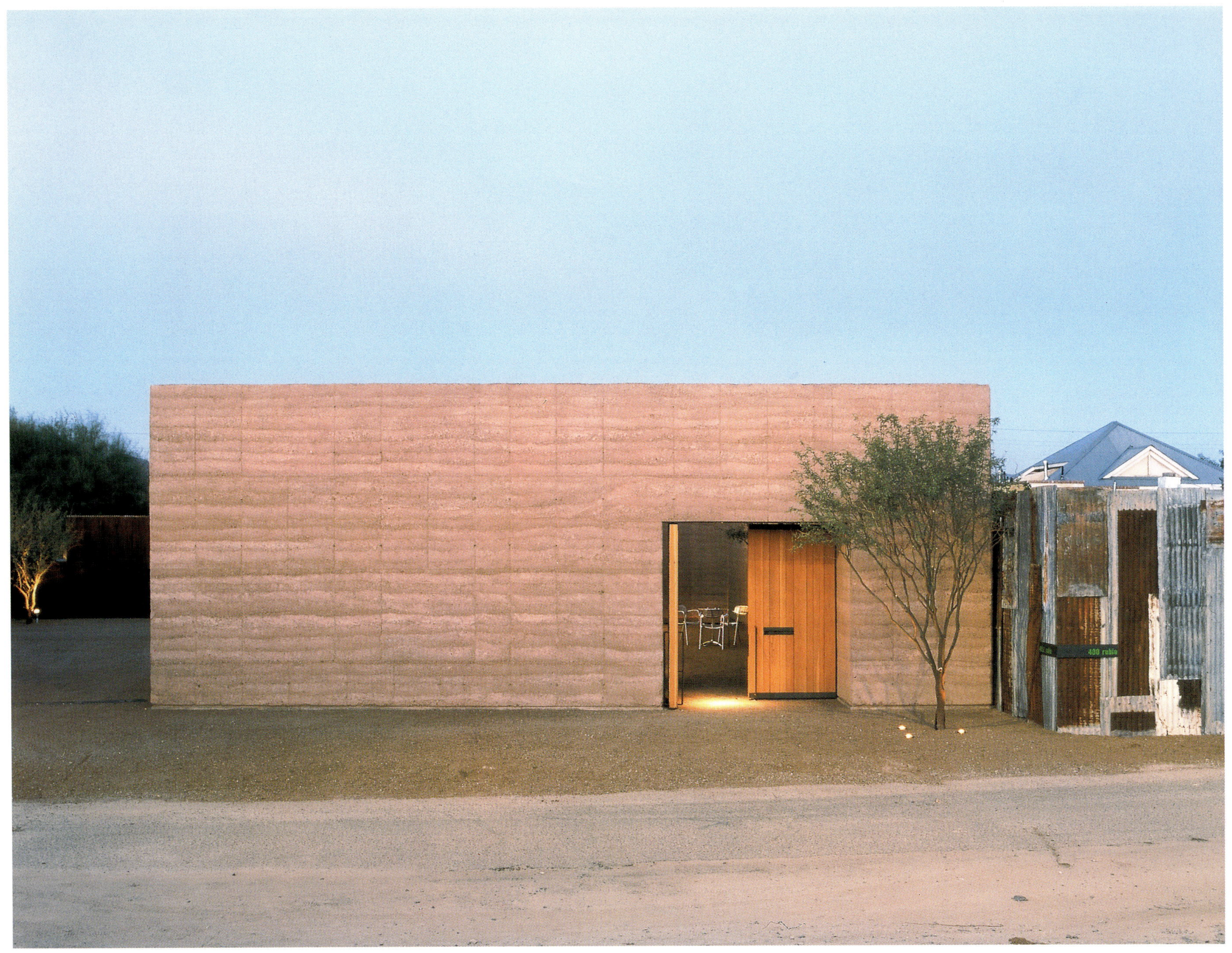

400 RUBIO AVENUE

Rubio Alley was once an active street with houses and businesses lining both sides. Today the richness of the larger Barrio Histórico fades into a bleak setting of vacant lots, fences, and dumpsters.

The studio presents itself as a monolithic block with a single deep opening and a pair of wooden gates. A single mesquite tree shades the approach and further marks the entry. Fourteen-foot-high rammed-earth walls rise from the boundaries of the site, a leftover portion of the property of the Convent Avenue Studios, to create a single introspective space.

Once inside the gates, one encounters another single mesquite tree, water trickling in a black steel pool, and the framed blue sky. A flush glass wall divides the space longitudinally into an exterior courtyard to the north and an interior workspace to the south.

This is a building of walls, but with blurred boundaries—earthen walls and a glass wall, all reaching to the sky. Like the sky, the reflective metallic ceiling seems to float between these walls. This quiet serene work space is a good place for us to burn the midnight oil.

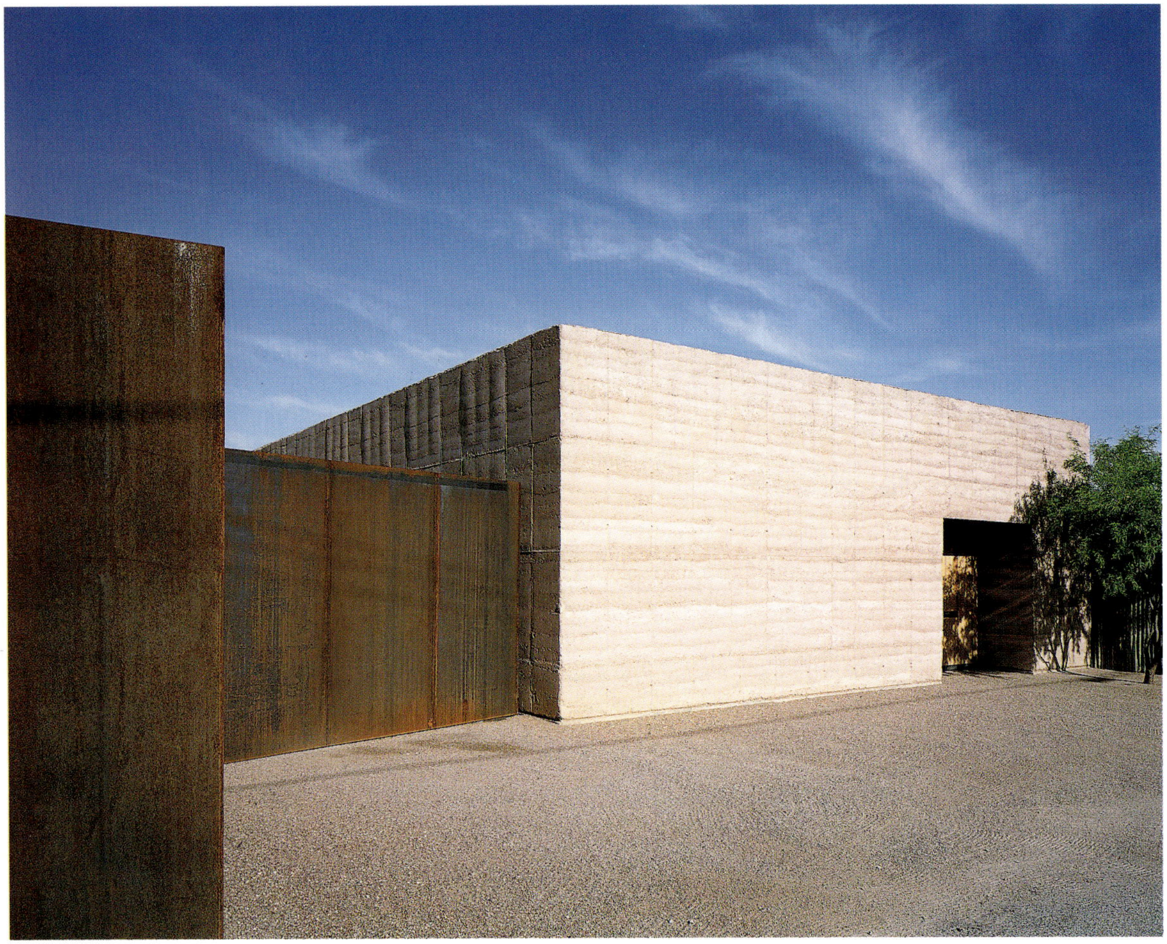

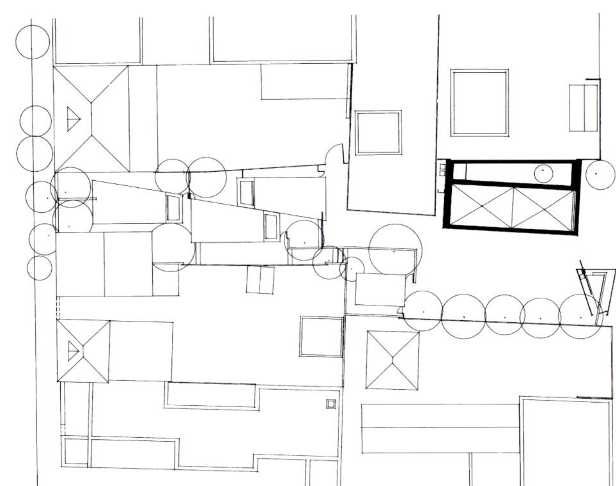
N

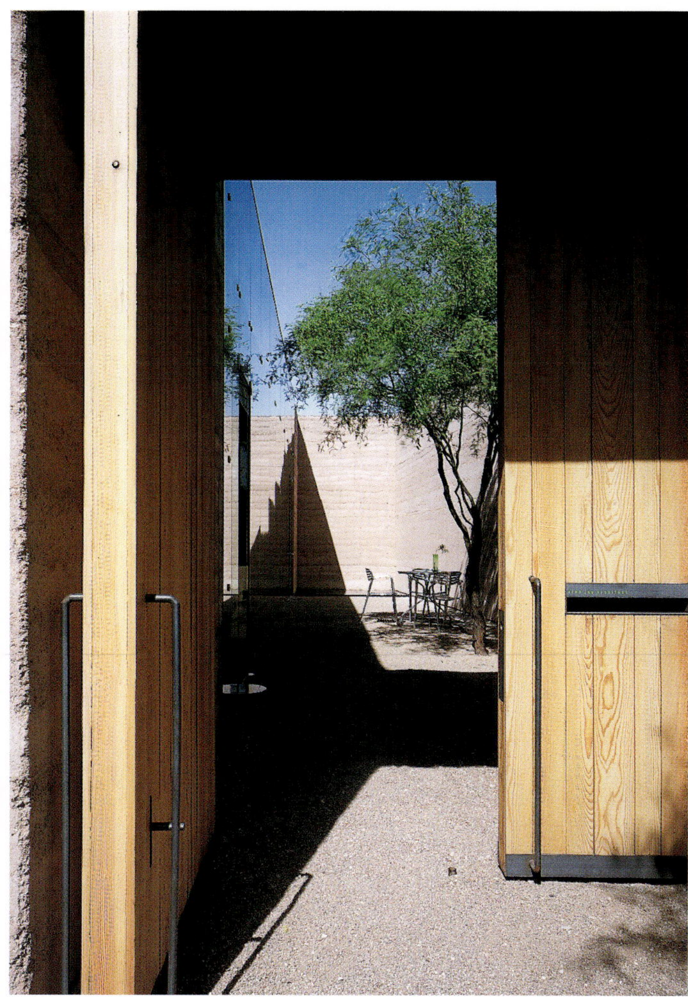

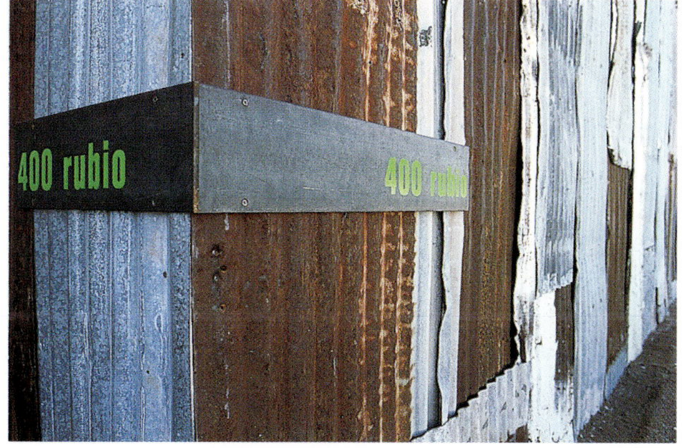
400 rubio
400 rubio

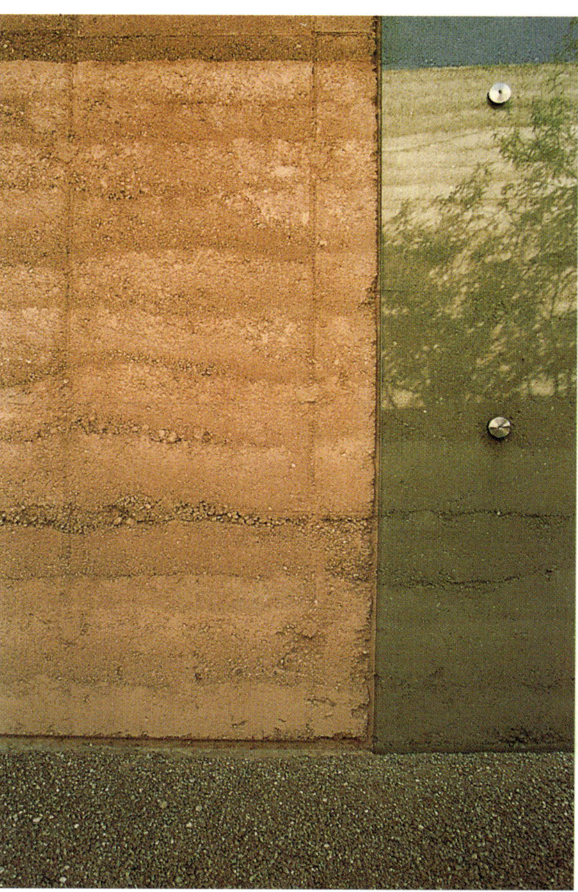

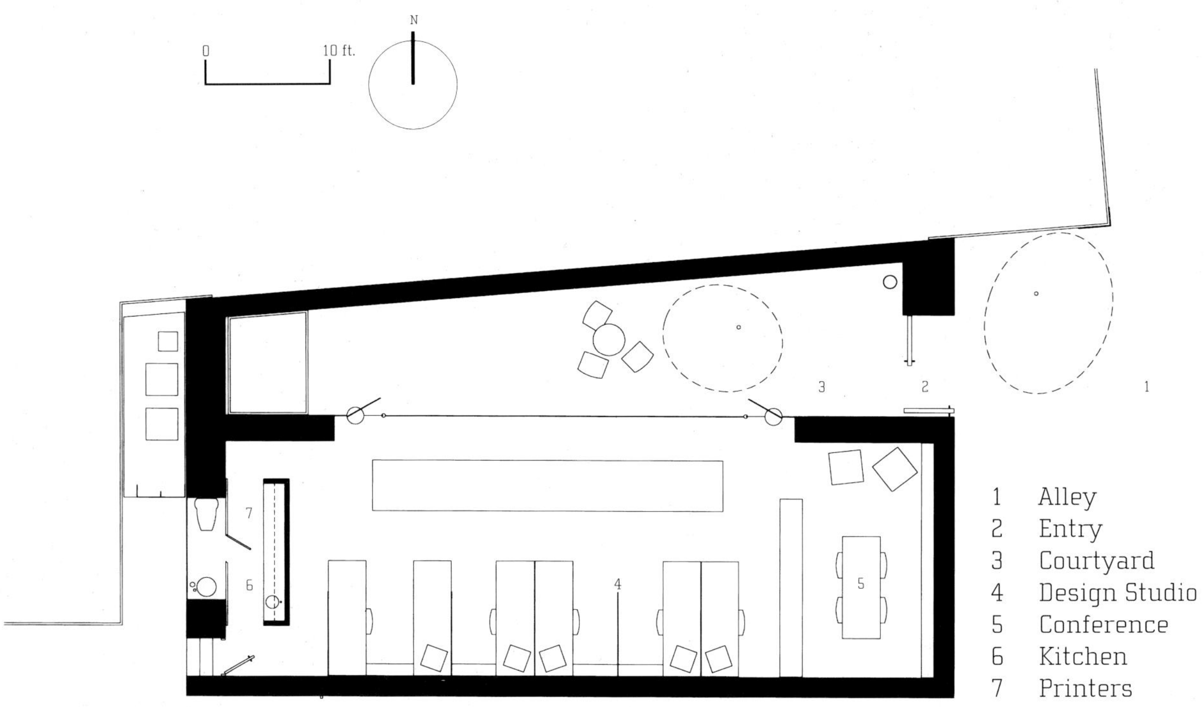
0
10 ft.
N
1 Alley
2 Entry
3 Courtyard
4 Design Studio
5 Conference
6 Kitchen
7 Printers

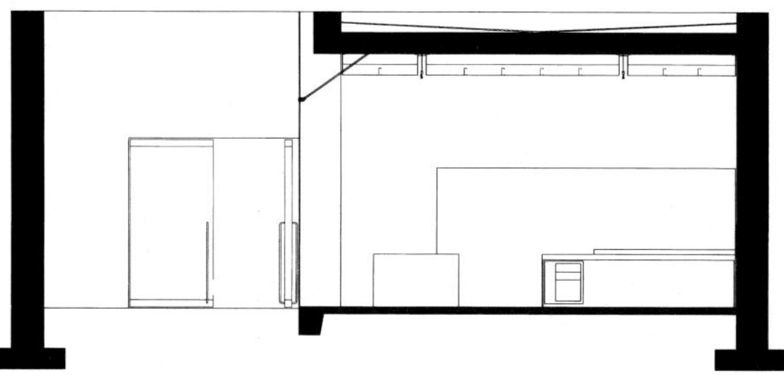

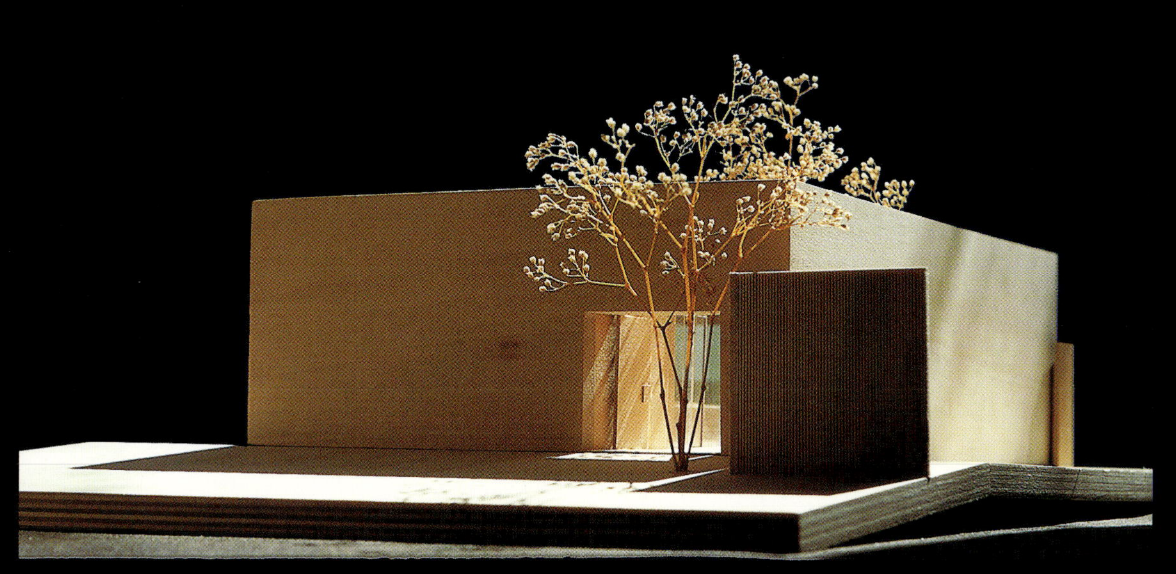

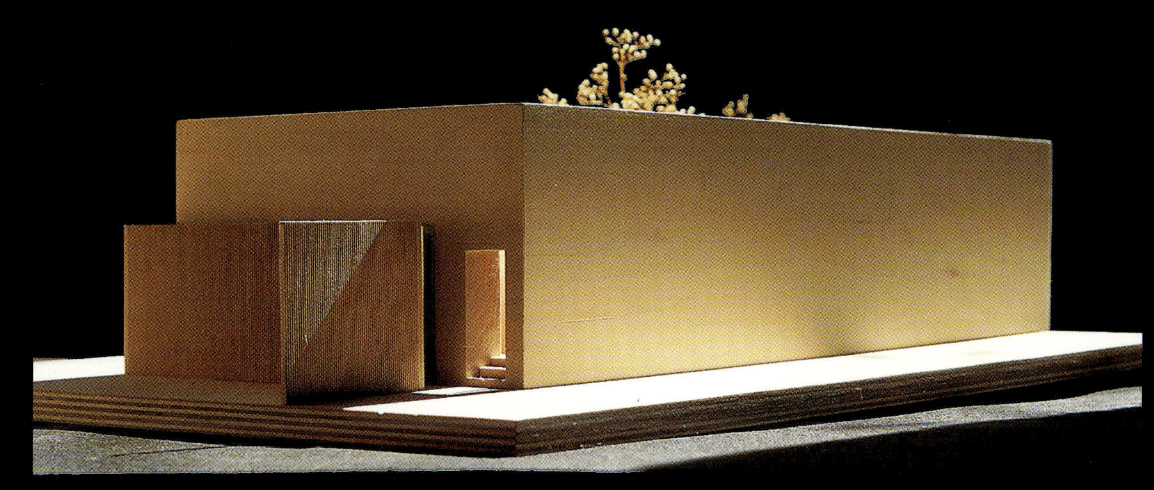

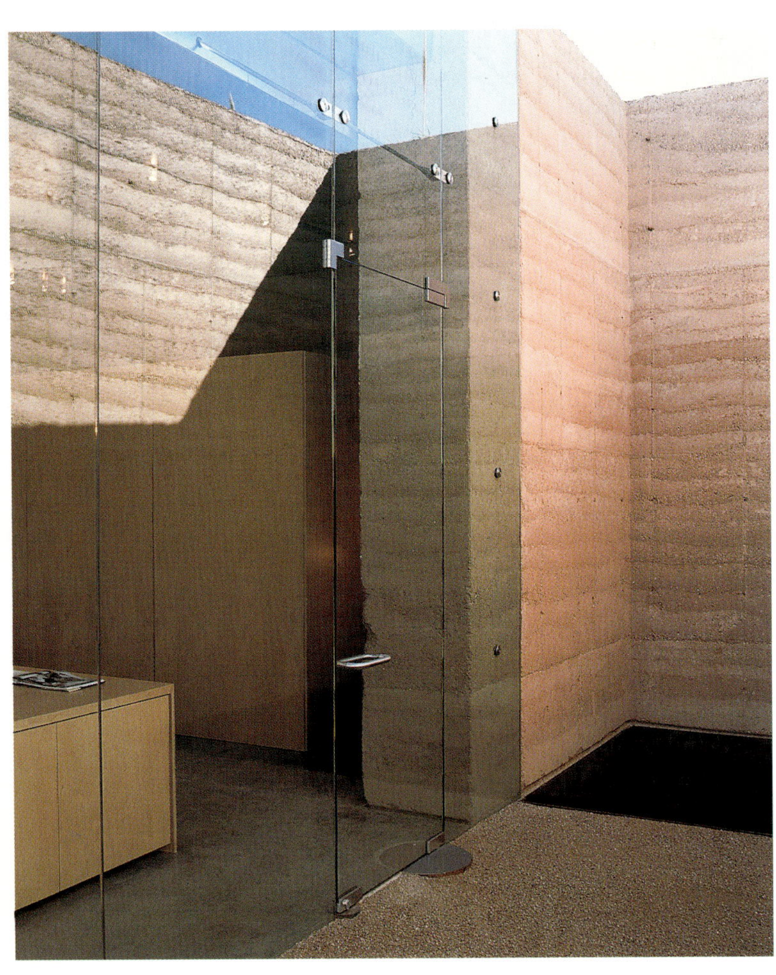

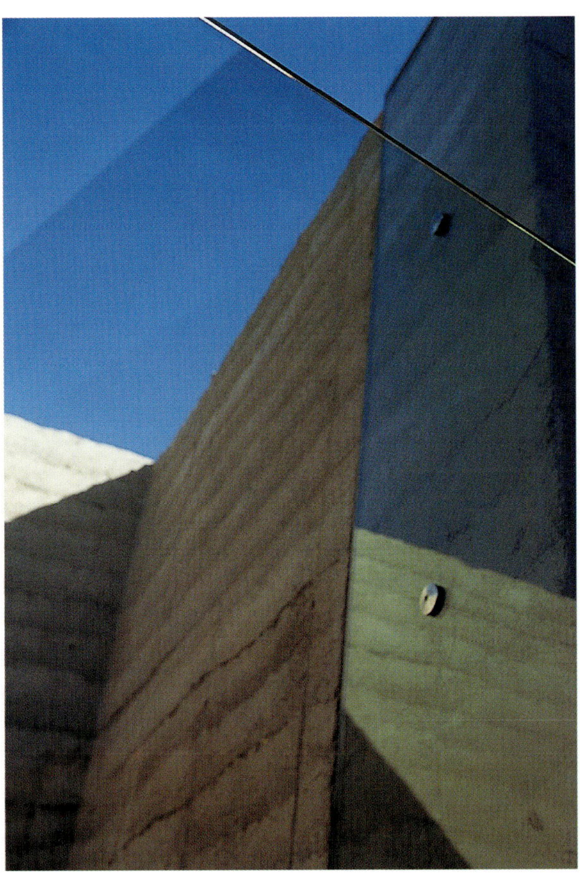

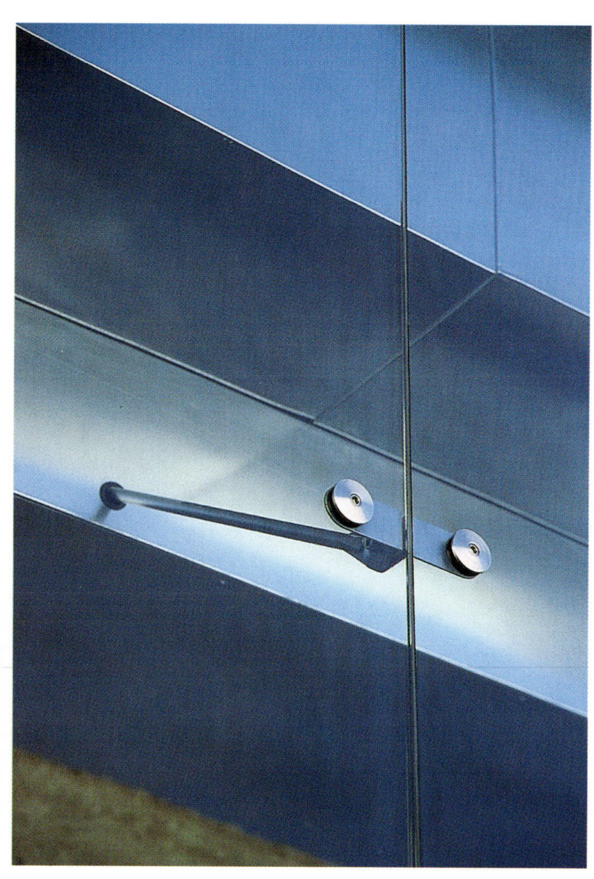

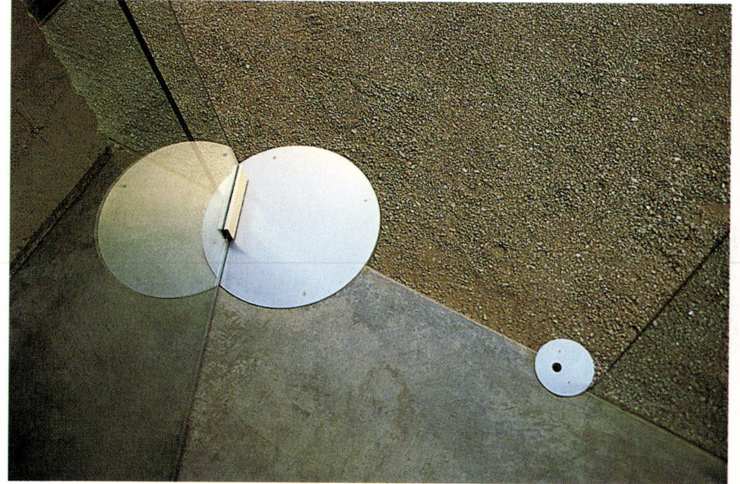

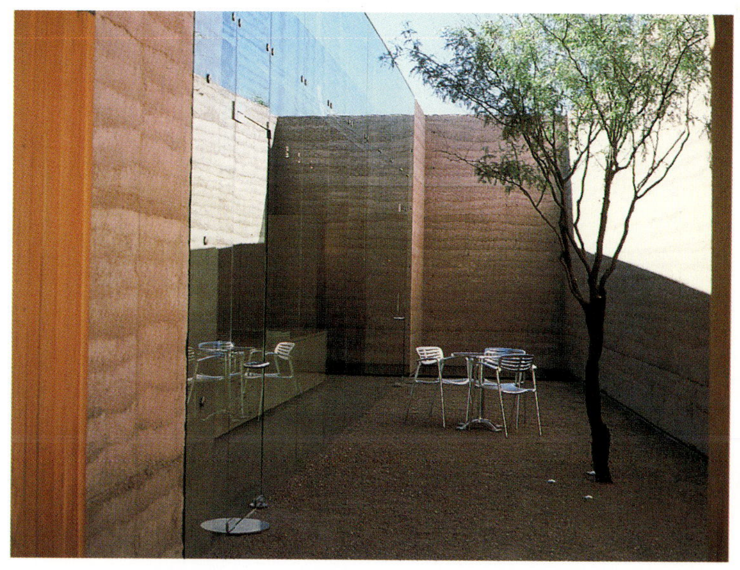

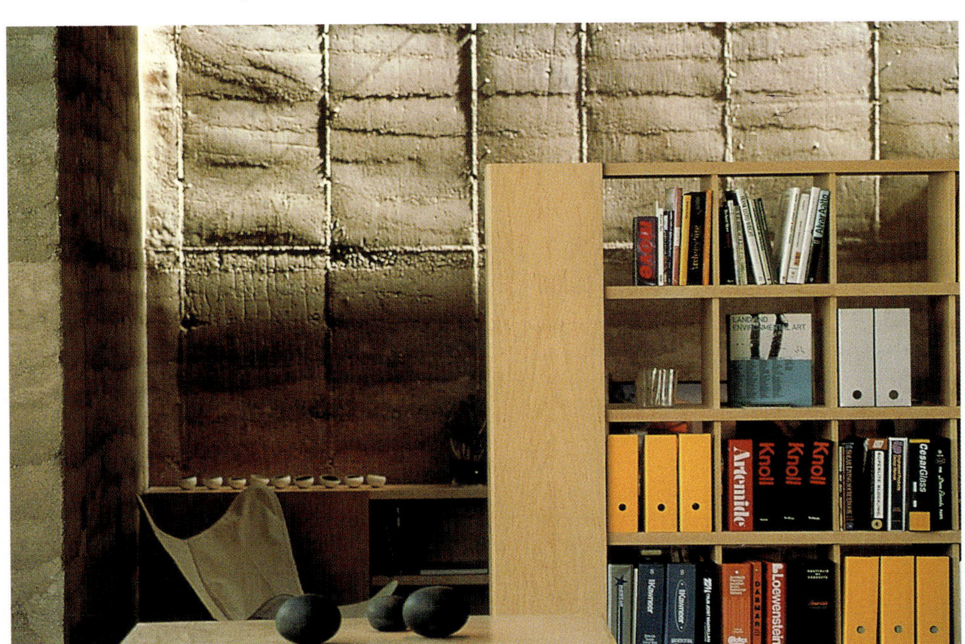
Artemide
Knoll
Knoll
Knoll
Loewenstein

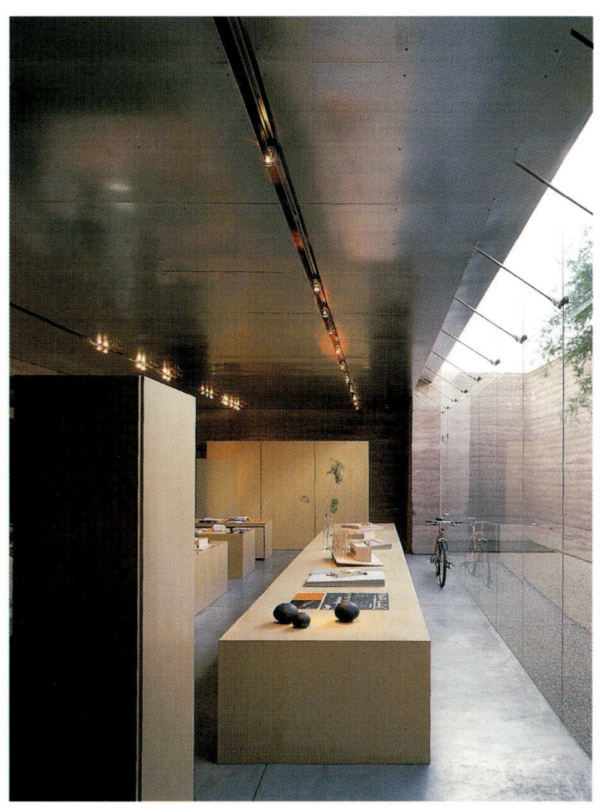

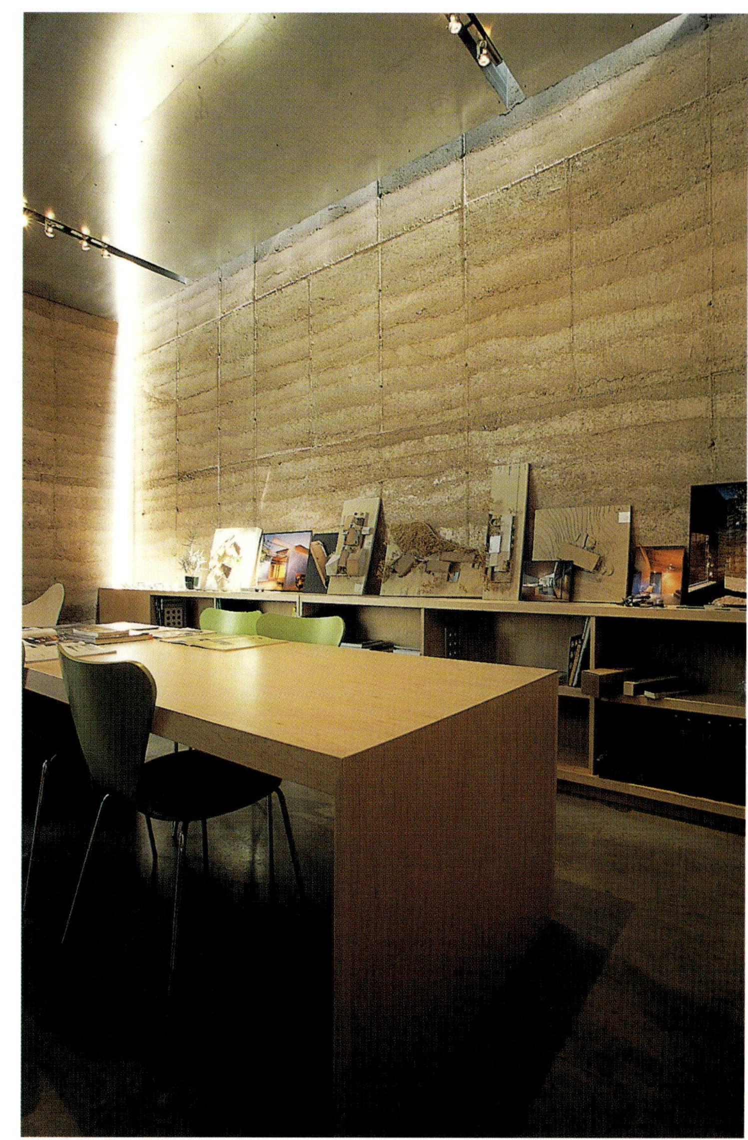

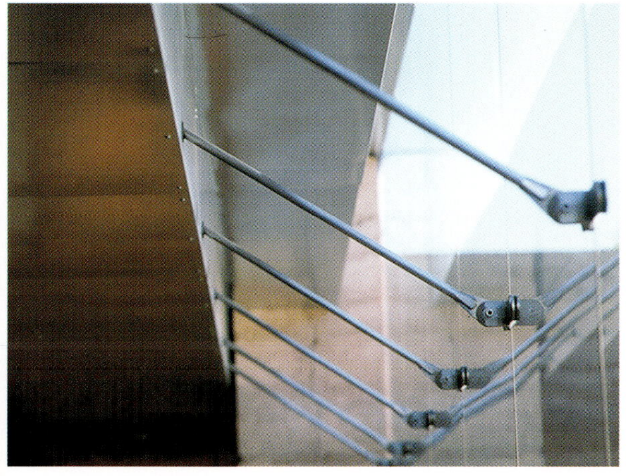

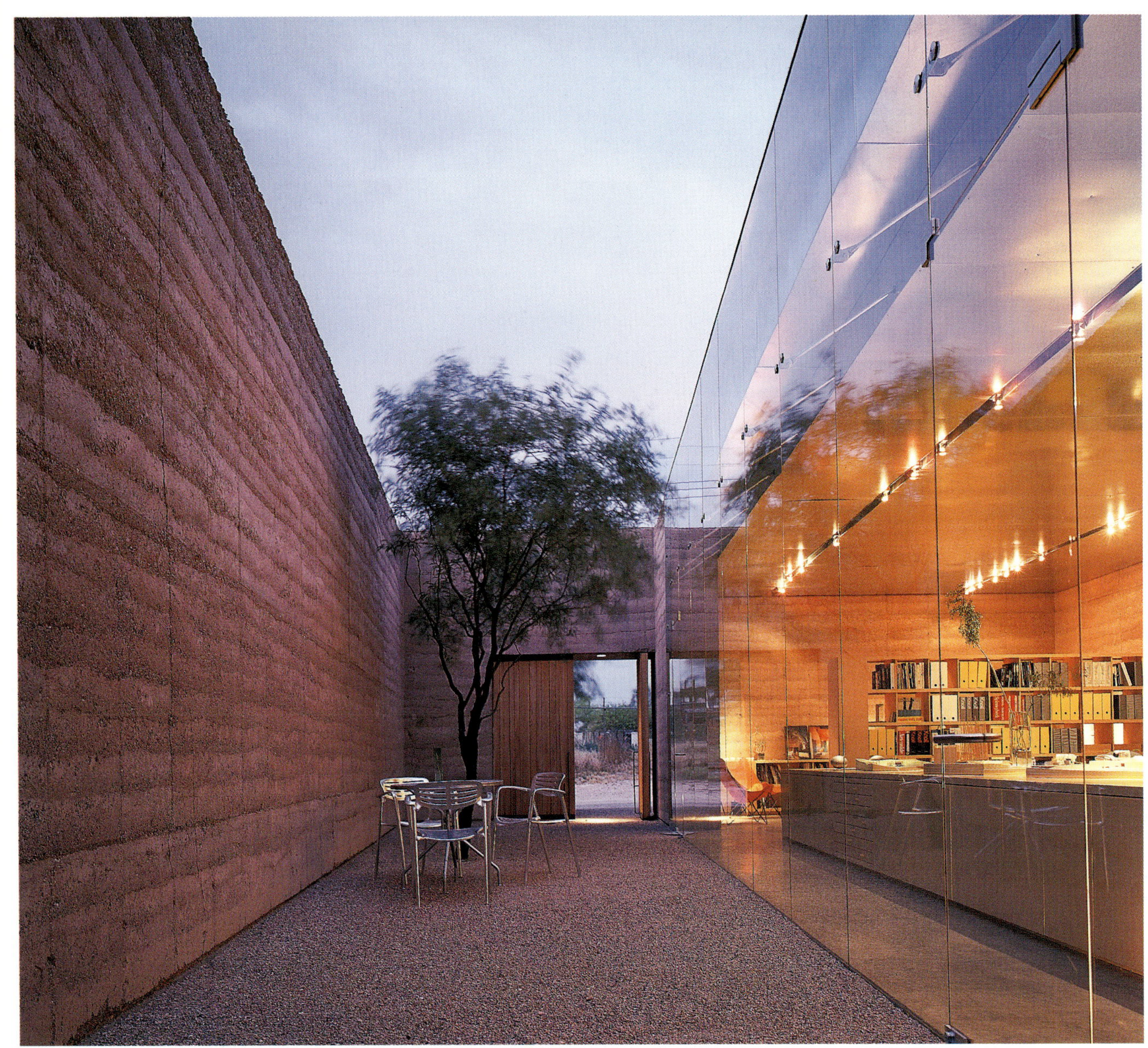

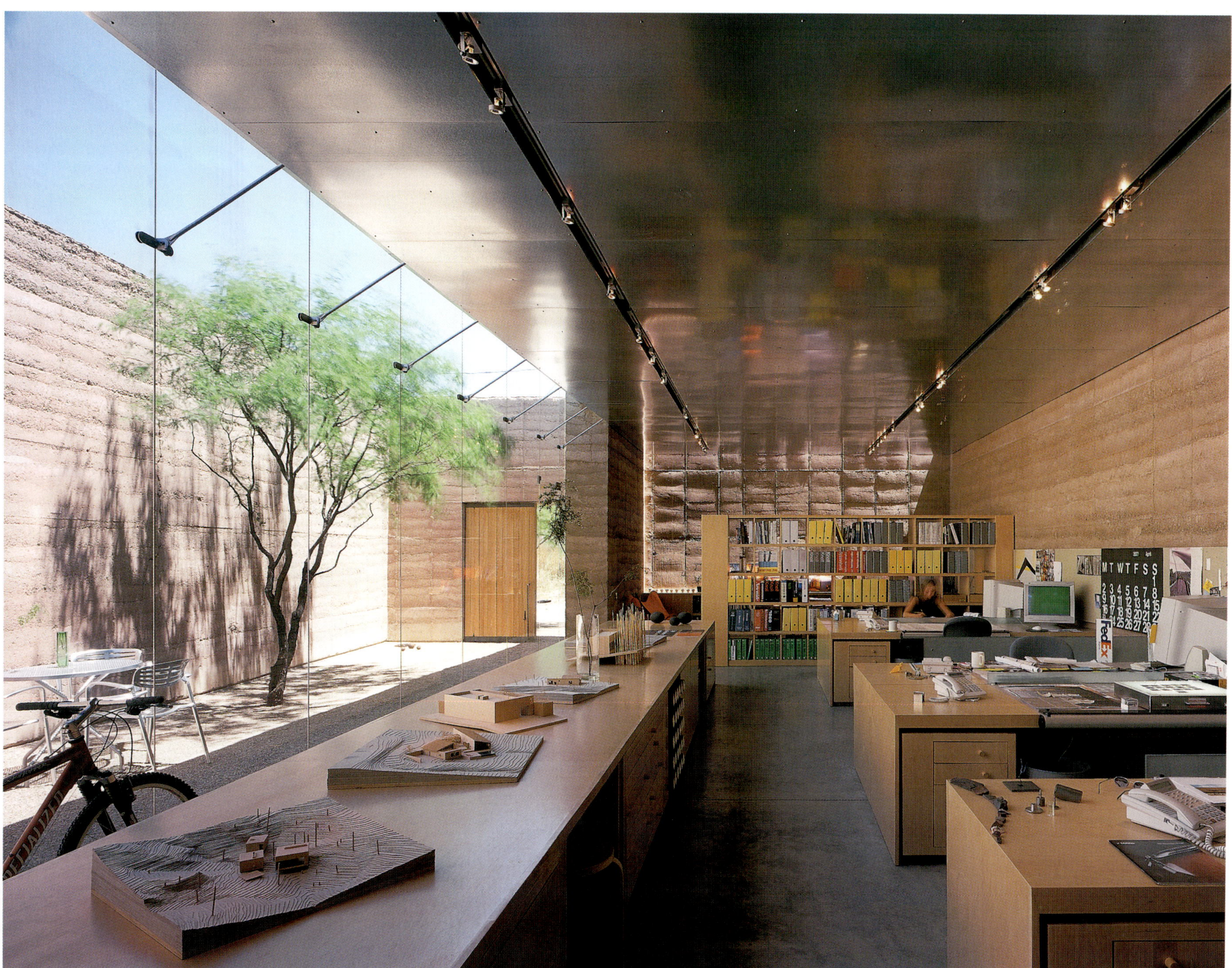
FedEx

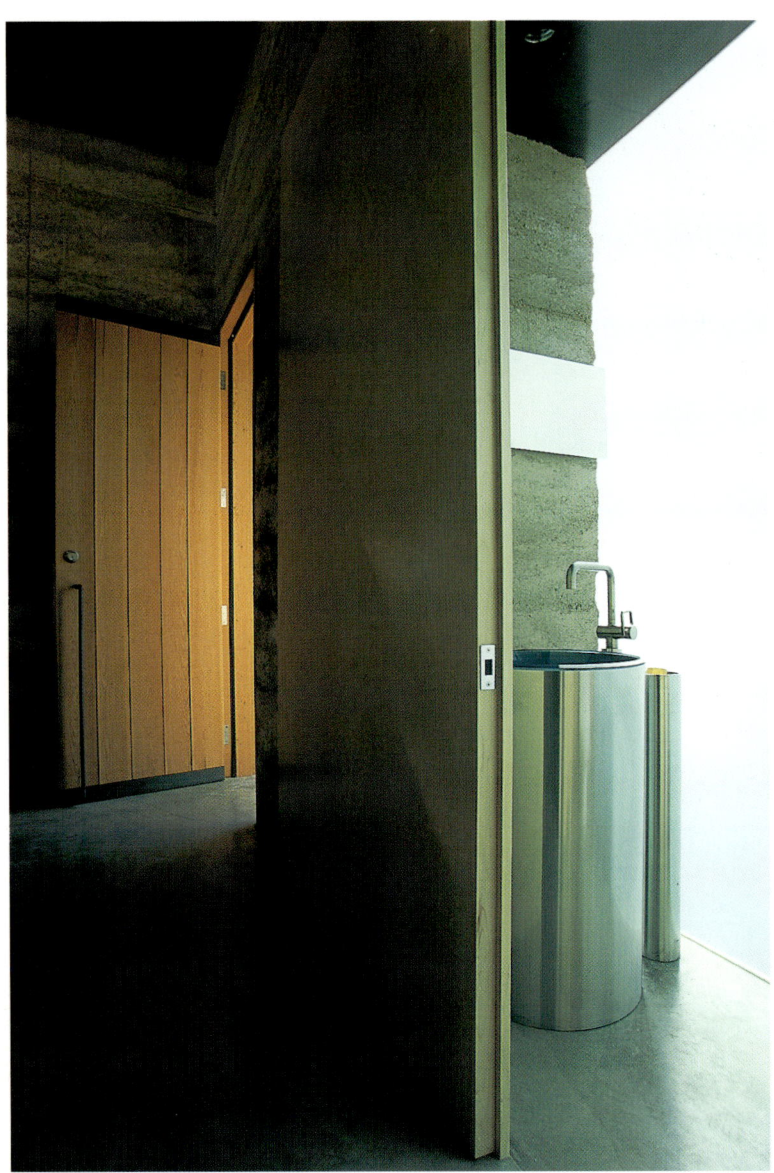

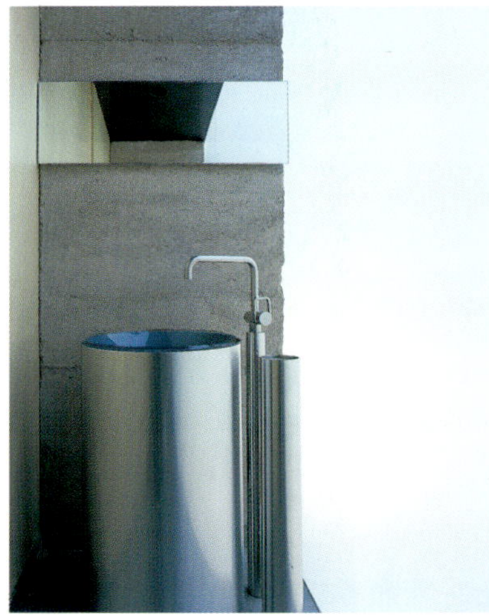

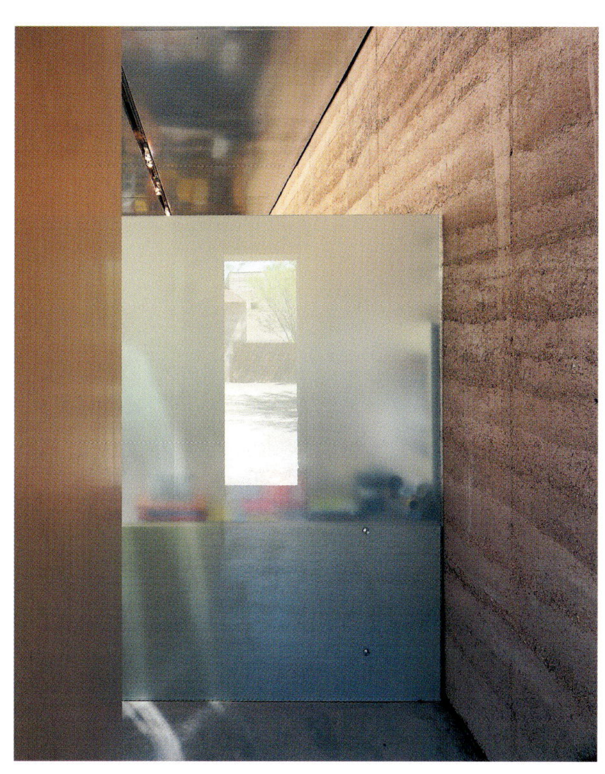

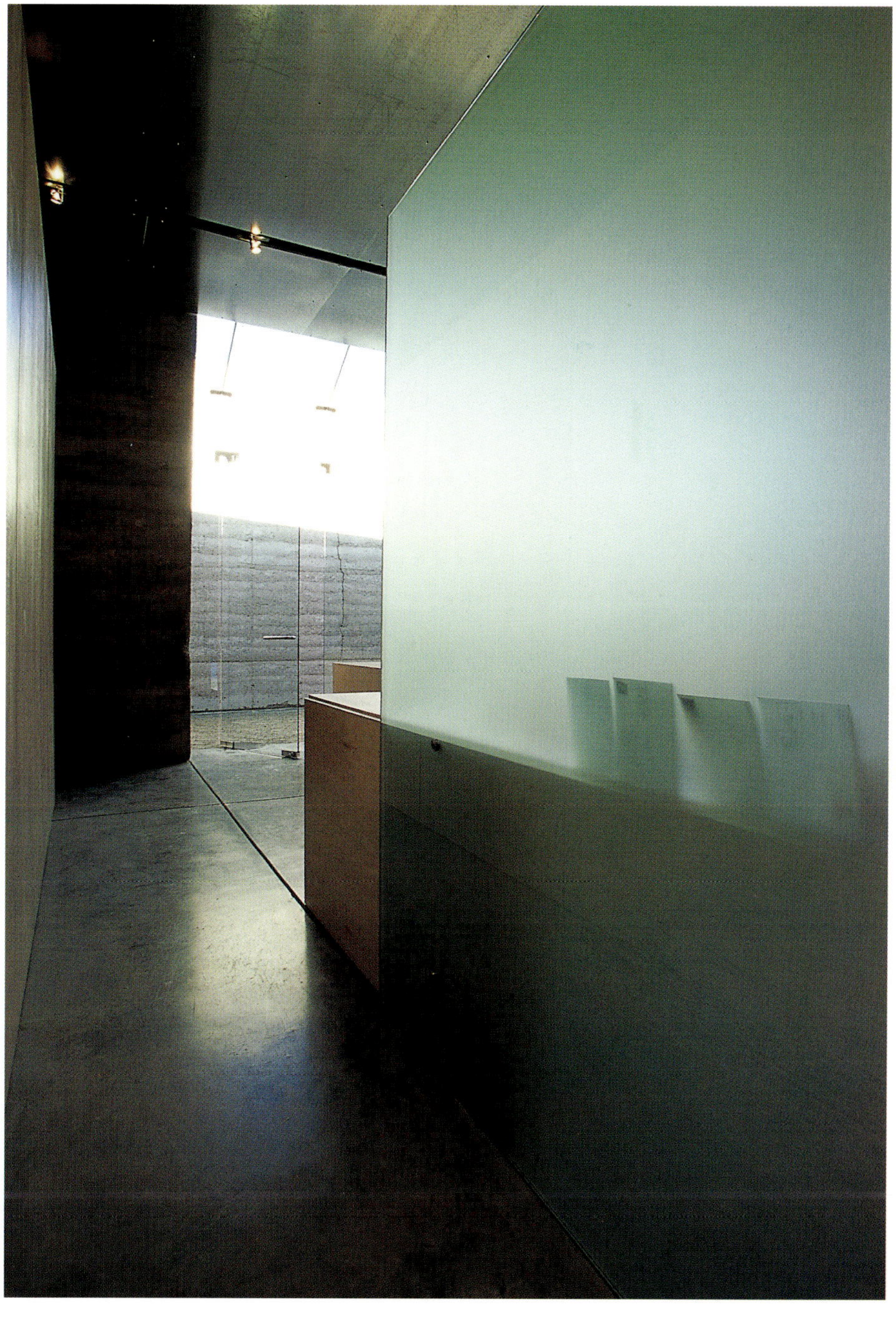

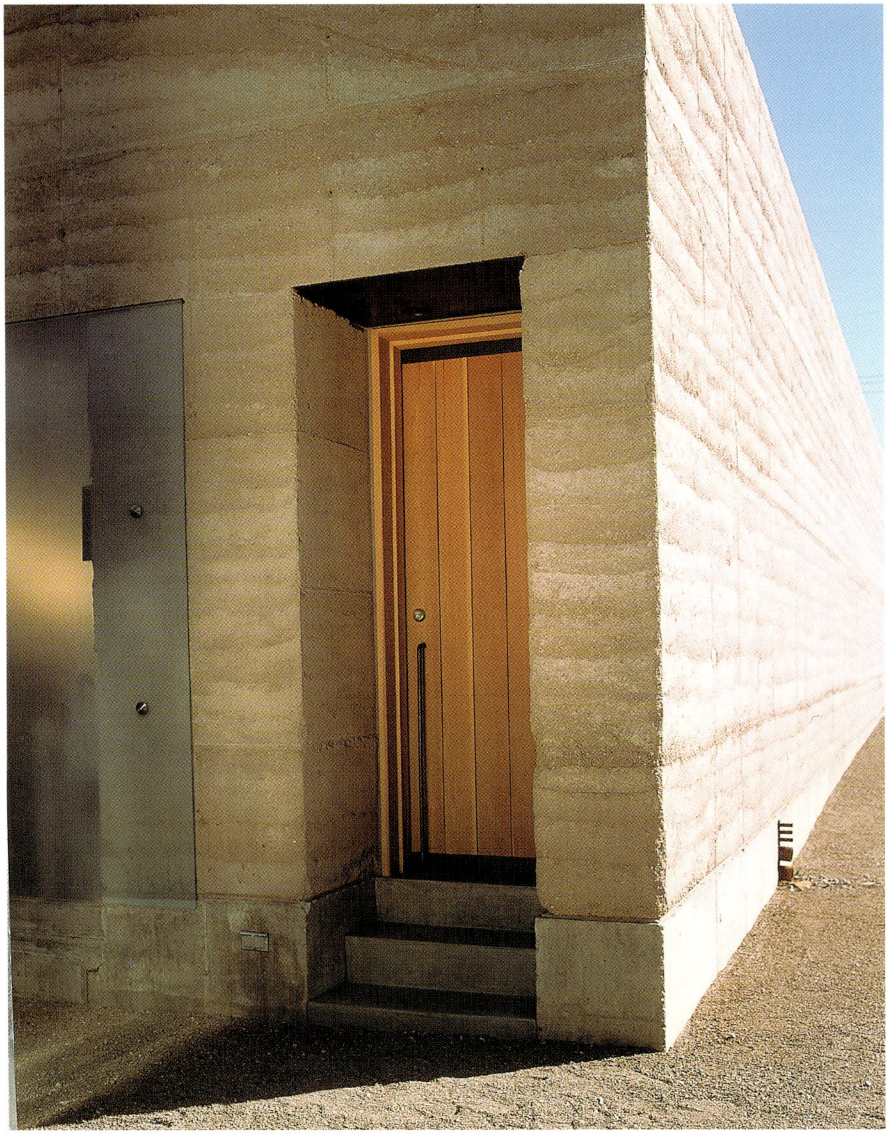

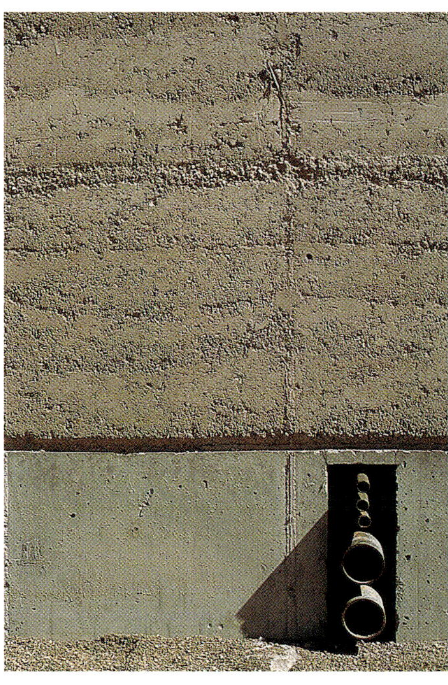

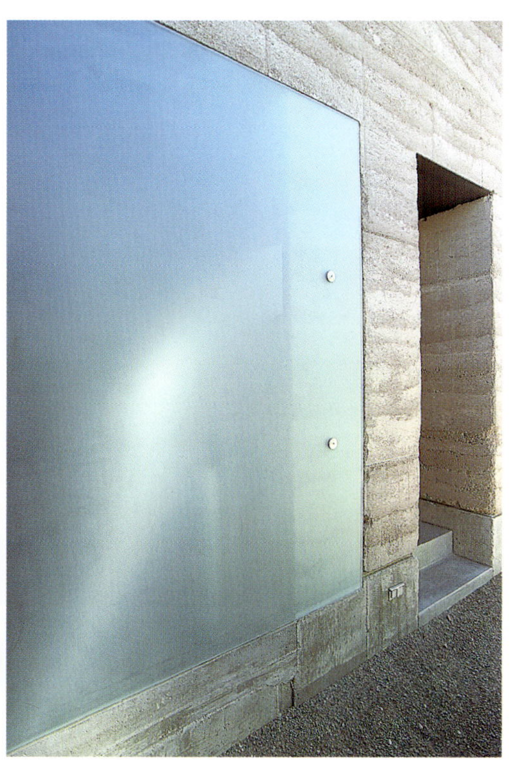

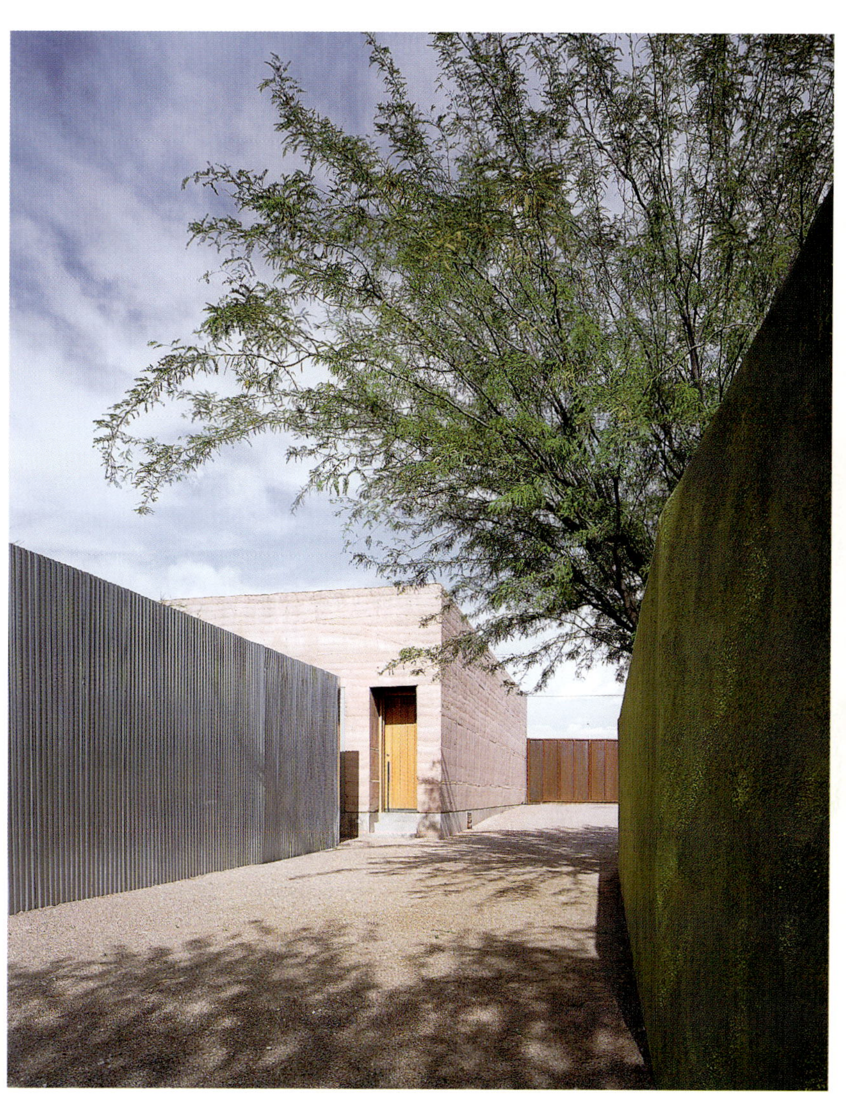

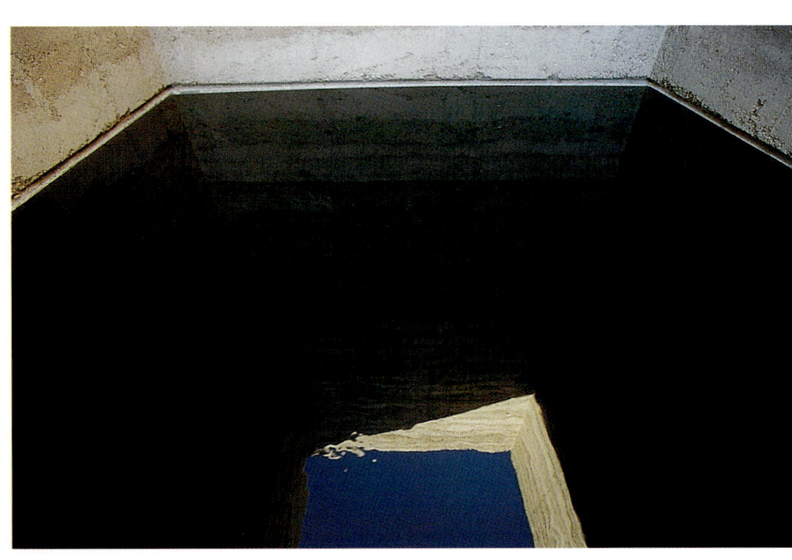

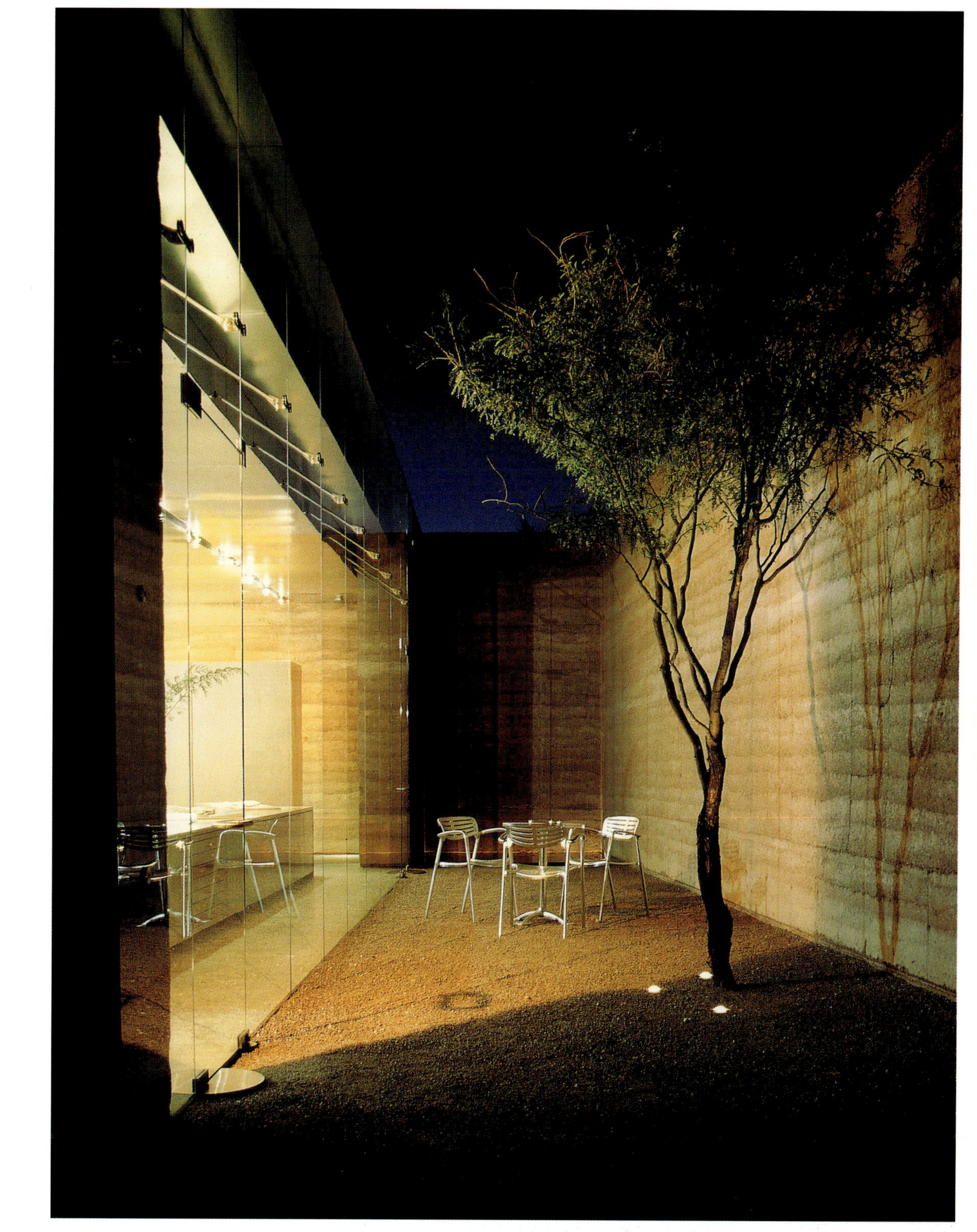

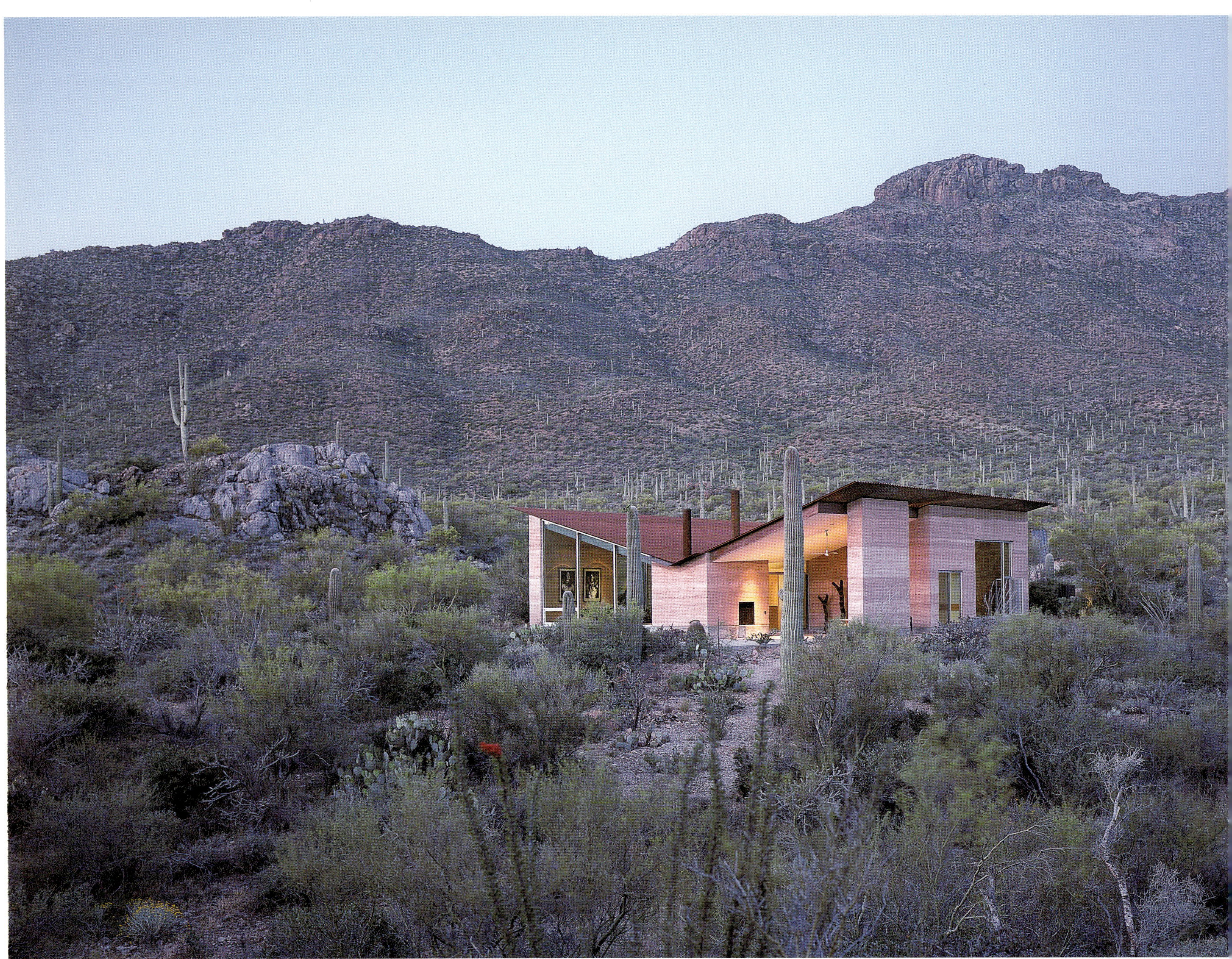

In a small valley surrounded by dramatic protected ridges, the house's secluded site is lush with Sonoran Desert flora and fauna. A singular object, alone with the elements, strives for respectful cohabitation within the natural balance of this fragile environment.

The compact whole has a butterfly roof shading, massive earthen protecting walls, and raw desert that meets its edges. North and south walls are two feet thick and rise to sixteen feet. The center roof valley slopes from eleven feet at the west entry to eight feet at the fireplace mass to the east, creating a softly warping roof form. A singular scupper directs water flow out and away from the building.

The house is divided longitudinally along the valley into two zones, with main house functions on one side and a guest space and porch on the other. Openings in the walls frame the owners' favorite views and sun-tracking events. The car parking is hidden away and a simple walkway, aligned axially with the central spine of the house, leads to the front door.

On the day we broke ground, a red tail hawk flew over to see what the big yellow thing was doing. I felt a sense of sadness and loss as I imagined her thoughts. Despite the awesome contradictions, my perception is that the house and site have begun to acquiesce.

TUCSON

MOUNTAIN

HOUSE

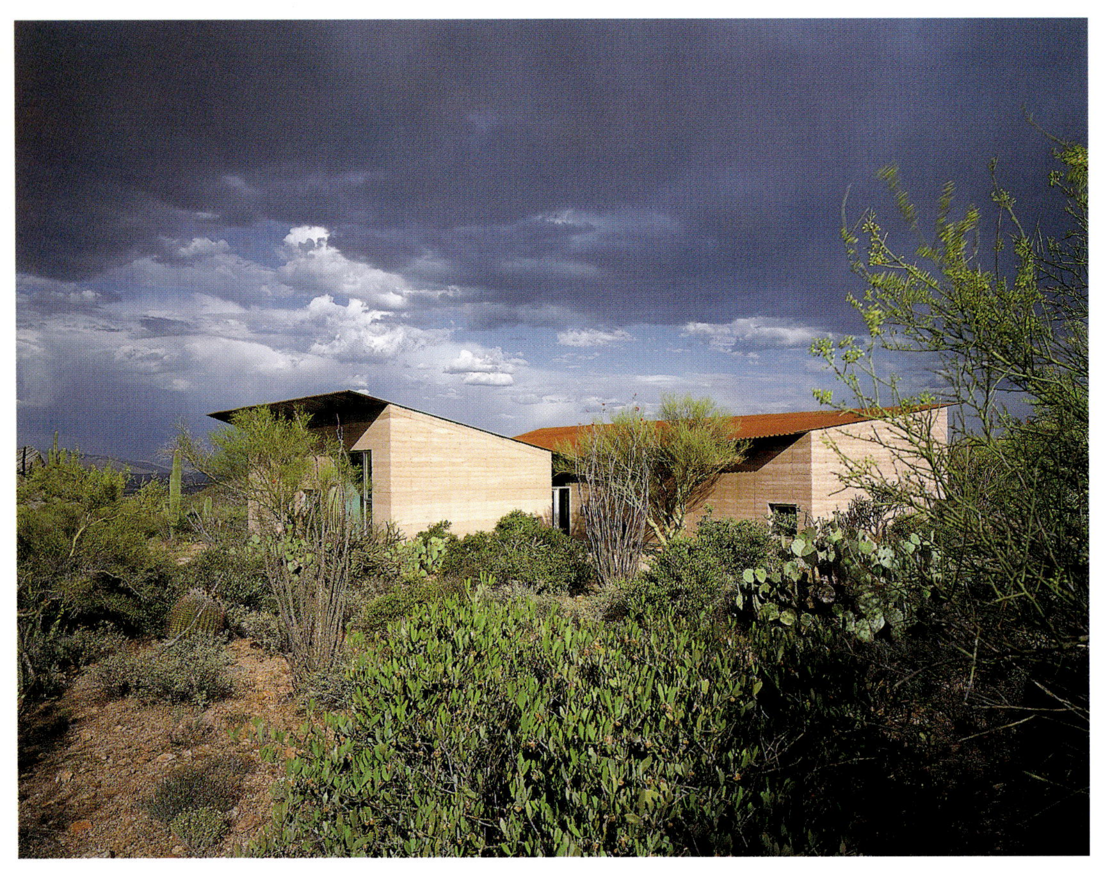

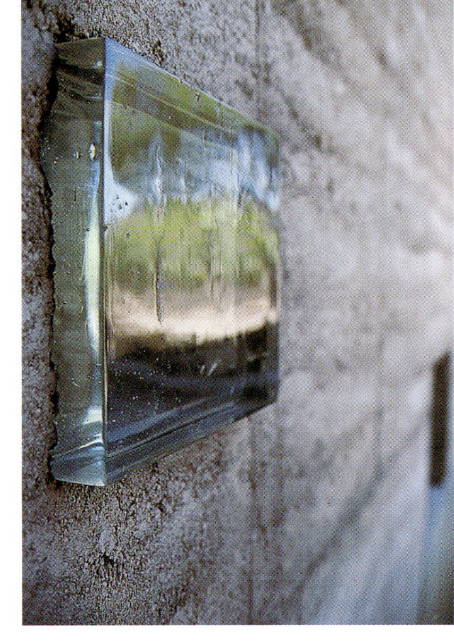

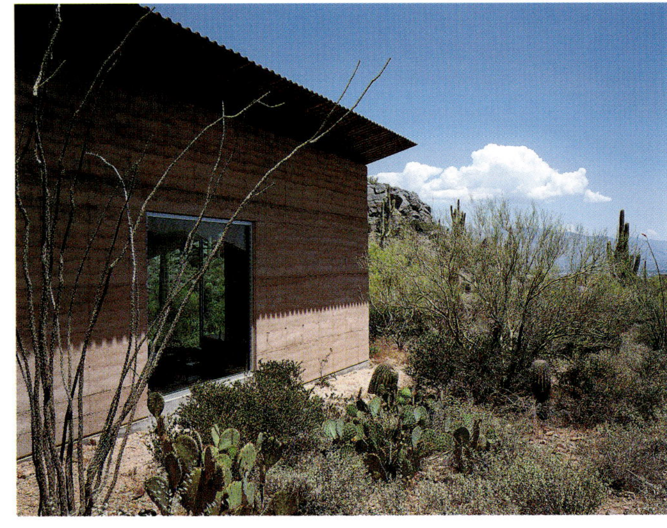

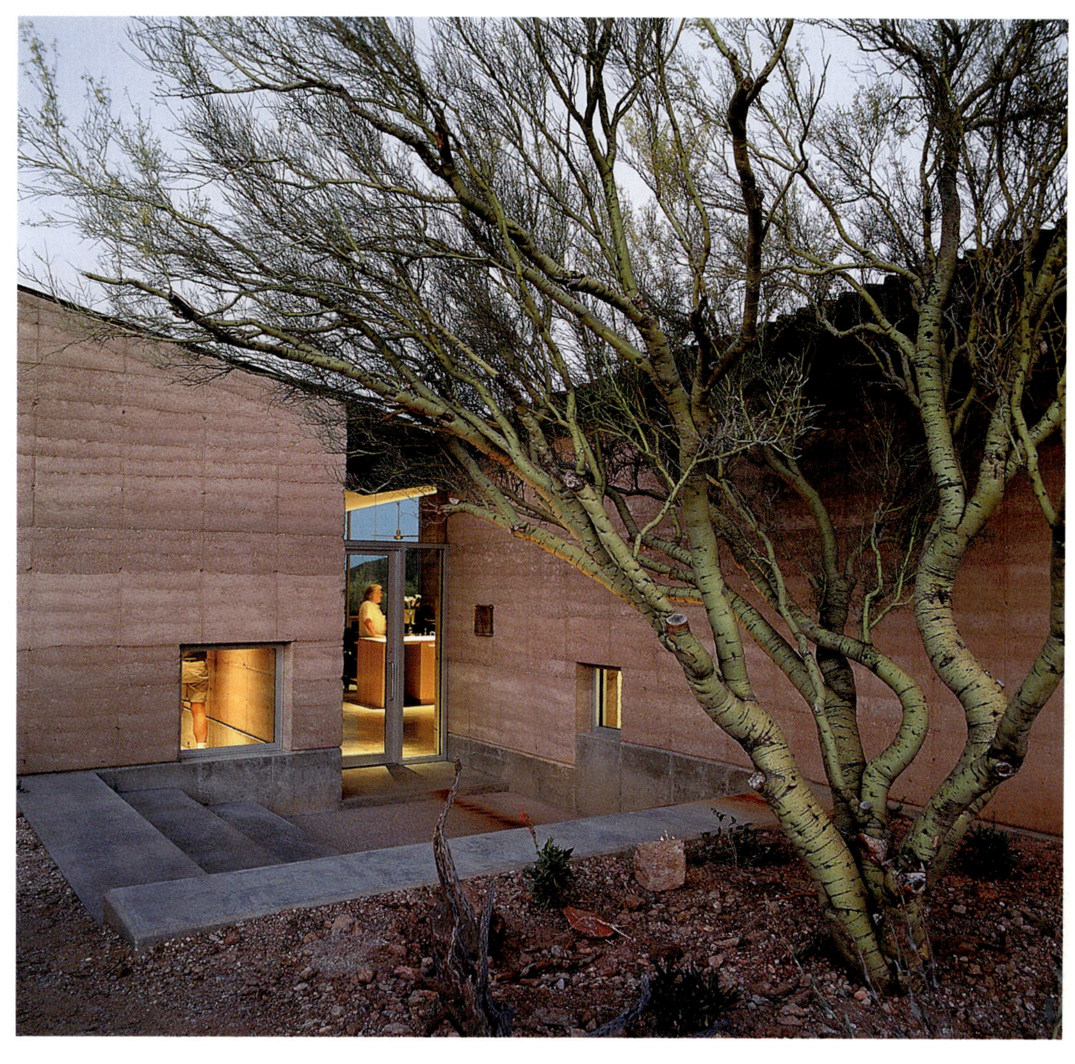

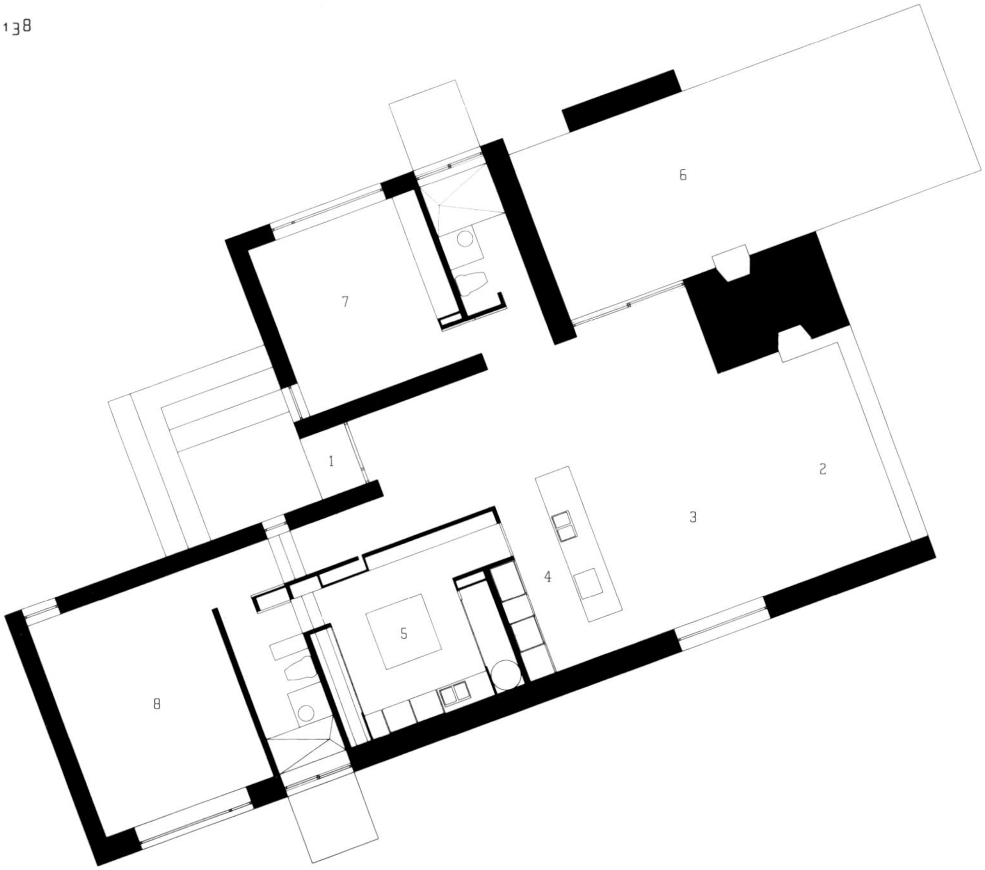

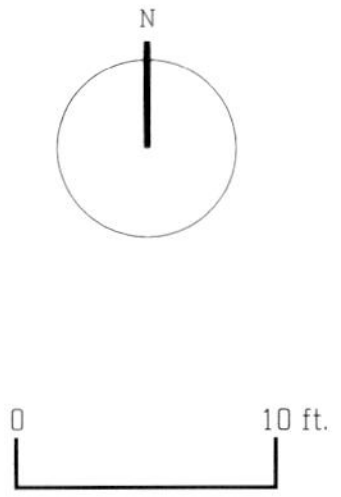

N

0 10 ft.

1 Entry
2 Living Room
3 Dining
4 Kitchen
5 Pantry
6 Porch
7 Guest
8 Bedroom

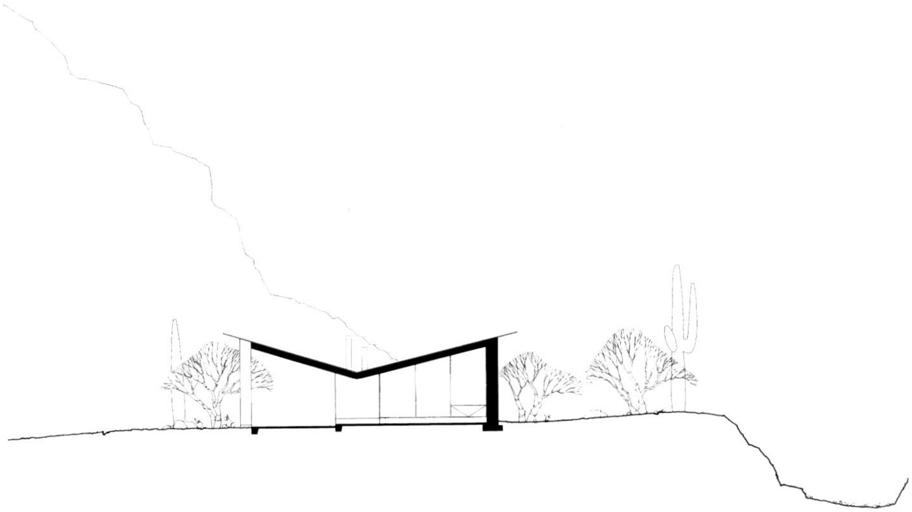

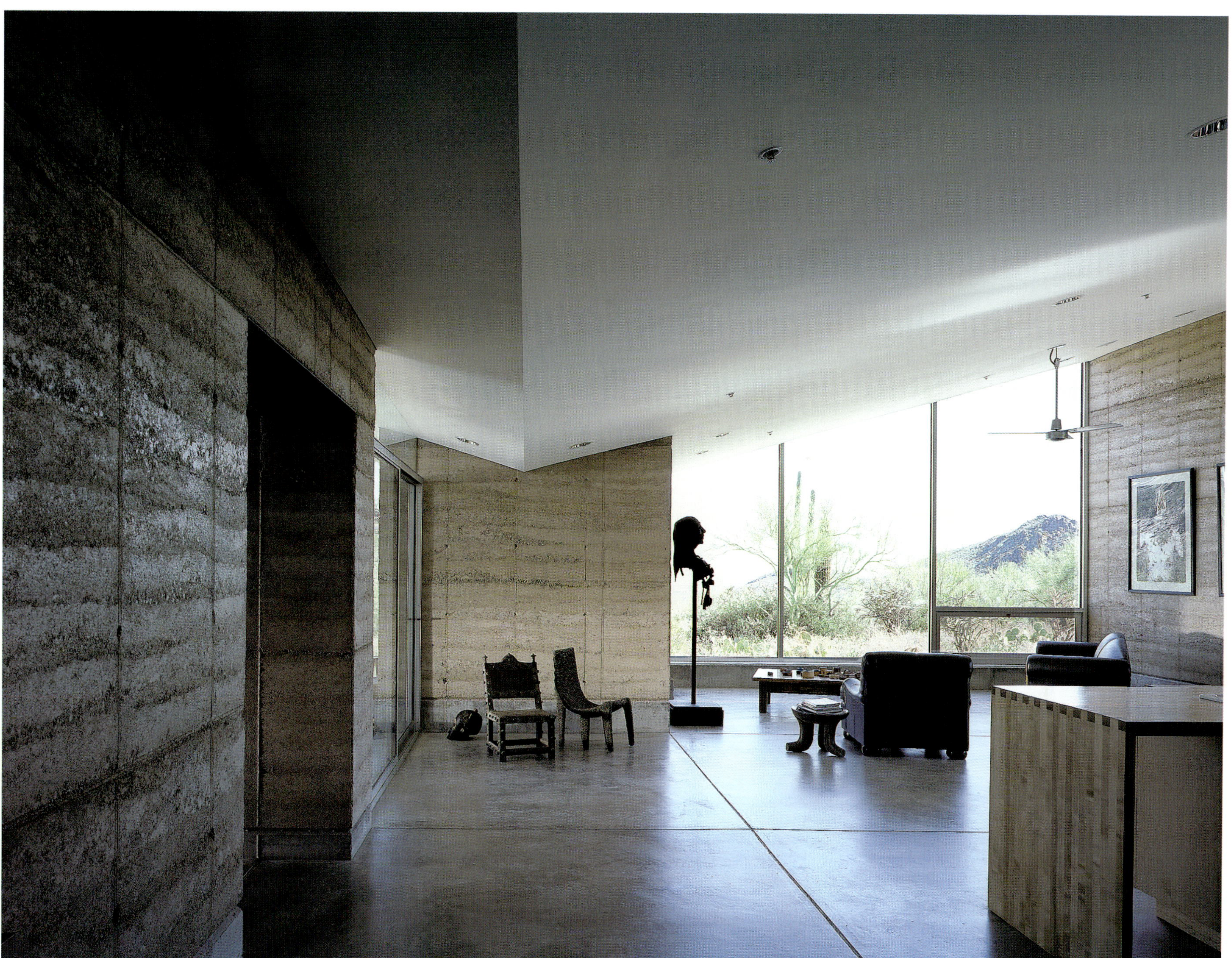

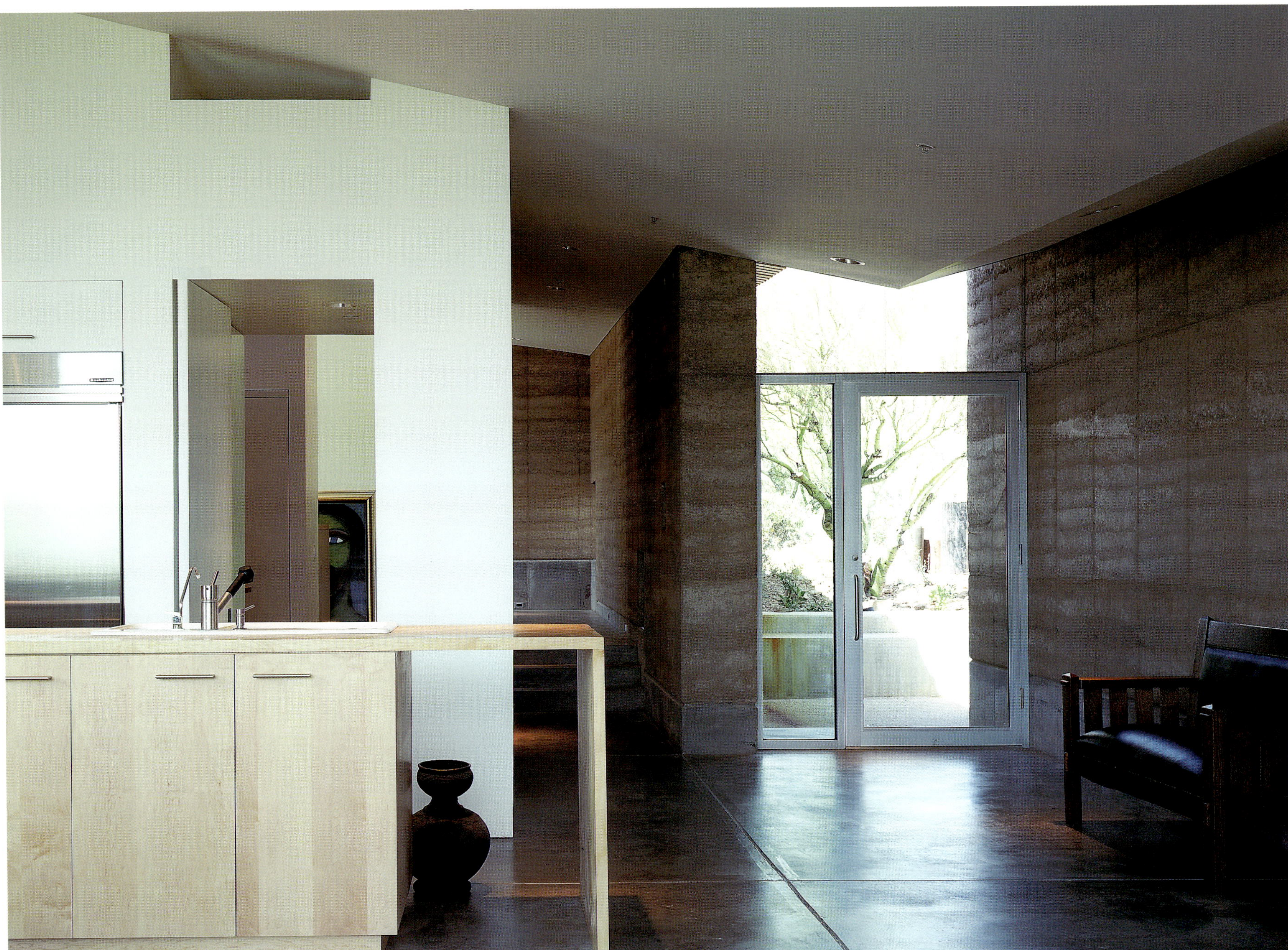

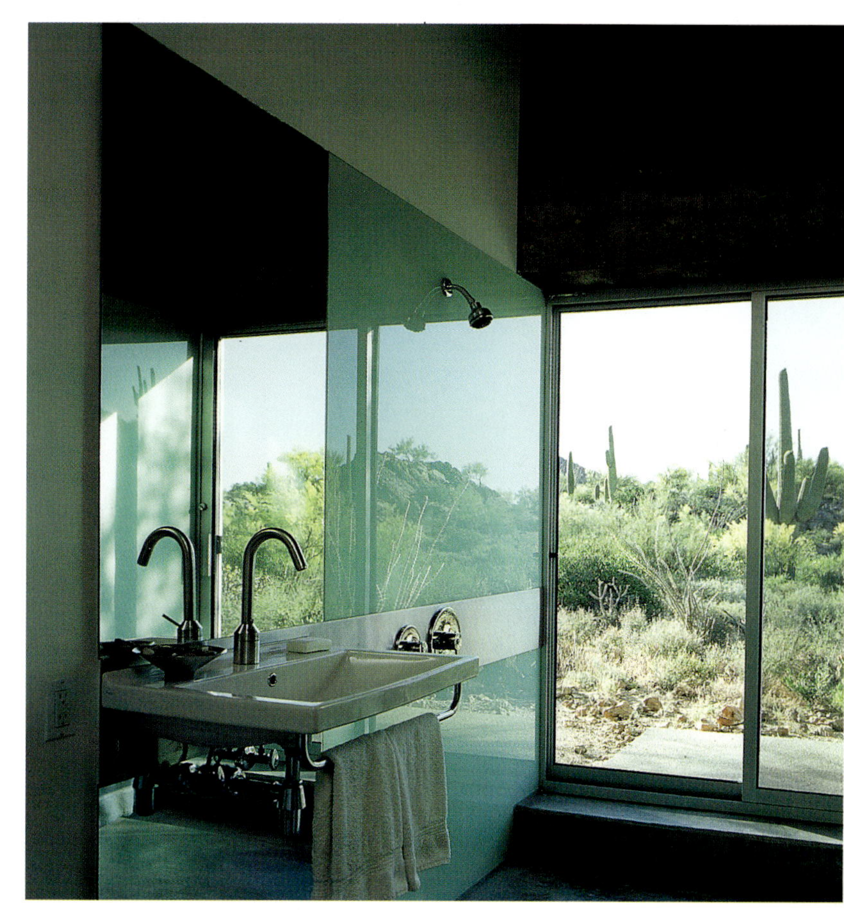

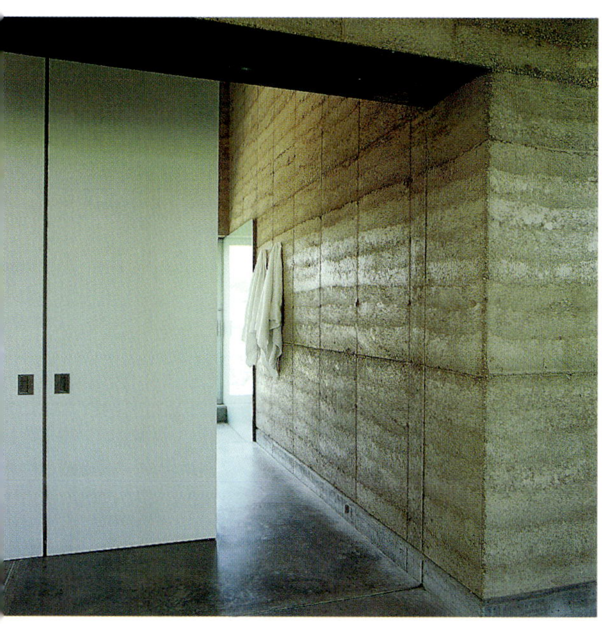

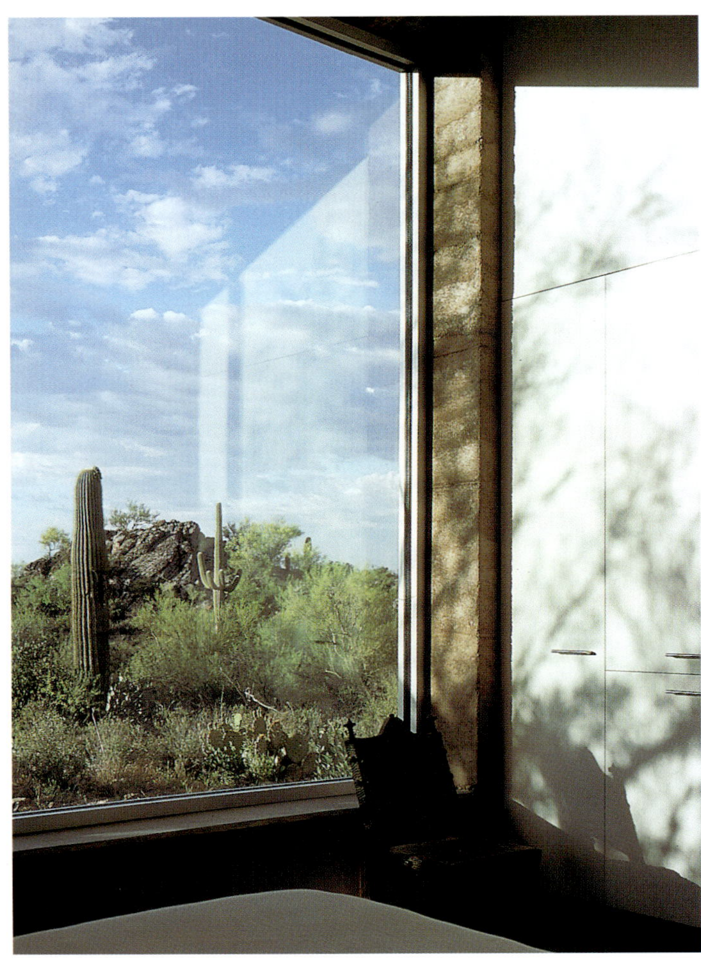

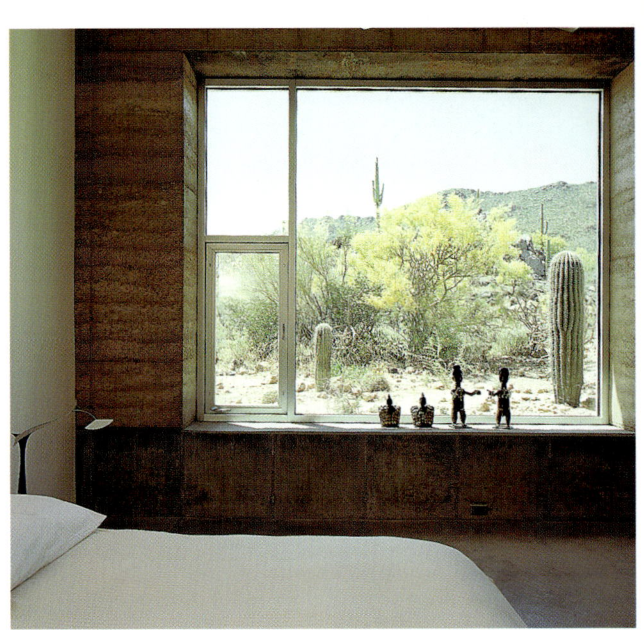

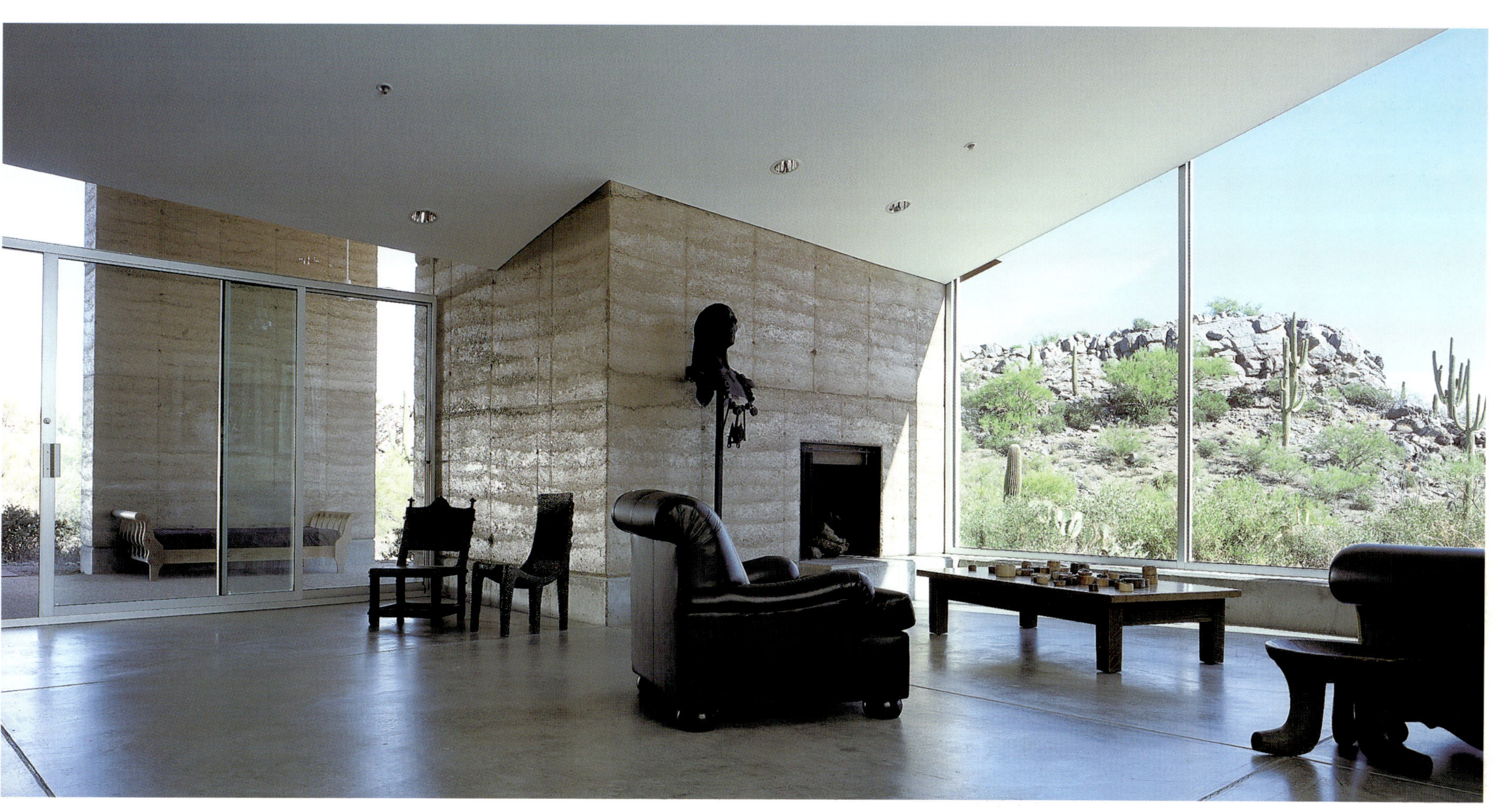

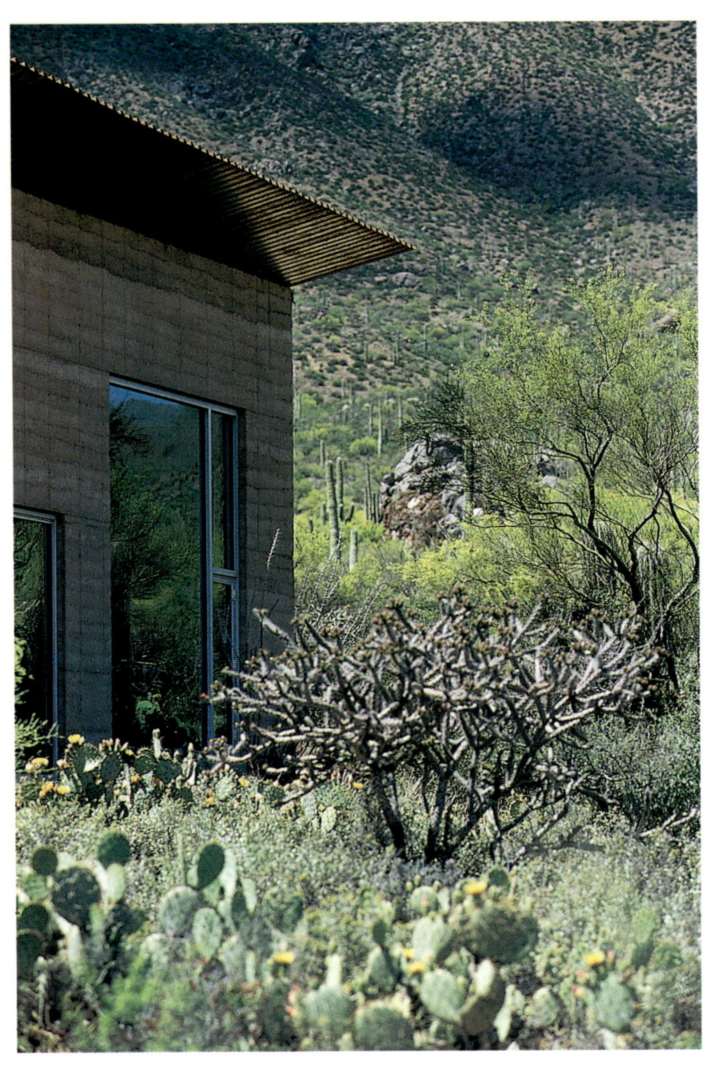

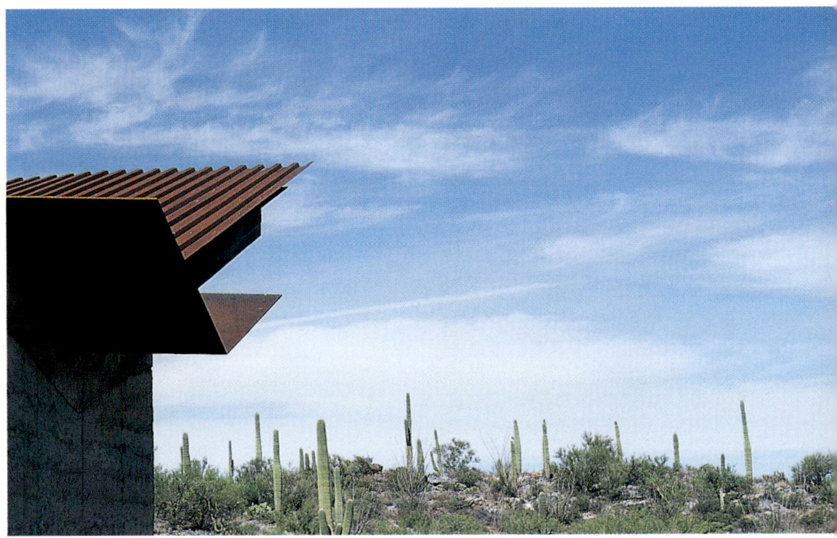

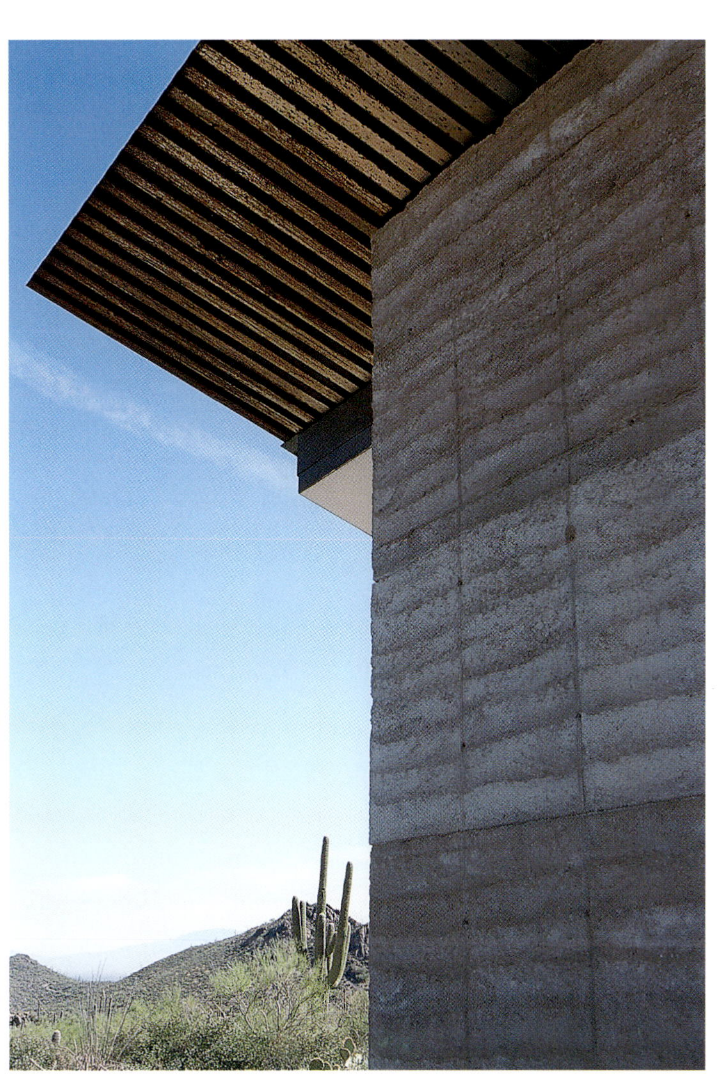

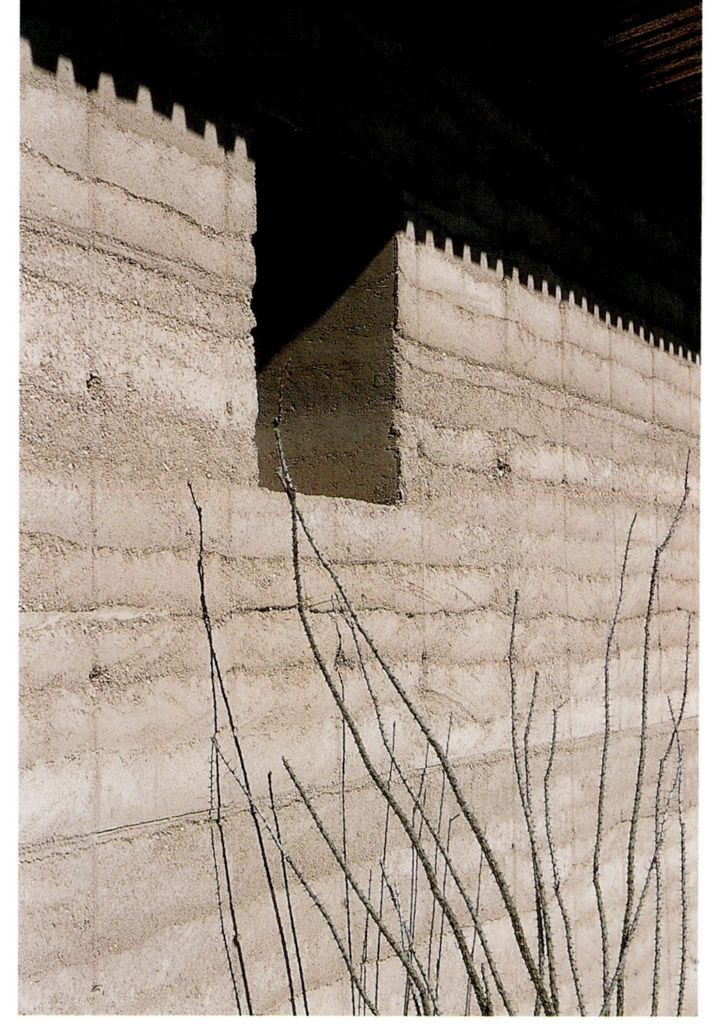

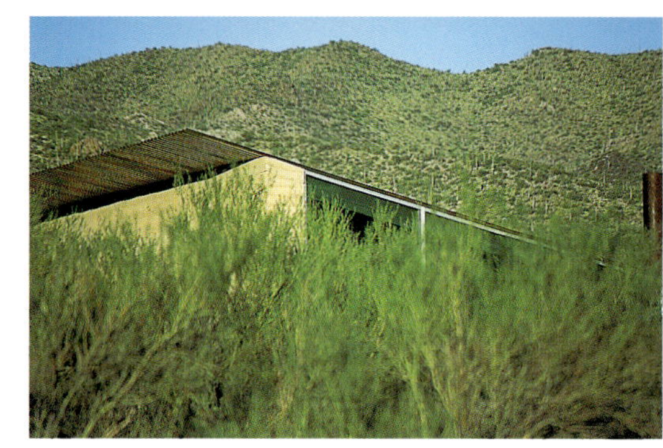

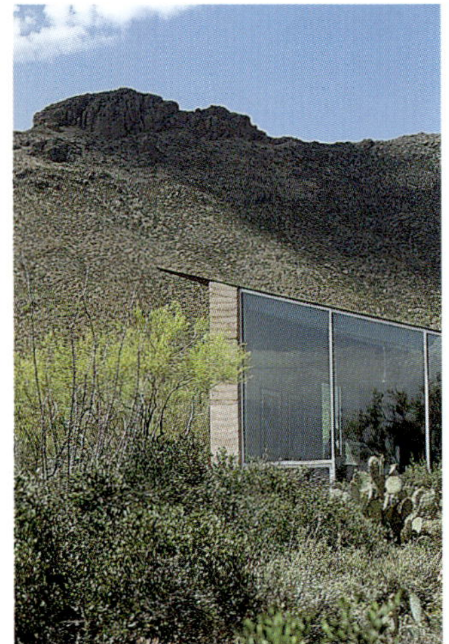

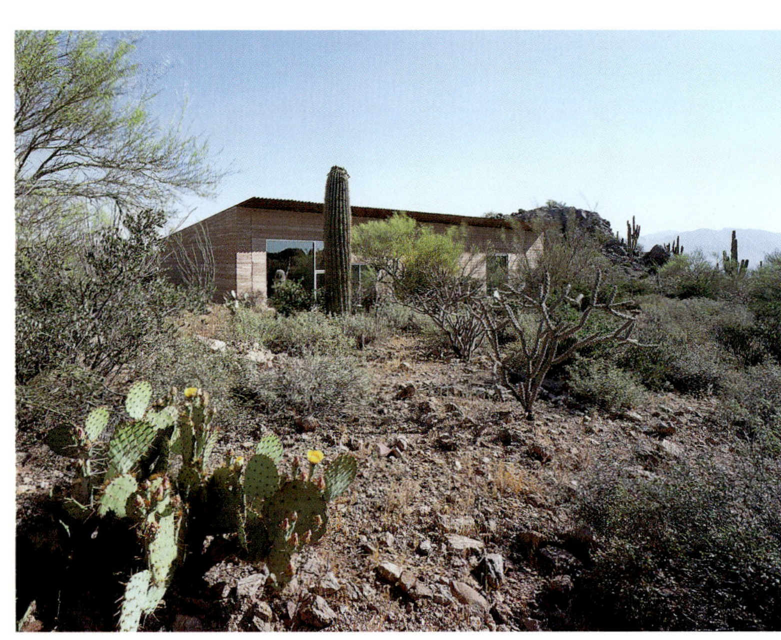

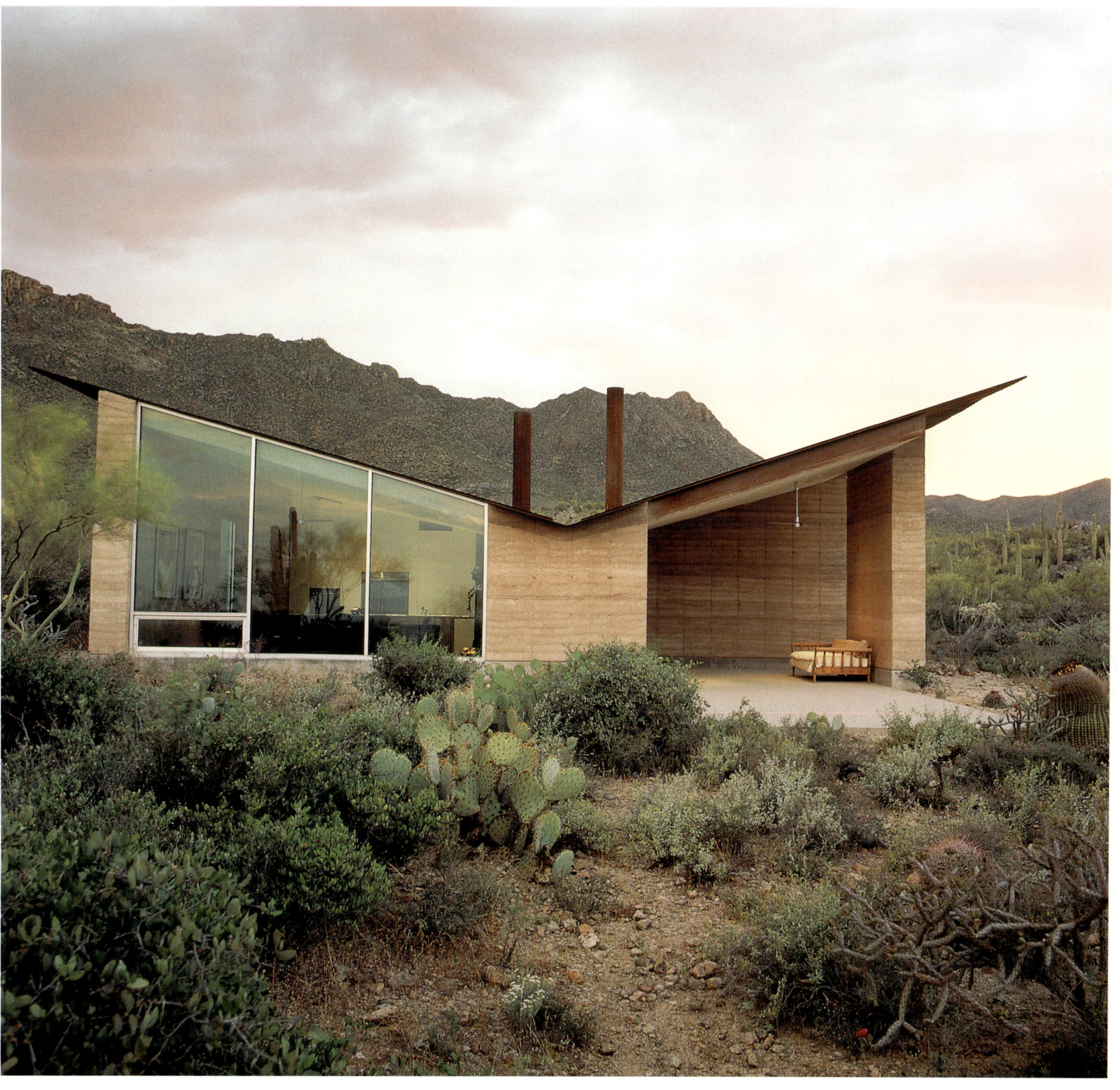

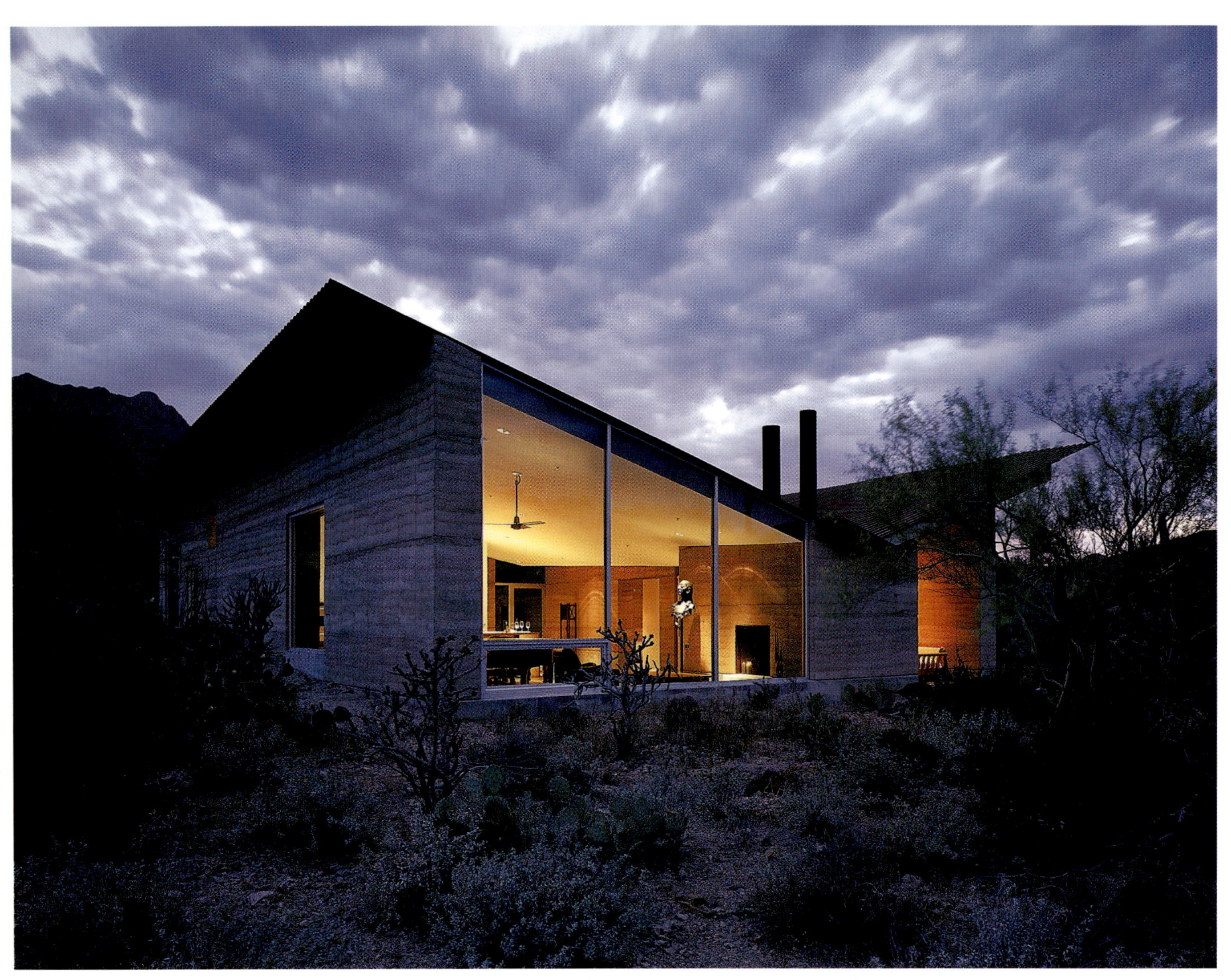

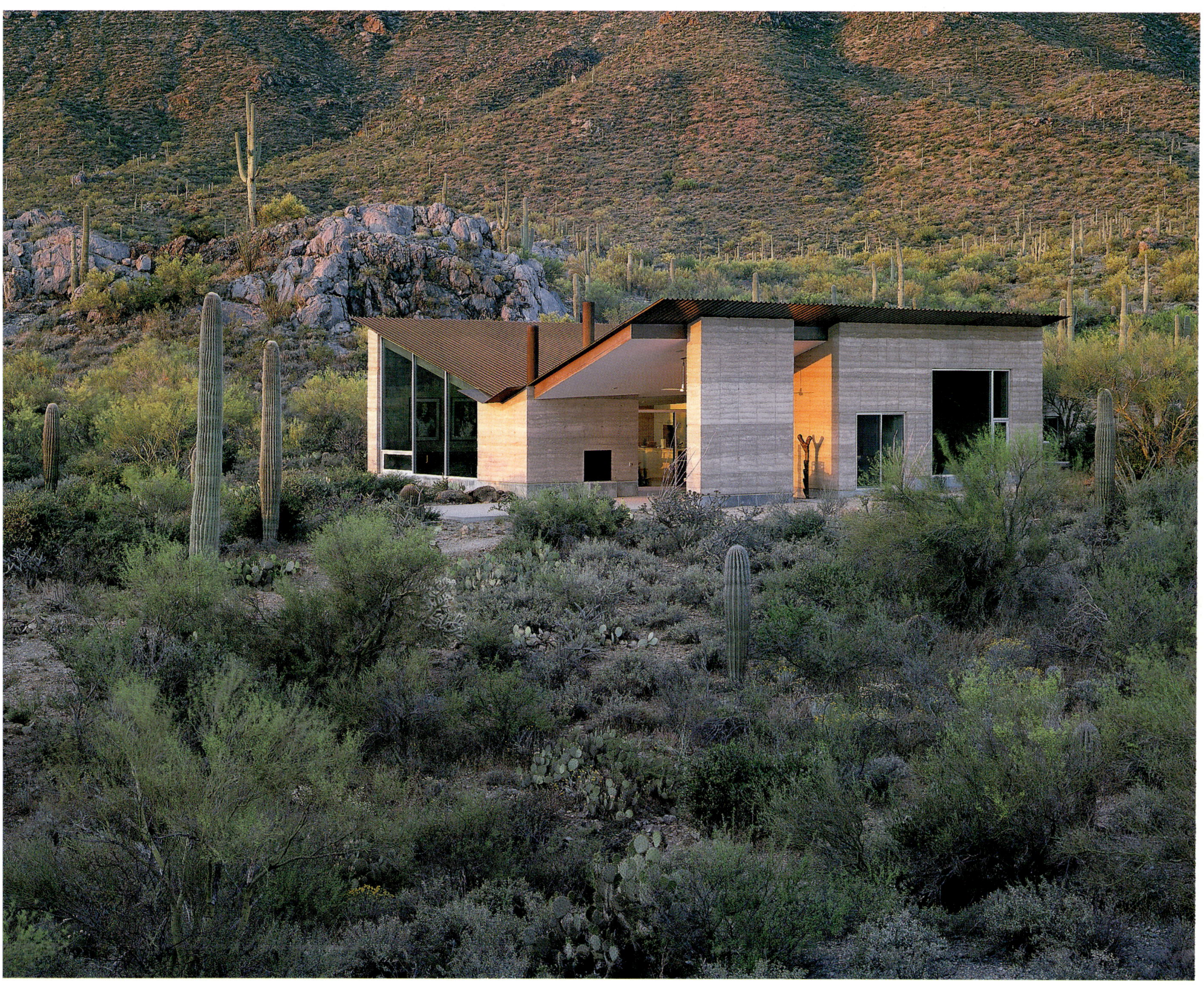

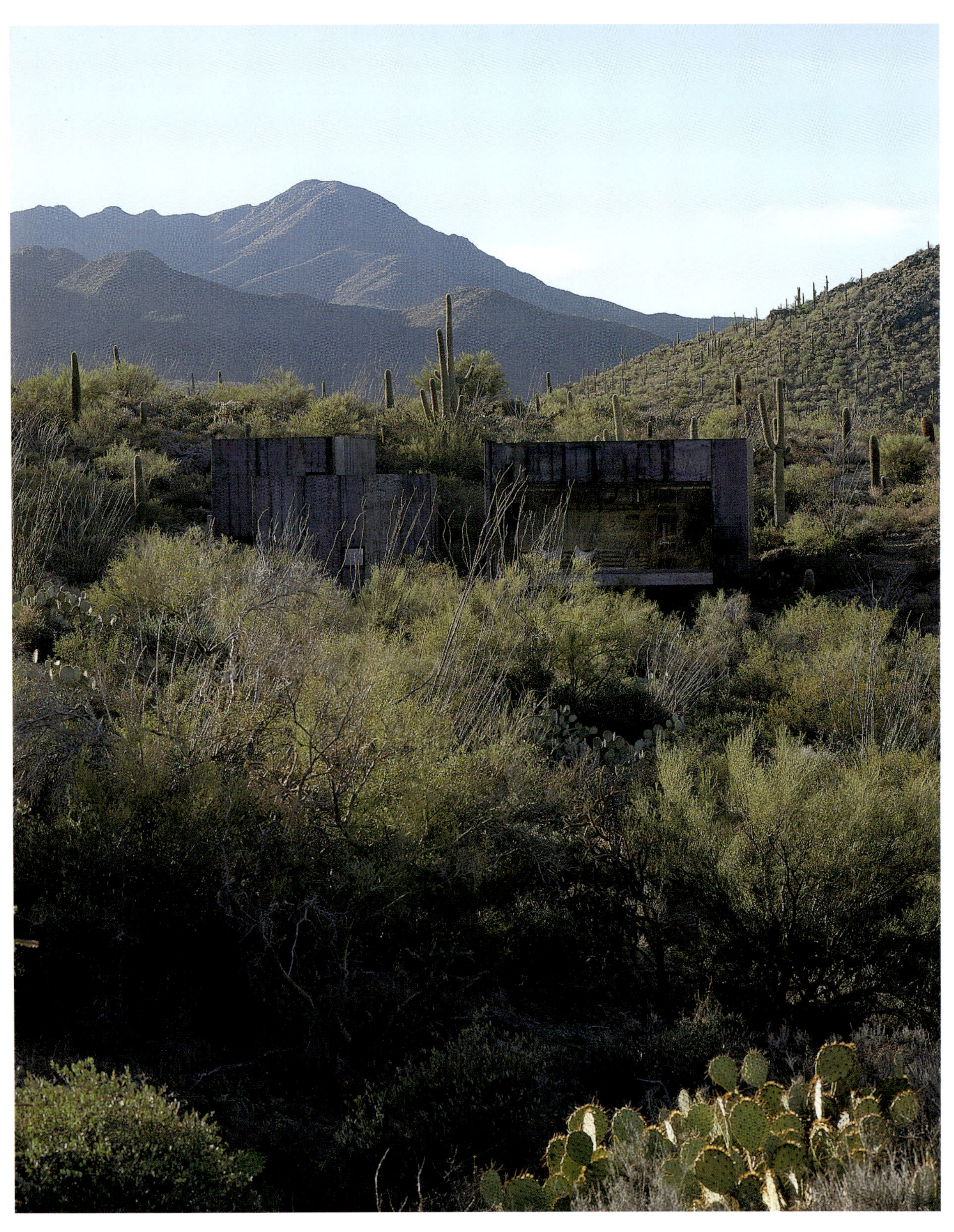

The three boxes have landed in their rightful place, nestled in a secluded bowl-like formation on the land, striving for low impact and equilibrium among the ancient saguaros. Opportunities for dramatic views surround the site. A singular view for each primary space was selected after studying possible orientations.

The house is divided into three zones. For the main living space there is an intense early evening view to the southeast. The setting sun highlights a large craggy rock hill; the low-lying landscape in the foreground is in the shadows of the mountains behind. As night falls, the city lights of Tucson emerge. For the bedroom, the rising sun illuminates a particularly stunning rock face at the top of the mountains to the southwest. The reflected light backlights the saguaros and ocotillo in the foreground. A still life of a rock outcropping and saguaro is for the small den.

To enhance the experience of each space and view, we gave the three zones individual boxlike structures with a single aperture from which to experience each sun-lighting event. Each box is elevated and one must walk on footpaths between them; this further reinforces the isolated experience. The fragility of the site also prompted this idea. Water and critters flow freely beneath.

Each box is framed and clad in plate steel on the exterior and maple veneer panels on the interior. A ventilated air space behind the steel skin allows heat to be exhausted via natural convection currents. Panels are articulated and fasteners exposed, asserting the applied-skin nature of the elevated box. Interior partitions are translucent glass and the kitchen island is plate stainless steel. Flush wooden sleeping decks cap each form. A small carport constructed of steel grating is tucked into a small depression in the entry hill above.

On the land the forms are elusive. Like a group of hunter's blinds, their presence remains nearly unnoticed from the surrounding areas.

CASA JAX

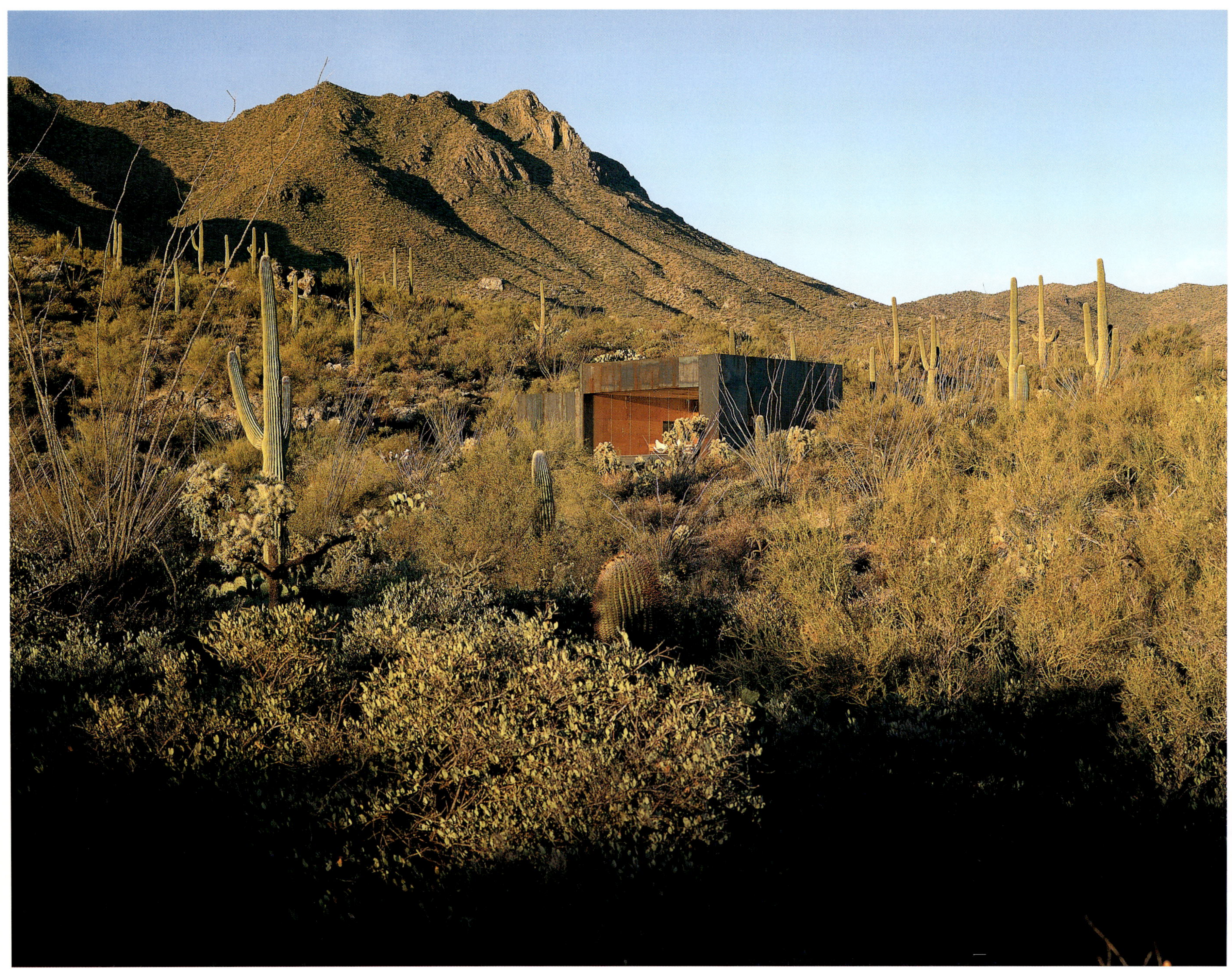

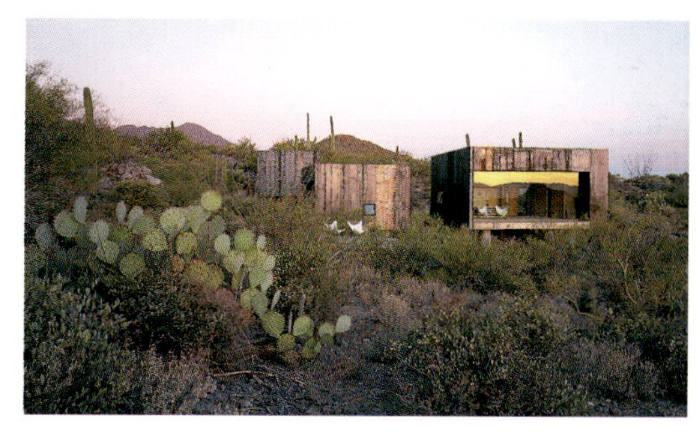

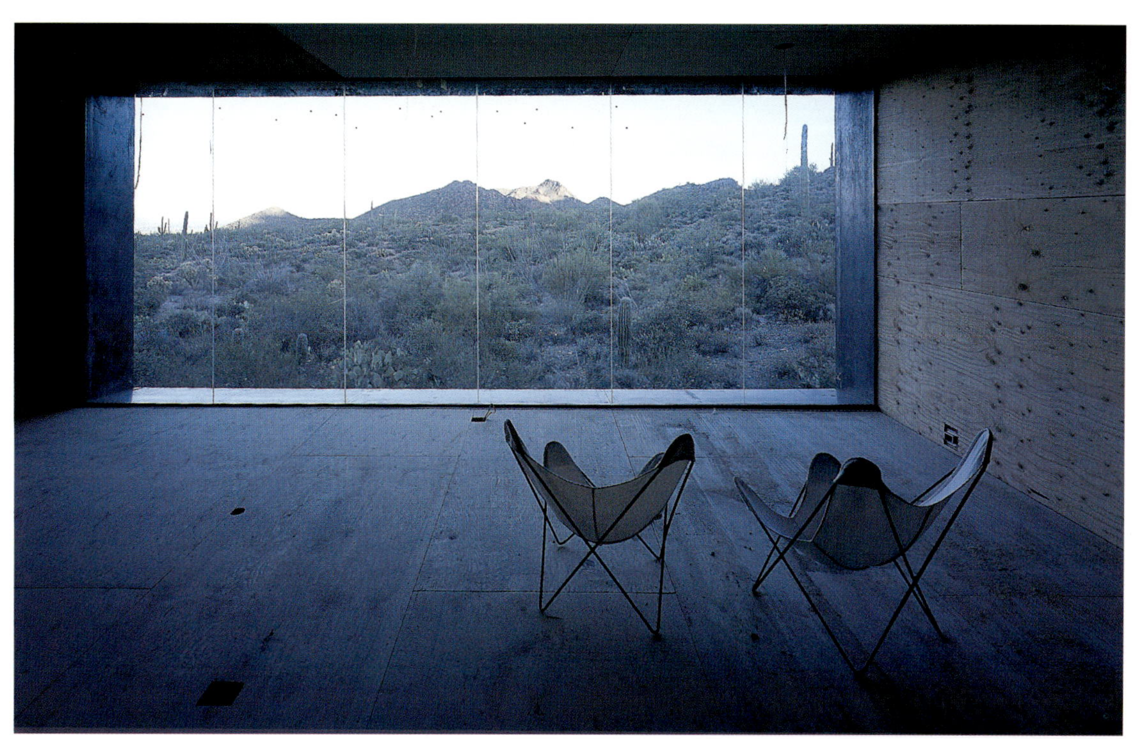

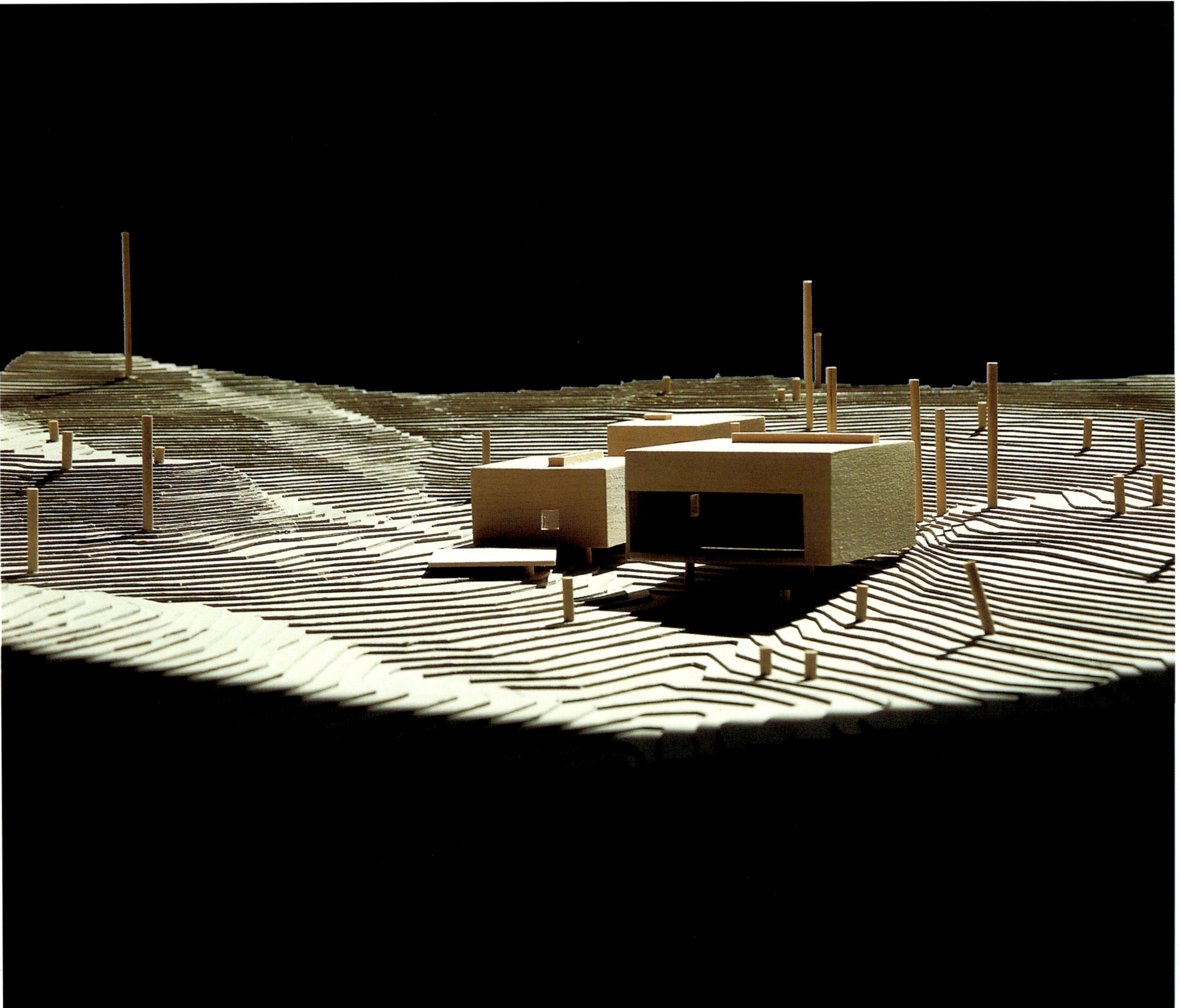

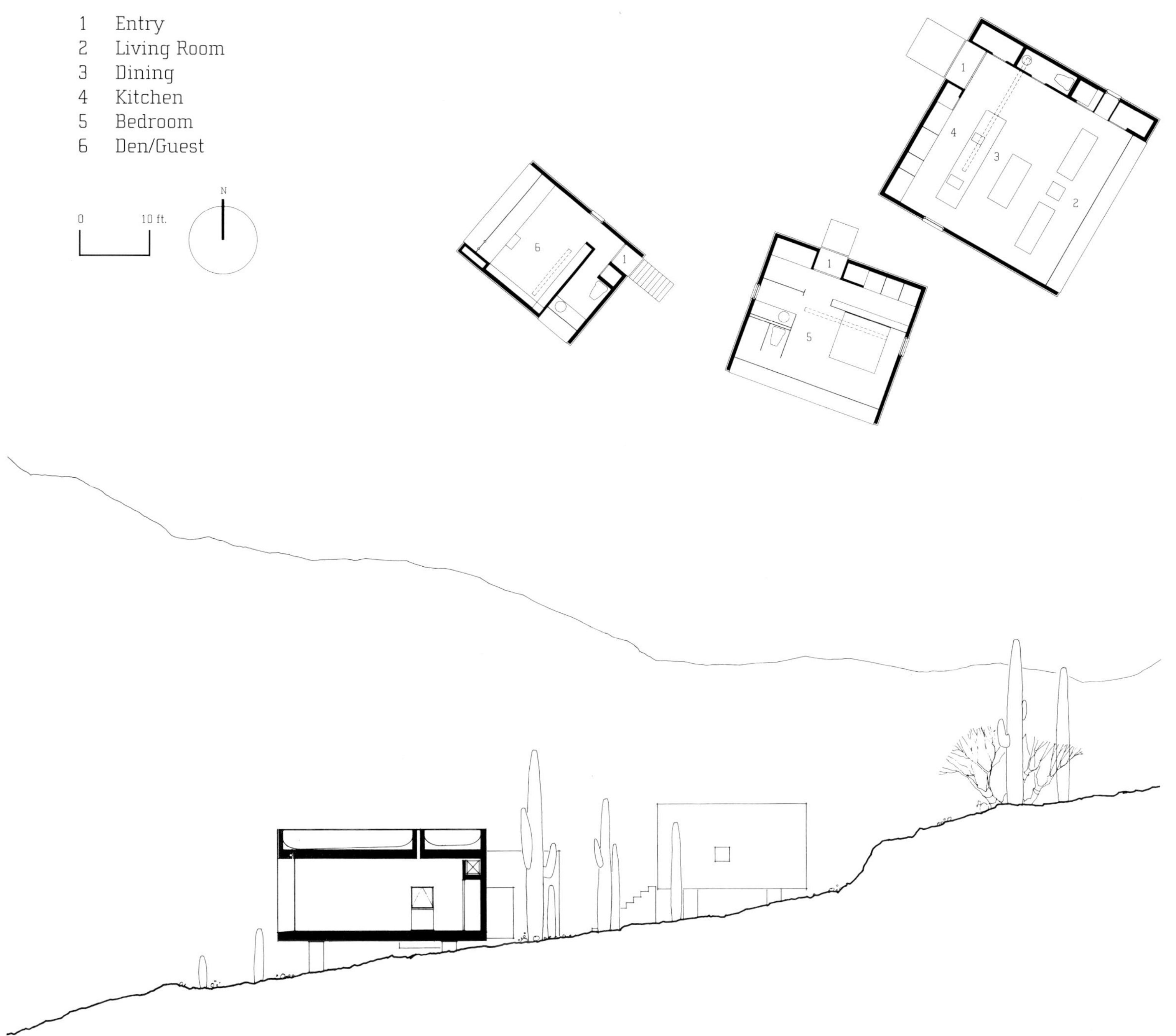
1 Entry
2 Living Room
3 Dining
4 Kitchen
5 Bedroom
6 Den/Guest
0
10 ft.
N

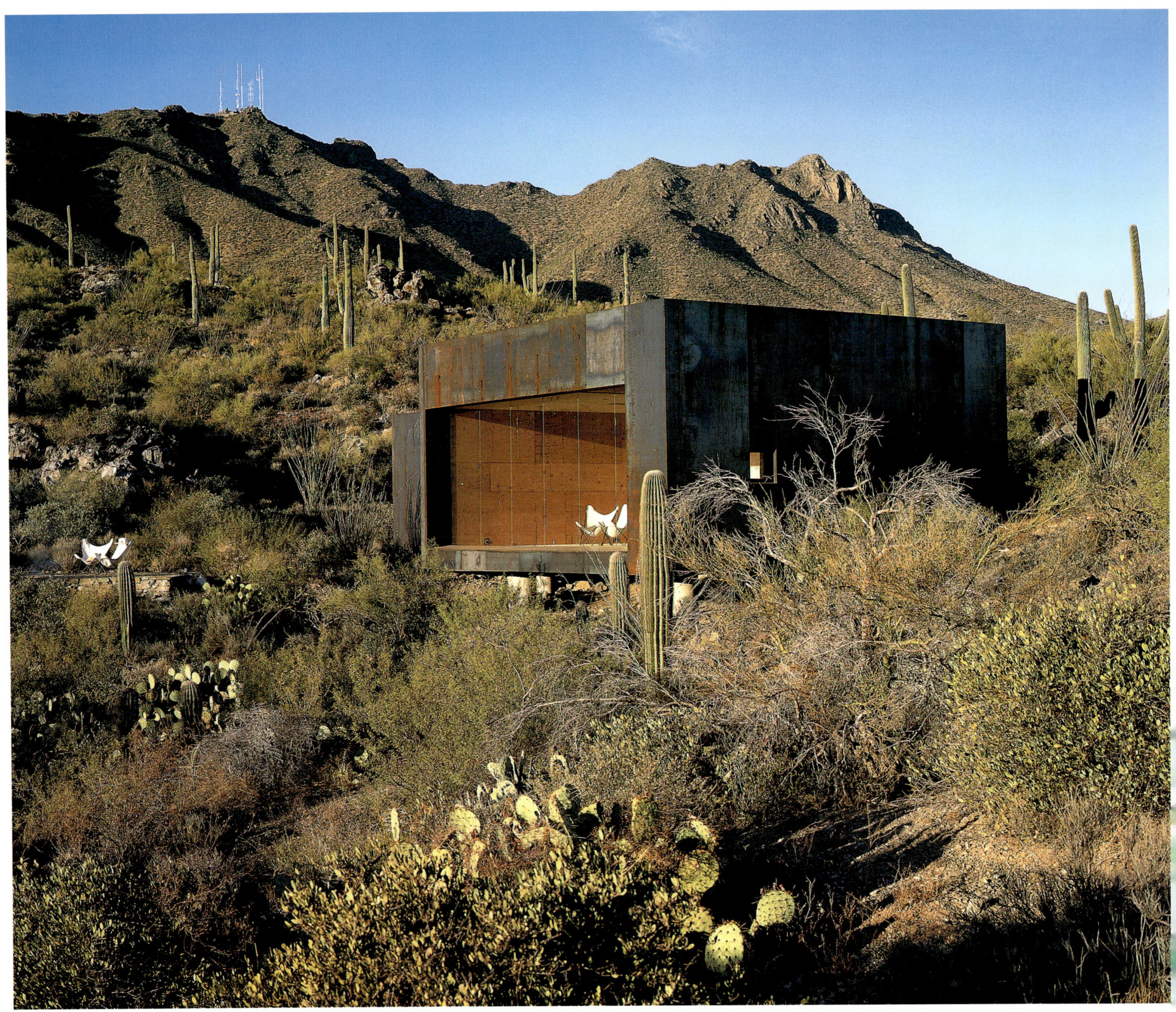

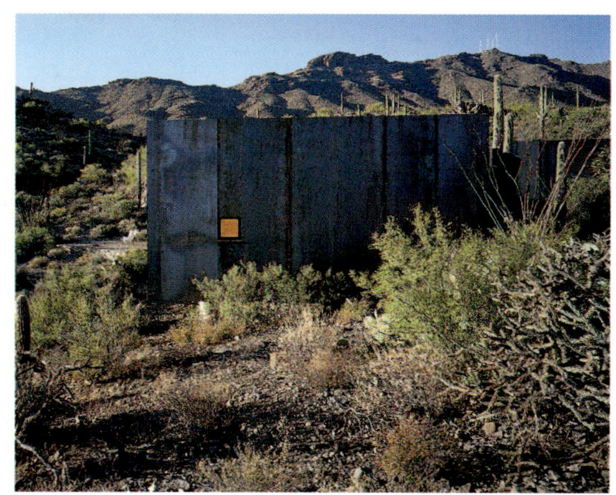

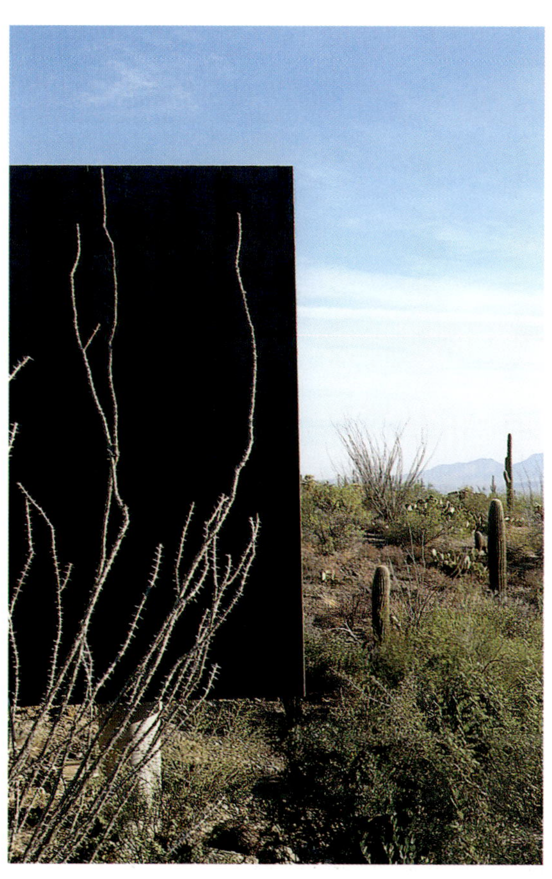

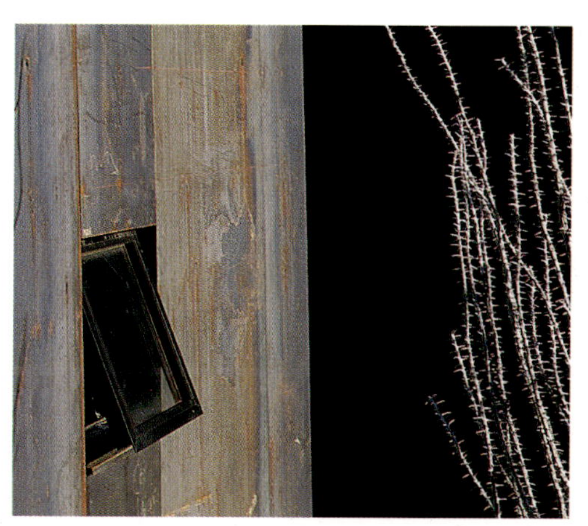

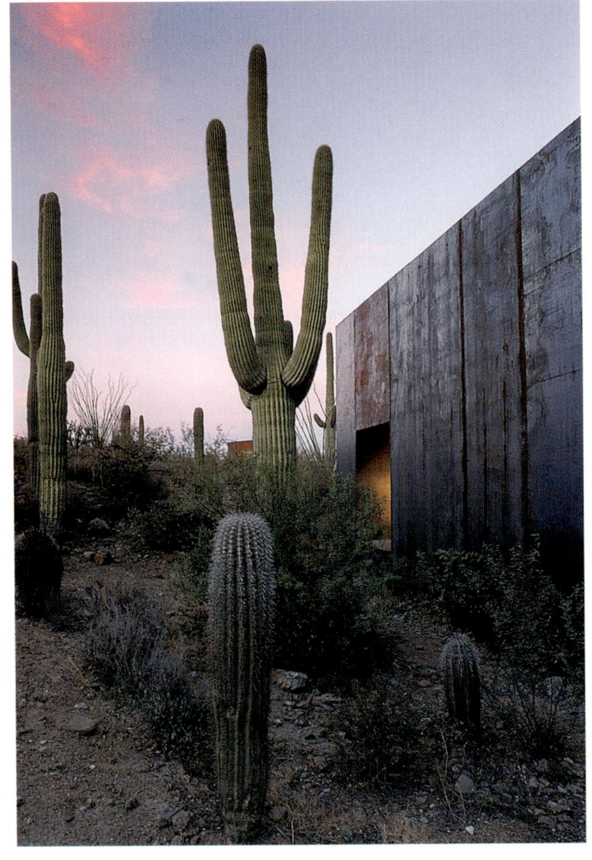

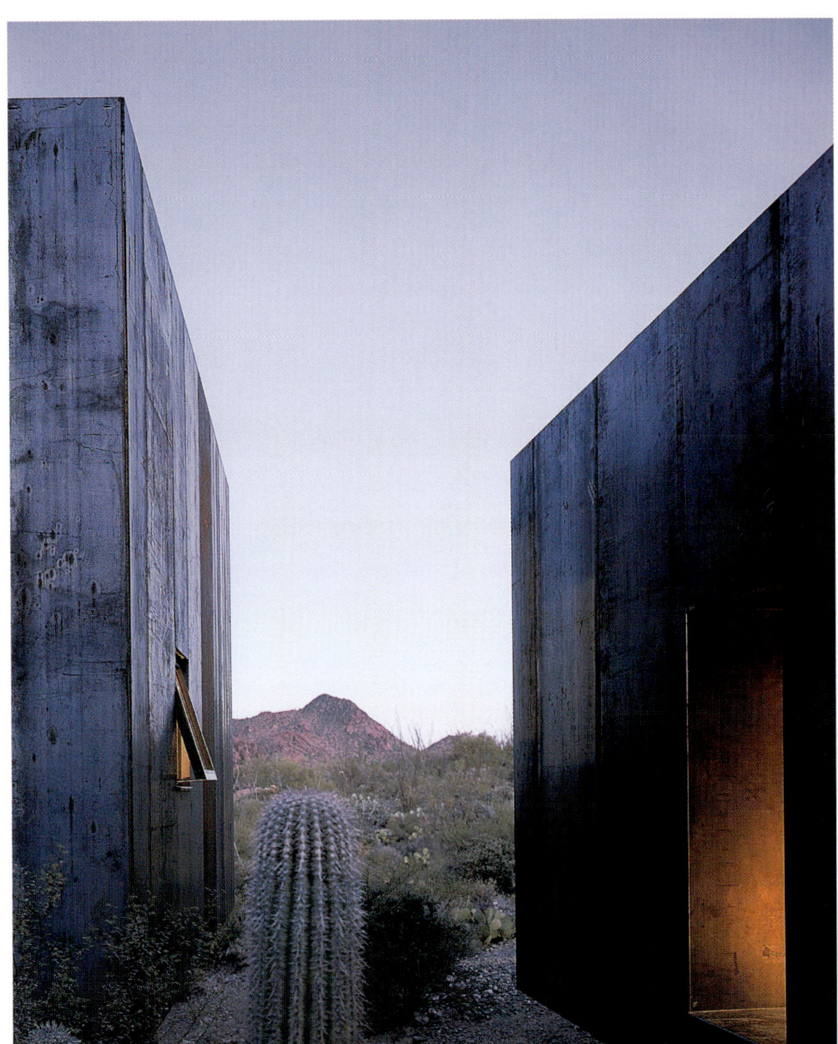

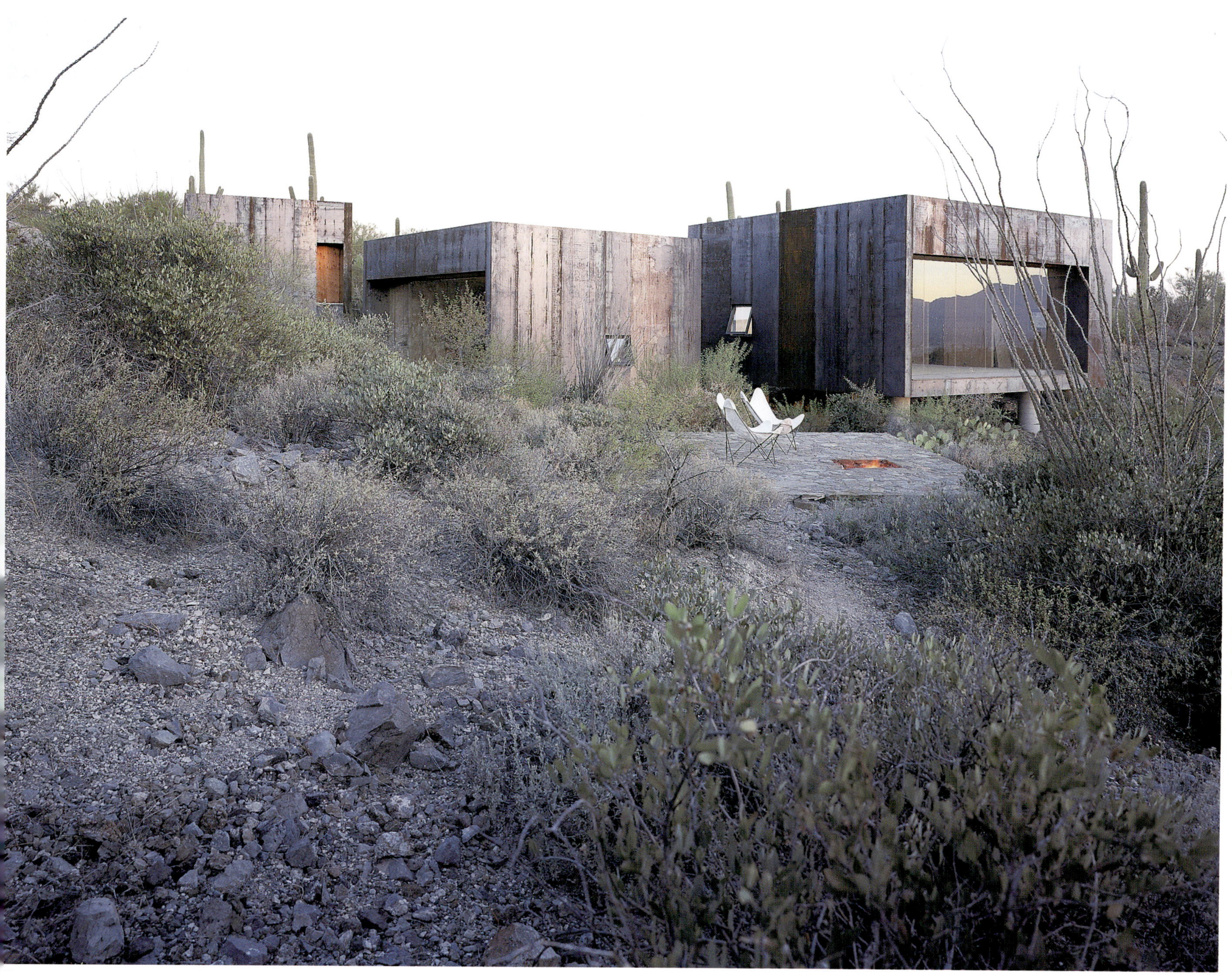

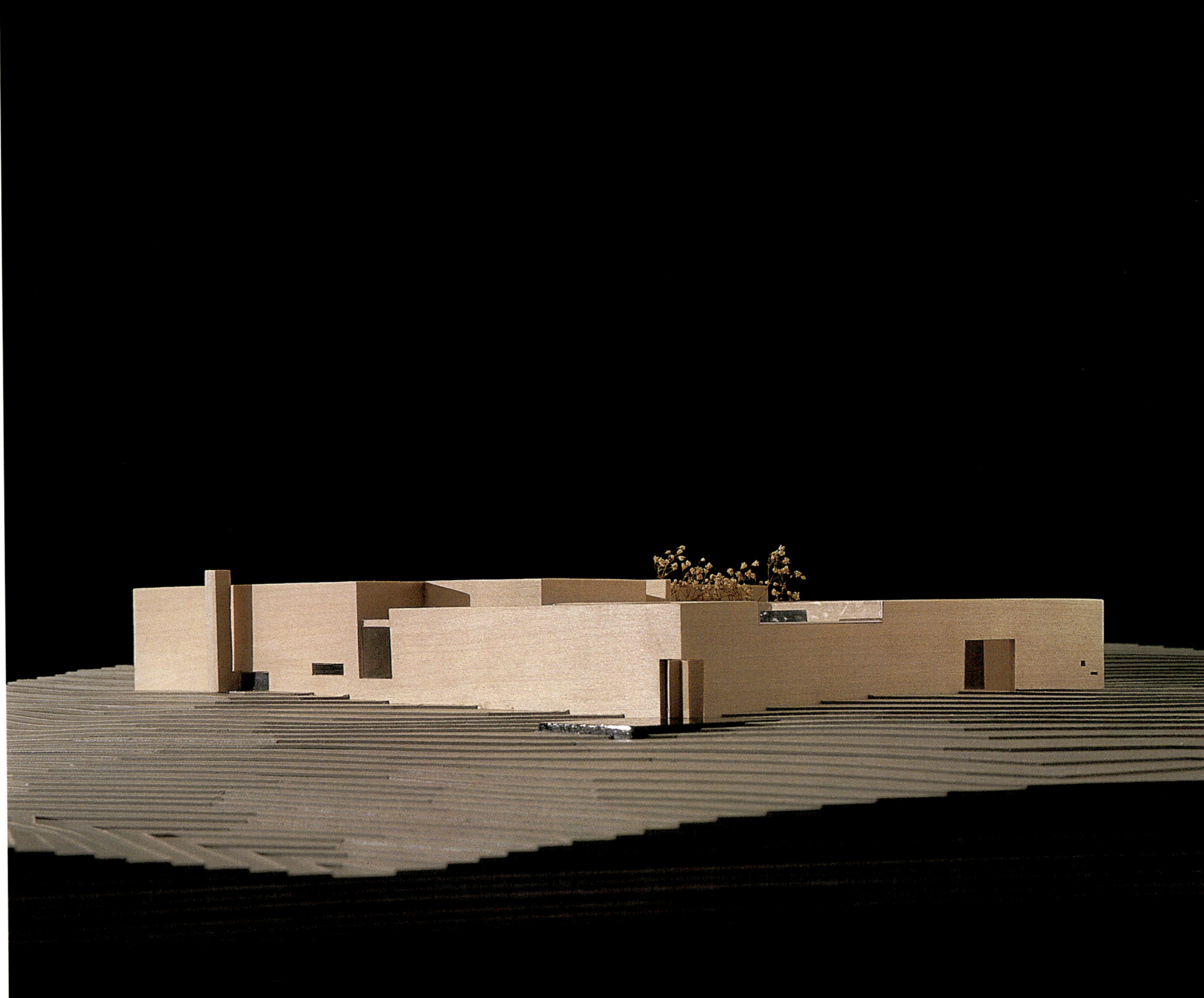

The one-acre site is in a gated housing community regulated by ill-conceived notions of desert living. Given the nature of the existing context, the design of the house is turned in on itself and contained within a singular walled form. It is an idealized version of the subdivision home.

One enters through the southwest corner, via a revolving steel gate, into a small dark chamberlike space. With very little light and the sound of slowly dripping water, it is a serene and silent space where the body and mind unconsciously slow and a sensory tuning in occurs, discarding the world outside. From this "decompression chamber," visitors ascend a terraced path in a canyon-like space under dappled light to a glass entry pavilion.

The main living spaces form an L around an exterior living courtyard. On the northeast corner, over a flush pool of water, the perimeter walls are parted, capturing the only available mountain view between the other houses in the community.

The structure of the buildings is post-tensioned concrete block with integral insulation. The interior surfaces match the exterior—lightly textured plaster. Walnut, stainless steel, sandblasted glass, and polished concrete complete the interior palette.

PIMA CANYON HOUSE

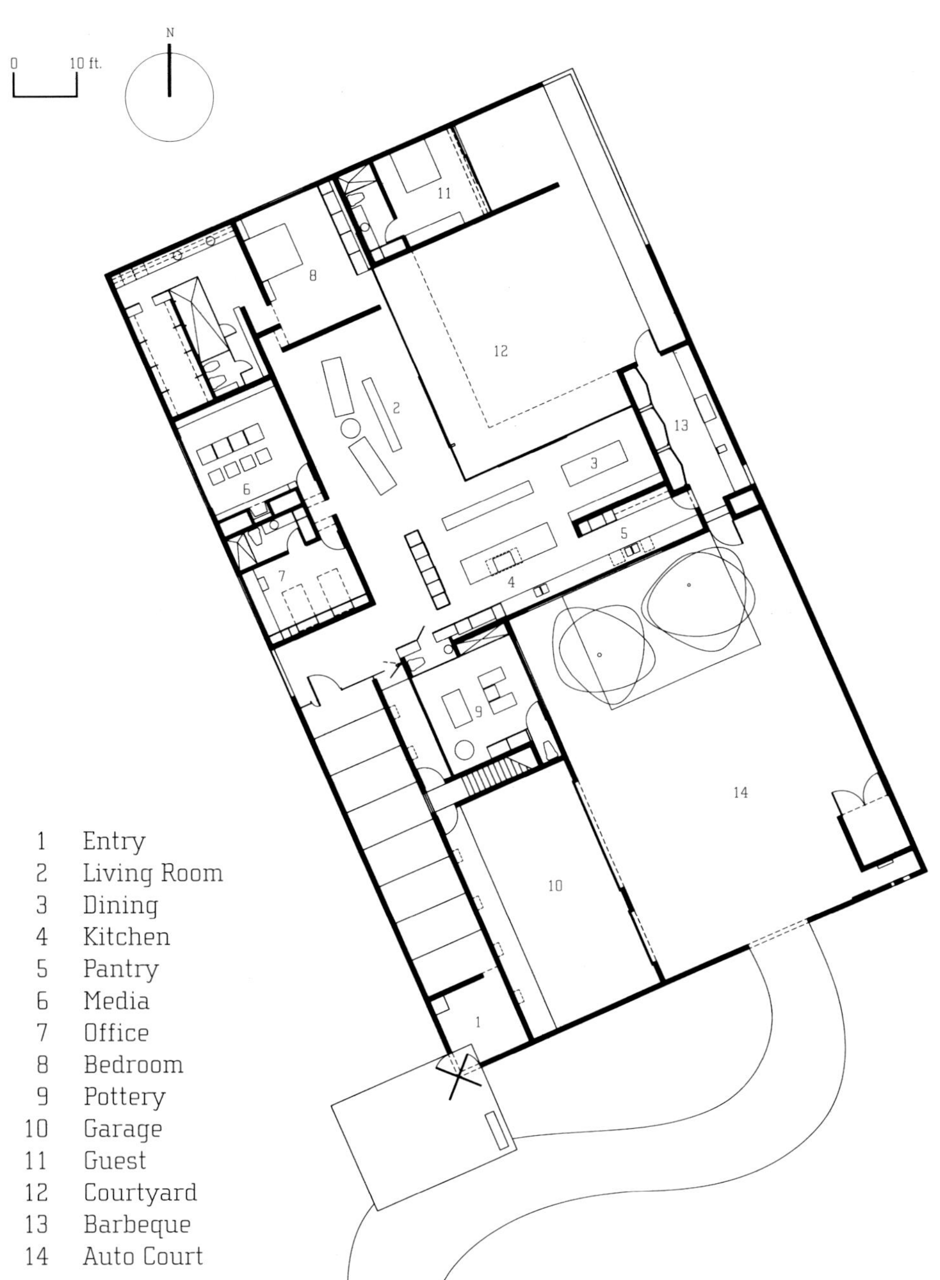
0
10 ft.
N
1 Entry
2 Living Room
3 Dining
4 Kitchen
5 Pantry
6 Media
7 Office
8 Bedroom
9 Pottery
10 Garage
11 Guest
12 Courtyard
13 Barbeque
14 Auto Court

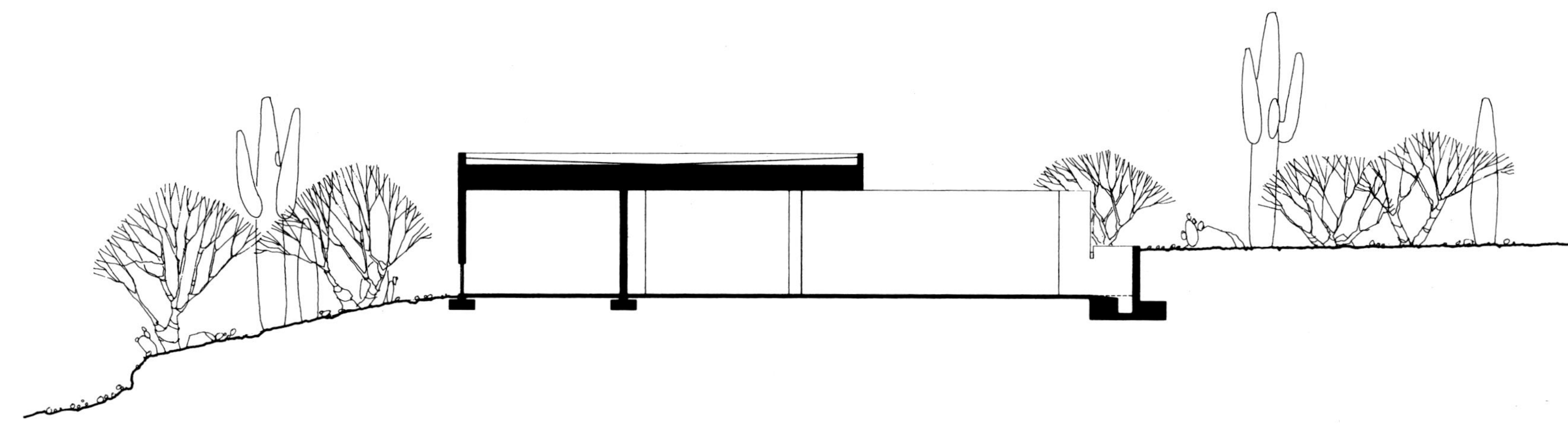

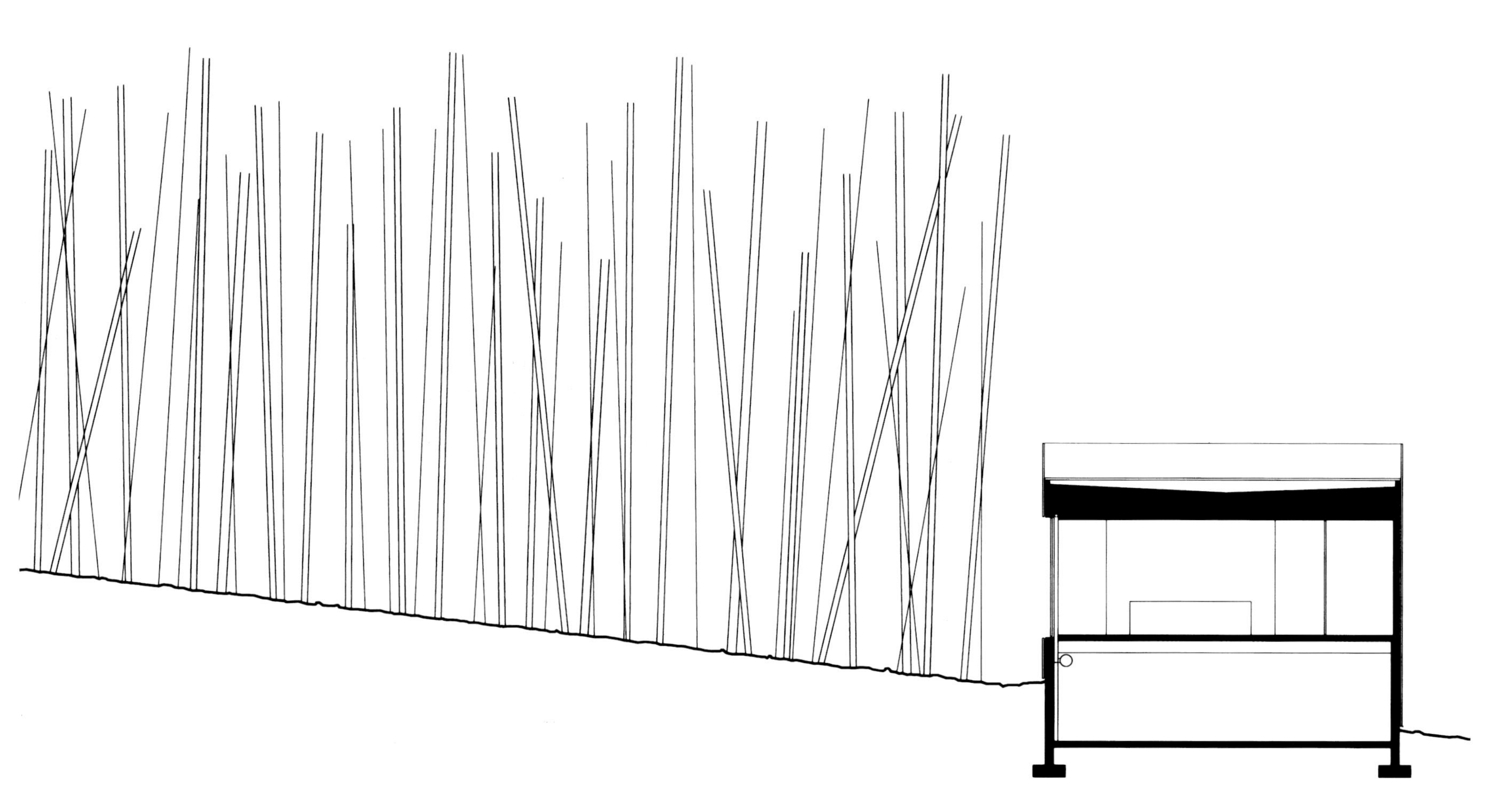

GREER CABIN

At nine thousand feet above sea level, the site is in a sloping open field at the edge of an aspen forest. The cabin is a functional box with garage, wood storage, and kennel below, two-bedroom open plan above, storage, service area, and bathrooms along the north, and a roof terrace. Two translucent glass forms that screen the bedrooms on the ends contain the stairways. The wood and steel frame structure sits on a concrete base. White interiors complement the vertical cedar exterior.

One continuous window wall to the south frames the view to the aspen forest—a pattern of vertical white lines. A pine forest about one hundred feet back provides a deep dark backdrop to the aspen, further enhancing the whiteness of their bark.

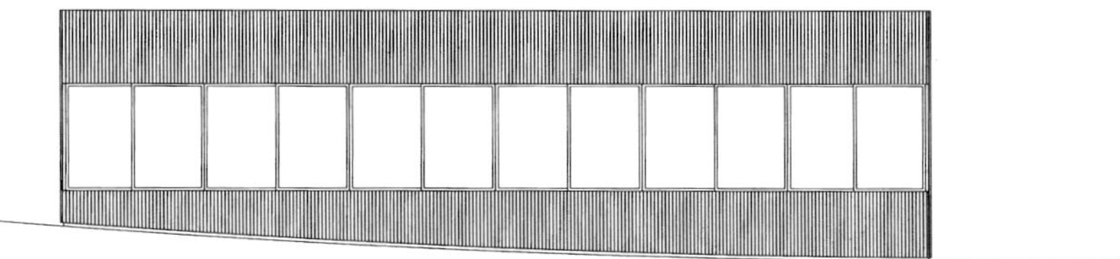

South elevation

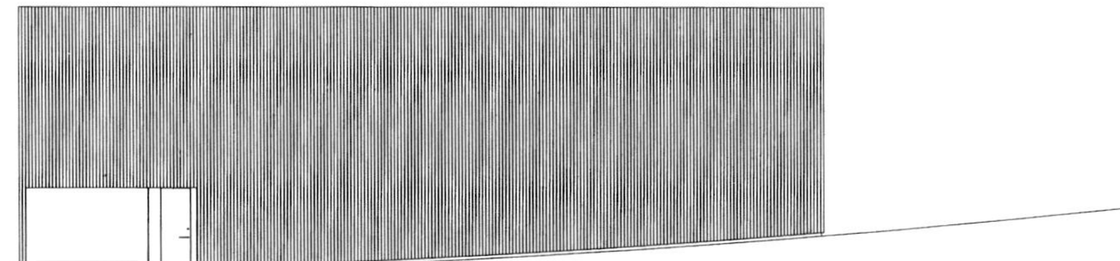

North elevation

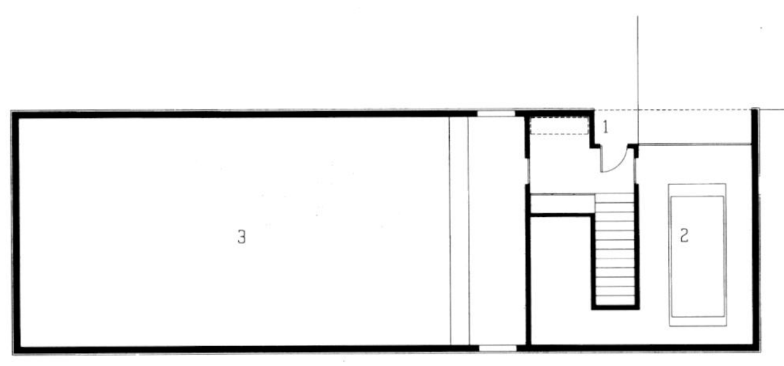

First floor

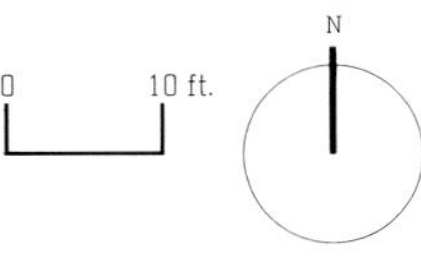

1 Entry
2 Garage
3 Basement
4 Living
5 Dining
6 Kitchen
7 Bedroom

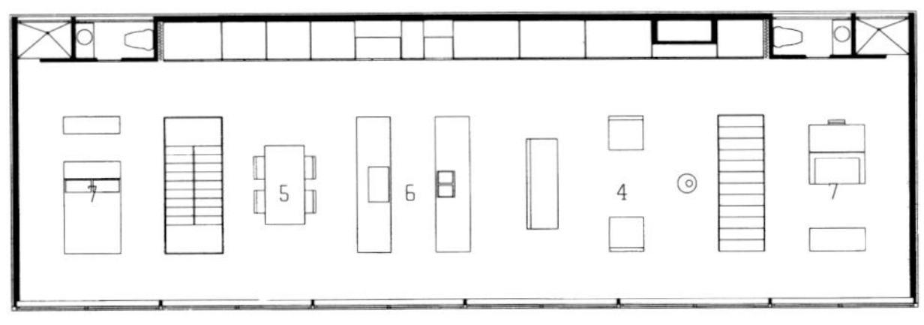

Second floor

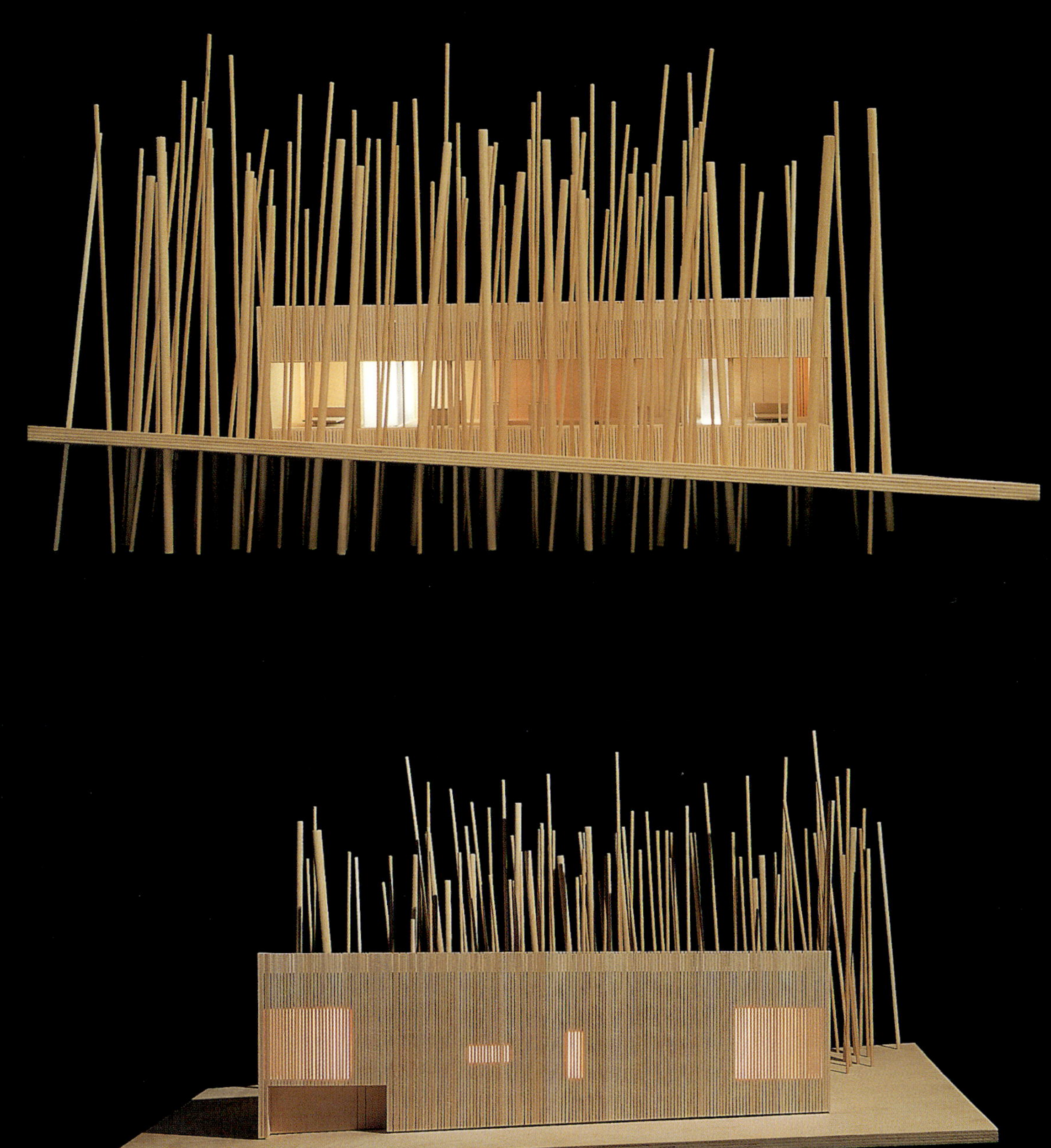

CREDITS

Project Credits

Convent Avenue Studios

Tucson, Arizona

Design:	1995
Construction:	1996–1997
Area:	existing casita: 600sf, new houses: 1000sf each, laundry: 200sf
Owner:	Rick Brezer, Sienna Funding Corporation
Project Team:	Rick Joy, Holly Damerell, Franz Buhler
Engineers:	Southwest Structural Engineers, Otterbein Mechanical Engineering
Builder:	Rick Joy Architects
Earth walls:	Rammed Earth Solar Homes
Adobe restoration:	Tony Guzman

Godat Design Studio

Tucson, Arizona

Design:	1997
Construction:	1997
Area:	2000sf
Owner:	Ken Godat, Godat Graphic Design
Building Owner:	H. Kelley Rollings, Trustee
Project Team:	Rick Joy, Andy Tinucci, Chelsea Grassinger, Franz Buhler, Eric Lunsford
Builder:	Rick Joy Architects

Catalina House

Tucson, Arizona

Design:	1997
Construction:	1997–1998
Area:	main house: 2600sf, porch: 650sf, garage/shop/guest: 1500sf
Owner:	Dr. John Palmer
Project Team:	Rick Joy, Andy Tinucci, Chelsea Grassinger, Holly Damerell, Franz Buhler
Engineers:	Southwest Structural Engineers, Otterbein Mechanical Engineering
Landscape:	Michael Boucher Landscape Architects
Builder:	Rick Joy Architects
Earth walls:	Rammed Earth Solar Homes

Tubac House

Tubac, Arizona

Design:	1998
Construction:	1999–2000
Area:	main house: 2700sf, garage/shop/guest: 1800sf, courtyards: 4400sf
Owner:	Warren and Rose Tyler
Project Team:	Rick Joy, Andy Tinucci, Chelsea Grassinger, Franz Buhler
Engineers:	Southwest Structural Engineers, Otterbein Mechanical Engineering
Landscape:	Michael Boucher Landscape Architects
Builder:	Rick Joy Architects

400 Rubio Avenue

Tucson, Arizona

Design:	1998
Construction:	1999
Area:	studio: 1400sf, courtyard: 700sf
Owner:	Rick Brezer, Sienna Funding Corporation
Project Team:	Rick Joy, Andy Tinucci, Chelsea Grassinger
Builder:	Rick Joy Architects
Earth walls:	Rammed Earth Solar Homes

Tucson Mountain House

Tucson, Arizona

Design:	2000
Construction:	2000–2001
Area:	main house: 2200sf, porch: 400sf
Owner:	Kevin Osborn and Robert Claassen
Project Team:	Rick Joy, Andy Tinucci
Builder:	Rick Joy Architects
Earth walls:	Rammed Earth Development

Casa Jax

Tucson, Arizona

Design:	1999
Construction:	2001–2002
Area:	1500sf
Owner:	Withheld
Project Team:	Rick Joy, Andy Tinucci, Chelsea Grassinger, Franz Buhler
Engineers:	Southwest Structural Engineers, Otterbein Mechanical Engineering
Builder:	Rick Joy Architects

Pima Canyon House

Tucson, Arizona

Design:	2000
Construction:	2001–2002
Area:	house: 5400sf, living courtyards: 2600sf, court: 2600sf
Owner:	Cecile Follansbee and David Grove
Project Team:	Rick Joy, Andy Tinucci
Engineers:	Southwest Structural Engineers, Caruso Turley Scott Engineers, [Integra-block] Otterbein Mechanical Engineering
Builder:	Rick Joy Architects

Greer Cabin

Greer, Arizona

Design:	2001
Construction:	2002
Area:	main level: 2000sf, garage/basement: 2000sf
Owner:	Withheld
Project Team:	Rick Joy, Andy Tinucci, Chelsea Grassinger, Chad Cornette, Dave Hardin
Engineer:	Grenier Structural Engineering
Builder:	RA Conley Constructors

Biographical Notes

1958–1976

- Born in Dover-Foxcroft, Maine on December 25
- Lived in Ipswich, Massachusetts until age twelve
- Attended high school in Old Town, Maine

1977–1984

- Studied music at the University of Maine and performed as symphony percussionist
- Performed as a drummer in various venues on the East Coast
- Worked part-time as a carpenter
- Studied color theory, sculpture, and photography at the Portland School of Art
- Married Jean Millen

1985–1990

- Moved to Tucson
- Studied Architecture at the University of Arizona
- Received Bachelor of Architecture

1991–1992

- First son Ethan was born
- Worked in the offices of William P. Bruder Architect on the design team of the Phoenix Central Library
- Designed and built own family house in Tucson

1993

- Became registered architect in Arizona and launched Rick Joy Architects, Ltd.

1994–1996

- Progressive Architecture Magazine Young Architects Award
- Arizona Home of the Year for Joy/Millen Residence
- Architectural League of New York Young Architects Award
- Second son Eli was born
- Lectured at Arizona State University

1997–1998

- Record House Award for Convent Avenue Studios
- I.D. Magazine Annual Design Award for Convent Avenue Studios
- Roy P. Drachman Award for Convent Avenue Studios
- Founding Board of Directors Member of Civatas Sonoran—Environmental Design Council of Tucson
- Lectured at University of Arizona and University of New Mexico

1999

- Lectured at Auburn University and Rural Studio in Alabama
- Exhibited work at GA Gallery in Tokyo

2000

- Architectural Review AR+D Emerging Architecture Award
- Architectural League of New York Emerging Voices Award
- I.D. Magazine Annual Design Award for 400 Rubio Avenue
- AIA Central Arizona Home of the Year for Catalina House
- Architectural League of New York Ten Shades of Green Exhibit
- Visiting professor at Harvard University and University of Arizona
- Visiting critic at Yale University
- Lectured at University of Minnesota, Taliesin West, University of Arizona, Architectural League of New York, AIA Las Vegas, University of Virginia, Harvard University, and University of Texas at Austin
- Exhibited work at GA Gallery in Tokyo

2001

- Record House Award for Tubac House
- AIA Arizona Honor Awards for Tubac House and 400 Rubio Avenue
- Member of PA Awards Jury
- Visiting critic at Massachusetts Institute of Technology and Washington University
- Member of LA/AIA California Awards Jury
- Lectured at University of Michigan, University of Arkansas, San Diego Museum of Contemporary Art, Texas Technical University, University of Texas at Houston, San Juan Capistrano Museum of Architecture, Virginia Technical University, Massachusetts Institute of Technology, University of California at Berkeley, State University of New York at Buffalo, Arizona State University
- Exhibited work at GA Gallery in Tokyo, University of Michigan

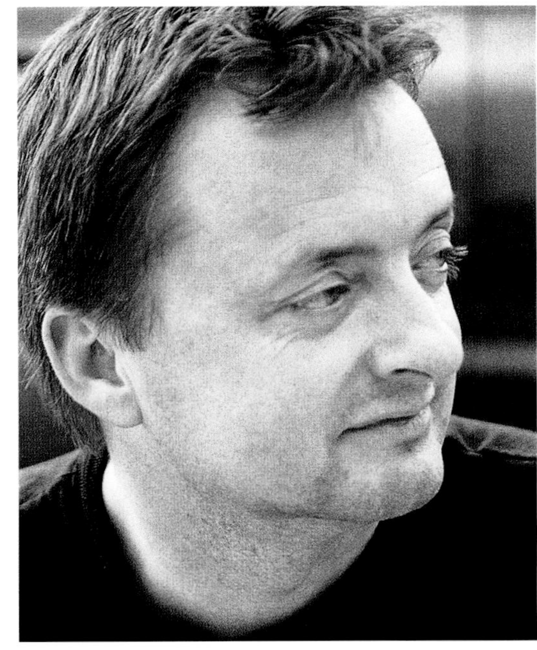

List of Associates
Rick Joy Architects
1993–2001

Andy Tinucci
Franz Buhler
Michio Vallian
Scott Woodward
Michael Elliot
Jared Fulton
Minette Martin
David MacGregor
Jane Schmitt
Ruth Mitchell
Carl Koski
Chad Cornet
Chelsea Grassinger
Dave Hardin
Doug Eure
Scott Semple
Michael Whitchurch
Kevin Burson
Maartje Steenkamp
Kami Witherspoon
Nina Tinucci
Rob Paulis
Michael Reinauld
Kevin Stewart
Curtis Eppley
Mathew Miller
Ben Holland
Jennifer Little
Michael Schwindenhammer
Holly Damerell
Nicole Herd
Evo Nellison
Fergus Scott

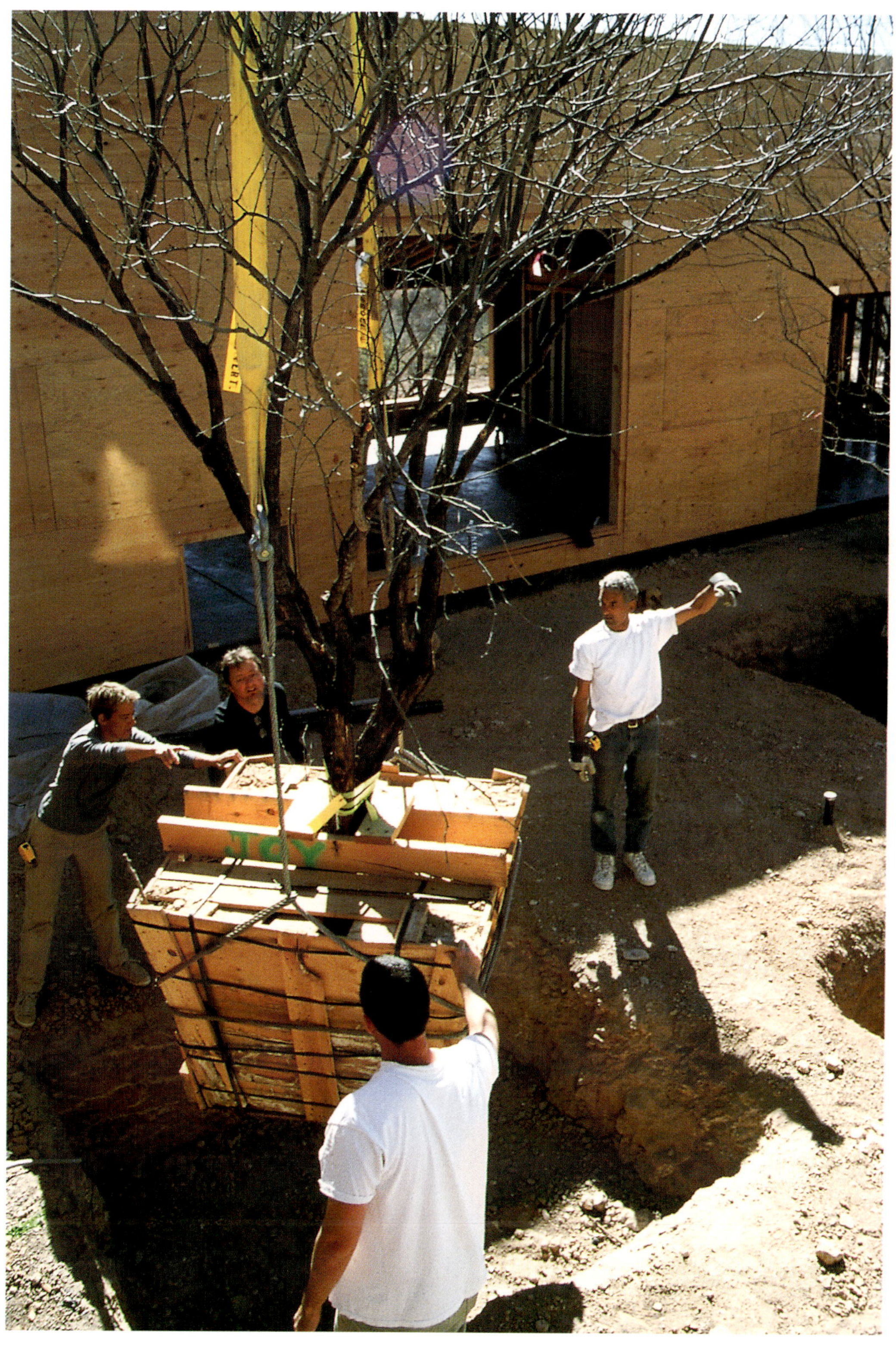

Selected Bibliography

1993

Fisher, Thomas. "Young Architects." *Progressive Architecture* (July 1993): 94–95.

1994

Miles, Candice. "Love's Labor Lavished." *Phoenix Home and Garden* 14, no. 7 (May 1994): 56–59.

1995

"Alqhuist Solar Retreat." *GA Houses* 45 (March 1995): 104–105.

1997

Architectural Record. *1997 Record Houses Virtual Reality CD-ROM*. New York: McGraw-Hill, 1997.

"Convent Avenue Studios." *L'architecture d'adujourd'hui* 312 (September 1997): 48–51.

Dixon, John Morris. "Convent Avenue Studios." *Domus* 796 (September 1997): 40–45.

"43rd Annual Design Review." *ID* 44, no. 5 (July/August 1997): 148.

"Joy/Millen Residence and Convent Avenue Studios." *GA Houses* 51 (March 1997): 140–157.

Ojeda, Oscar Riera. *The New American House 2: Innovations in Residential Design and Construction*. New York: Whitney Library of Design, 1997.

Pearson, Clifford. "Record Houses." *Architectural Record* 185, no. 4 (April 1997): 71–75.

"Walker Residence." *GA Houses* 52 (April 1997): 76.

Walker, Thom. "Old and New Reside Together." *The Arizona Daily Star*. 8 June 1997.

1998

Begley, Laura. "Desert Storm." *Wallpaper* 11 (May/June 1998): 152–165.

Giovannini, Joseph. "Earthwork." *Architecture* 87, no. 12 (December 1998): 90–97.

Giovannini, Joseph. "Modern's Many Faces." *Metropolitan Home* 30, no. 2 (March/April 1998): 71–74.

Lowe, Charlotte. "The Joy of Architecture." *Tucson Monthly* 1, no. 6 (February 1998): 48–53.

Lowe, Charlotte. "180 Tons and What Do You Get?" *Tucson Guide Quarterly* 16, no. 1 (Spring 1998): 82–86.

Seal, Margaret. "Twist of Lime." *The Architectural Review* 204, no. 1221 (November 1998): 47–49.

"Tyler Residence and Palmer-Rose Residence." *GA Houses* 55 (March 1998): 82–85.

1999

"Jack's House." *GA Houses* 59 (February 1999): 96–97.

Mostaedi, Arian. *The Home Office*. Barcelona: Carles Broto and Josep MaMinguet, 1999.

Palmer Residence. *Domus* 816. (June 1999): 20–26.

Palmer/Rose Residence. *GA Houses* 60 (June 1999): 70–79.

Sakamoto, Timothy K. "Planet Architecture." *In-D Digital Magazine* 2 (1999).

Seal, Margaret. "Joy Unconfined." *Architectural Review* 105, no. 1228 (June 1999): 76–77.

Trulsson, Nora Burba. "The Tucson Tempo." *Sources in Design* 4, no. 3 (Spring 1999): 34–35.

2000

Al-Sayed, Marwan. "The Weight of Modernity." *CITY AZ.* (January 2000): 58–63.

Davey, Peter. "Emerging Architecture." *Architectural Review* 108, no. 1246 (December 2000): 47–49.

"Design Review 2000." *ID* 47, no. 5 (July/August 2000): 147.

LeBlanc, Sydney. *The Architectural Traveler: A Guide to 250 Key 20th-Century American Buildings.* New York: W.W. Norton & Company, 2000.

Lee, Uje. *Context 3 Korea* 196 (September 2000): 94–135.

Lorenzo, Soledad. *The American House Today.* Barcelona: Carles Broto and Josep MaMinguet, 2000.

Makovsky, Paul. "New Architecture Faces the Future." *Metropolis* 19, no. 7 (April 2000): 74–75. See also photo essay by Amy Steiner, 100–105.

"Osborn/Claassen Residence." *GA Houses* 63 (March 2000): 140–141.

Patterson, Ann. "Earth Art." *Phoenix Home and Garden* 20, no. 7 (May 2000): 92–95.

Pope, Nicolas. *Experimental Houses.* New York: Watson-Guptill Publications, 2000.

Underwood, Max. "400 South Rubio." *Architecture* 89, no. 1 (January 2000): 78–83.

2001

Amelar, Sarah. *Bauwelt* 41 (2 November 2001): 16–21.

Amelar, Sarah. "Record Houses." *Architectural Record* 189, no. 4 (April 2001): 138–147.

Brown, Patricia Leigh. "Coyote Neighbors, Lightning Views." *New York Times,* 1 February 2001.

Edwards, Nick. "Top Talent." *Wallpaper* 40 (July/August 2001): 112.

Ho, Cathy Lang and Raul A. Barreneche. *House: American Houses for the New Century.* New York: Universe, 2001.

"Jones Cabin." *GA Houses* 66 (March 2001): 78.

McCoy, J. J. "10 Goals for Green Design." *Washington Post*, March 2001.

"Tubac House." *Architecture + Urbanism* 371 (August 2001): 107–111.

"Osborn/Claassen Residence." *GA Houses* 67 (April 2001): 118–125.

Pichel, Xose Manuel Rey. "Rick Joy in Arizona." *Obradoiro: Revisita do Colexio Official de Arquitectos de Galicia* 29, no. 01 (2001).

Sanza, Paolo. "A Butterfly in the Desert." *Hauser* (September/October 2001): 62–69.

Slessor, Catherine. "Touching Nature." *Architectural Review* 120, no. 1253 (July 2001): 46–49.

Truelove, James Grayson and Il Kim. *The New American House 3: Innovations in Residential Design and Construction.* New York: Whitney Library of Design, 2001.

Truelove, James Grayson and Nora Richter Greer. *Hot Dirt Cool Straw.* Washington D.C.: Harper Collins, 2001.

Trulsson, Nora Burba. "Office Politics." *Sources in Design* (Spring 2001): 34–46.

Viehweg, Boyd. "Synonyms of Simplicity." *I–15: Life Accelerated* (Spring 2001): 76–77.

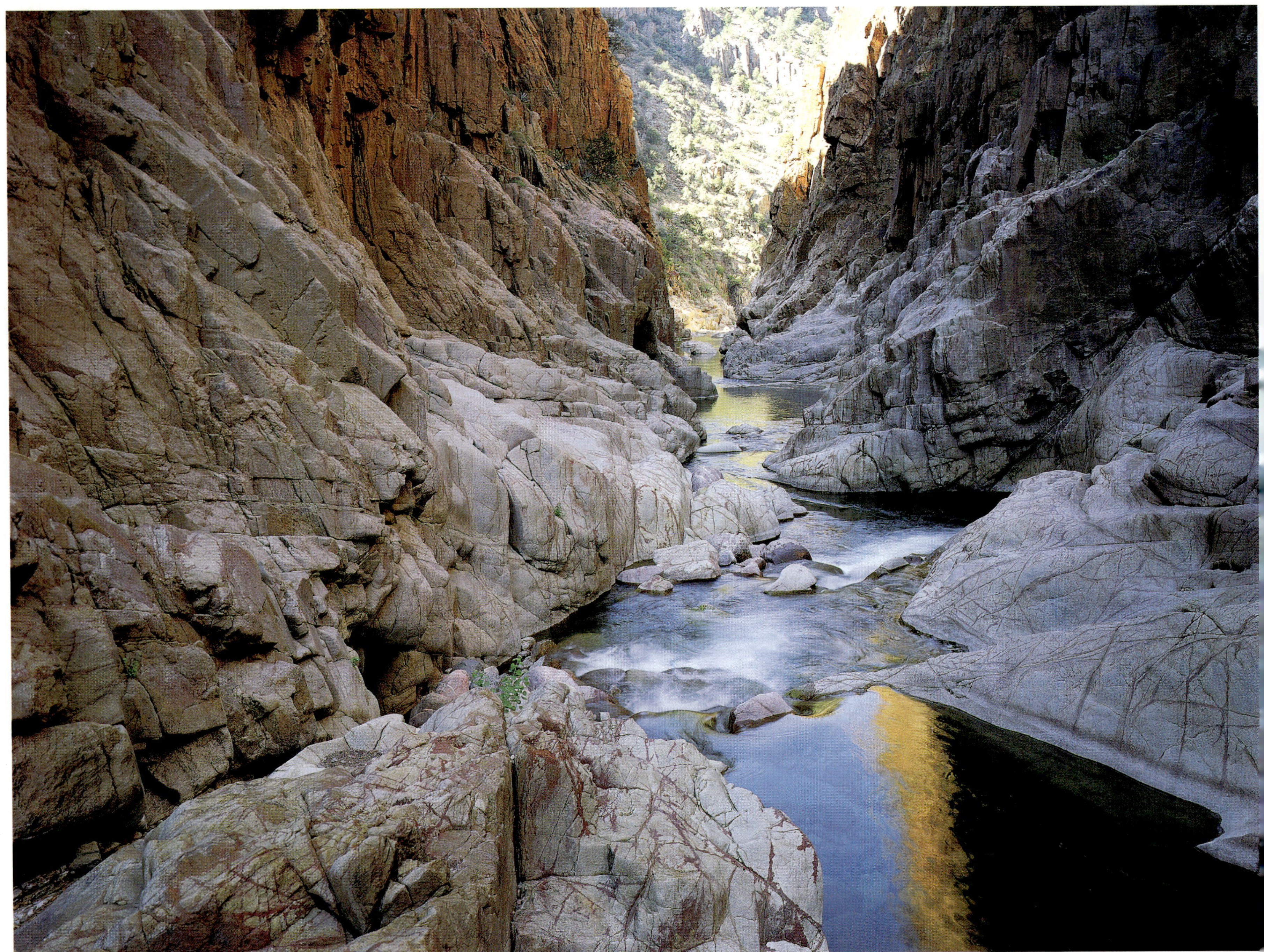